Great Accomplishment

Rangjung Yeshe Books • www.RANGJUNG.COM

Great Accomplishment

Teachings on the Drubchen Ceremony

Padmasambhava, Chokgyur Lingpa, Jamgön Kongtrül,
Joykyab Rinpoche, Tulku Urgyen Rinpoche,
Orgyen Topgyal Rinpoche, and Lama Putsi

Translated from the Tibetan by Erik Pema Kunsang
with Gyurme Avertin

Edited and Compiled by Marcia Dechen Wangmo
with Michael Tweed

Rangjung Yeshe • Boudhanath, Hong Kong & Esby

RANGJUNG YESHE PUBLICATIONS
Flat 5a, Greenview Garden,
125 Robinson Road, Hong Kong

ADDRESS LETTERS TO:
Rangjung Yeshe Publications
Ka-Nying Shedrub Ling Monastery
P.O. Box 1200, Kathmandu, Nepal

www.rangjung.com

1 3 5 7 9 8 6 4 2

FIRST PAPERBACK EDITION PUBLISHED IN 2013
Printed in the United States of America

Distributed to the book trade by:
North Atlantic Books & Random House, Inc.

Publication data: ISBN 978-962-7341-82-6 (pbk.)

Ocean of Amrita.
Light of Wisdom, Vol. III, Padmasambhava, Chokgyur Lingpa, Jamyang Khyentse
Wangpo, Jamgön Kongtrül & Joykyab Rinpoche

Translated from the Tibetan based on the teachings of Kyabje Tulku Urgyen Rinpoche
by Erik Pema Kunsang (Erik Hein Schmidt) with Gyurme Avertin.

Edited by Michael Tweed and Marcia Binder Schmidt.

Photo courtesy of Oscar Fernandez

FIRST EDITION

CONTENTS

CONTENTS

PREFACE

Marcia Dechen Wangmo

Preferring to practice alone, I have always found it difficult to engage in the annual drubchen practices at the monasteries in Nepal. To me, there was just too much color, noise, and people jostling for position and blessings. Moreover, in the monasteries in Nepal, a temporarily more important or wealthy sponsor always squeezed us Westerners out of our seats, even if we had diligently come to practice every day. So, in the midst of the sublime mandala, destructive emotions abounded in my small mind, and I decided it was better to practice alone on the mountainside and avoid all the squabbling, pressure, and complications.

I love sadhanas and practice them daily, so my inability to handle my reactions was a bit of a contradiction, especially in that I considered myself to be a decent meditator. So why did I react differently whether in a crowd or in solitude? My mind is in both places, and if I cannot control it in a group, a religious one at that, then what is the point of identifying oneself as a practitioner at all? I have seen many great Dzogchen meditators, like Kyabje Dilgo Khyentse Rinpoche, preside over many drubchens, unmoved from *rigpa,* so I did have a clear example of how one could practice.

In any event, for many years I opted to stay away from such public rituals and practice on my own instead. All of that changed when I started to be in the company of Orgyen Topgyal Rinpoche, to work on completing the *Light of Wisdom*[1] series and the *Tukdrub* drubchen text, and begin to really learn what drubchen was all about. Suddenly, what previously seemed a burden was a great joy and I began to travel around the world to participate in drubchens. Of course, I always appreciated interacting with sublime beings in the development stage practices, but now I was having a really good time doing it, aside from the sheer exhaustion and complete sensory overload.

It started with a comment by Dzongsar Khyentse Rinpoche about his friend Orgyen Topgyal, where he quoted him saying, "The Vajrayana path is basically achieving enlightenment while having fun." My appreciation was also nurtured by performing drubchens at the Rigpa Centers in the West, where order and discipline was the code of behavior, and no wild people or self-important individuals could unseat me. So, in a way, the environment was protected. I certainly did not need to fear for my life with people pushing and stampeding for blessings. But aside from these seemingly small-minded factors, being in the company of many similar-type practitioners and handpicked lamas and monks who knew what they were doing truly inspired me.

And then there were the explanations and teachings, which brings me to this book. They are not new and not something that I had not already studied, but somehow now they hold so much more meaning for me. I experientially appreciated that when serious practitioners come together, replete with their buddha natures, even though covered by temporary obscurations, the power of such a gathering is magnified, and we can collectively accomplish something.

I film the circumambulating of the main mandala repeatedly; it resonates with my gypsy nature. The colors of the streamers waved in space to gather the blessing by realized practitioners is magnetizing and awesome. When I watch the films afterward, each time I witness individuals who know exactly what they are doing, and it is impressive. We too can connect with that blessed energy by one-pointedly engaging in these group assemblies with our fellow yogis and yoginis, who become a support to stabilize awareness in a vivid and heartfelt way. Fortunately, there are many centers in the West that afford the opportunity to connect with drubchens, where the main shrine people and chant masters are Western, and women perform in lama dance as well. I truly rejoice in all this profound Dharma activity that has helped break away at my shell of close-mindedness.

By studying and coming to understand some aspects of the practice and the perfection of those carrying it out correctly, my appreciation for and devotion to the skillful means of Vajrayana has increased, and the next phase is to actually embody it. So, for right now, being the frivolous type, I am enjoying having a really good time, and if I can share that enthusiasm with you, it makes me all the more joyful. Sit back, read, and learn about all the beauty and deep meaning in drubchen, and when you can join one, it will be one of the best choices you will ever make.

INTRODUCTORY TEACHINGS ON THE RITUAL OF GREAT ACCOMPLISHMENT

Tulku Urgyen Rinpoche

Please read this teaching with the proper motivation of bodhichitta, the mind of enlightenment, and with the intention of putting the teaching into practice for the benefit of all sentient beings who have been our own mothers.

Great accomplishment is a translation of the Tibetan term *drubchen* [sgrub chen]. In accordance with the Vajrayana system, this group practice consists of three stages: development, recitation, and completion. Moreover, it incorporates the four aspects of approach, full approach, accomplishment, and great accomplishment. When you participate in a drubchen, you should imagine that the outer vessel, our world, is a celestial palace, and its inner contents, all the inhabitants of this world, are pure beings; all sounds, whether animate or inanimate, and all voices, whether human or animal, are the resounding of mantras; and your own thoughts, emotions, and mental movements, as well as those of all other beings, are the inconceivable wisdom of vajra mind. In short, all that appears, exists, and resounds in this world, all male and female beings, all of our thoughts and emotions should be considered as pure wisdom without the slightest trace of impurity.

The main principle of Vajrayana path is pure perception or sacred outlook. However, this does not mean superimposing something unreal onto the way things are; the true nature of things actually is primordially pure. However, the vajra body, speech, and mind have been obscured by our habitual patterns of thinking, so that the indestructible vajra body is obscured by conceiving a body of flesh and blood, the unceasing vajra speech obscured by our ordinary voice, and the changeless vajra mind by our constant conceptualizing.

In the Vajrayana system, there are always three aspects: symbol, meaning, and sign. So there is a lot of symbolism that we must try to understand.

The five elements of the outer world—earth, water, fire, wind, and space—are actually the nature of the five female buddhas. They are known as "the spaces of the five consorts." It is said that the earth element is Lochana, the water element is Mamaki, the fire element is Pandaravasini, the wind element is Samayatara, and the space element is Dhatvishvari. Therefore, from the very outset, these five elements have, in fact, been the five female buddhas. Furthermore, our body is the mandala of the buddhas in that the five minor elements exist internally as the constituents of our physical body. In principle, these two are the same in that our flesh and bones are the earth element, the blood and liquids are the water element, the body's warmth is the fire element, our breath is the wind element, and the body's cavities are the space element.

Similarly, sentient beings are composed of the five aggregates or skandhas. These five aggregates are originally pure because, primordially, all sentient beings are composed of the five male buddhas: the aggregate of form is Vairochana, the aggregate of sensations is Ratnasambhava, the aggregate of conceptions is Amitabha, the aggregate of formations is Amoghasiddhi, and the aggregate of consciousnesses is Akshobhya. This is how things actually are, yet we have continually wandered in samsara because we have not recognized the fact of primordial purity. Instead, confused and bewildered, we are constantly engaging in deluded experience.

The body is also known as "the mandala of the three bases of completeness," meaning that the qualities of these three bases already exist within us. The first base, the aggregates and elements, acts as the basis for the male and female tathagatas. As mentioned above, our five aggregates are the five male buddhas and our five elements are the five female buddhas. The second base, the sense bases or ayatanas (literally, "avenues for experience"), acts as the basis for the eight male and eight female bodhisattvas, namely the pure aspect of the eight groups of consciousnesses and the eight objects of these consciousnesses. The third base, called the views and times, acts as the basis for the male and female gatekeepers. The four views are those of permanence, nothingness, ego, and concepts. The four times are the past, present, future, and timelessness. We also have what are known as the six poisons—the negative emotions of greed, attachment, aggression, jealousy, delusion, and arrogance—but in their pure aspect they are the six *munis* or sages.

We possess the tathagatagarbha, the enlightened essence, which is like pure gold, but we have fallen into confusion, which is like gold becoming tainted by impurities. Similarly, possessing the deities of the three bases of completeness is like possessing pure gold, but not recognizing it as such is like gold being concealed by dirt.

The Buddhist path is simply purifying our perception of those mistaken views that obscure the truth, which is the purpose of all the practices. If we weren't already endowed with this pure gold, but instead possessed mere brass, we could polish and clean all we wanted, but the brass would never turn into gold. Nevertheless, since we already have a divine nature, if we engage in the development, recitation, and completion stage practices, which act like a polish, we can purify our obscurations and truly realize the dharmakaya.

The Vajrayana system has many techniques and few difficulties, but it is meant for people of higher capabilities. However, because each of us possesses the enlightened essence, when a large group participates in a drubchen, many enlightened essences are gathered together in one place, and practice will be more effective. If we have recognized and realized our enlightened essence, then circumstances will be perfect; but even if we have not, when we participate in the ritual and stay within the environment, there will still be great benefit.

As for the basic structure of the ritual itself, because there are one hundred peaceful and wrathful deities, no less than one hundred people should participate when performing a drubchen of these deities. Each morning begins with the lineage supplication and so forth. Next, since Vajrayana practices like this encompass all three Buddhist vehicles, an important aspect of the preliminary verses is the taking of refuge, which embodies all the Hinayana teachings. Following this, we always arouse bodhichitta, or the mind of enlightenment, which embodies the Mahayana teachings. So you can see that we never practice "only Vajrayana," for Hinayana and Mahayana are always included.

After refuge and bodhichitta, a torma, known as a *gektor*, is offered to any obstructing forces. Obstructing forces are fabricated by our own dualistic concepts. When we have dualistic concepts, which are confusion resulting from ignorance, we have already fabricated demons and negative forces. In order to appease them, a symbolic torma is peacefully taken outside, then any remaining obstructors are commanded to leave, and finally those stubborn ones who refuse to leave are dispelled in a subjugating manner.

Next, in order to consecrate the offering articles, environment, practitioners, and so forth, we enact bringing down the splendor of wisdom blessings. After that, offerings are made. Offerings do not refer only to the few articles placed on the shrine, such as water and rice, for on their own these would not be very effective. Rather, by means of emanating countless offering goddesses, each of these articles must be multiplied to fill the skies, bringing benefit to all beings everywhere.

The inner offerings are "medicine," namely amrita, rakta, and torma. These are symbolic representations of the three poisons of aggression, passion, and delusion. By offering our three poisons, we empty samsara because the three poisons are what create samsara. Finally, the secret or ultimate offering is the experience of our enlightened essence.

On the first day of the drubchen, the preliminaries include drawing the boundary line for the retreat. This boundary also has outer, inner, and secret aspects. The outer boundary is demarcated when the lamas walk around and erect the four poles with inscriptions. These inscriptions remind the four guardian kings that, at the time of Lord Buddha, they promised to protect the teachings and all future practitioners; so we are reminding them of their commitment, and request them to guard and protect our place of practice.

First, digging a hole in the ground in front of the monastery creates the inner boundary; a torma is then thrown into it, covered with earth, and stepped on. By doing so, ignorance, our lack of recognition of the enlightened essence, is symbolized as a demonic force that is now subjugated and pressed down into a state of oblivion until all thoughts and dualistic concepts have been obliterated. Having done this, our first thought should be the awakened attitude of bodhichitta. We make the wish that this demonic force be reborn in the first assembly of the Enlightened One. Hence, even though this action might appear wrathful, it is actually an expression of compassion.

The third boundary, known as the secret boundary, is the liberation of *rudra*. Rudra is symbolic of the negative force that obscures our vajra body, speech, and mind. These are sometimes called the apparent rudra of body, the semi-apparent rudra of speech, and the inapparent rudra of mind. These three are what should be liberated, which means our ignorance is freed into the expanse of wisdom.

Once the boundary has been completed, the ritual known as "the deity preparation" is performed. First, the celestial palace is erected. On the left side of the shrine hall, there is a platform on which the vajra master carefully measures and draws lines, and square plates with colored powder are placed, representing the celestial palace of the deities. There are three kinds of mandala representations; the best is composed of colored sand, the next best a drawing on canvas, and the third best is heaps of grain. Colored sand or powder is used to symbolize that the phenomenal world was first created from atoms or particles. Next comes the vase preparation, in which we visualize the entire mandala with its celestial palace of the deities inside the actual vase. Thirdly is the article preparation, which is consecration of the articles that are used for the four empowerments of Vajrayana: the vase, secret, wisdom-knowledge, and word empowerments. There is also consecration of the articles that represent vajra body, speech, and mind. Next comes what is called "bringing down the splendor of blessings." After that, the ceremony is brought to an end for the first day. The next day, the main part of the practice will begin and continue for seven days, ending on the ninth day. The first day is the preparatory practices, as mentioned above, and the last day is taking the siddhis, so a drubchen is nine days in total.

On each of the following days, the daily preliminaries of the lineage supplication, refuge, bodhichitta, and so on are repeated, followed by the main part of the practice, which is the visualization of the celestial palace and the deities. This begins with the three samadhis: the samadhi of suchness, the all-illuminating samadhi, and the seed-syllable samadhi. Imagining that everything in the universe, including all beings, dissolves into emptiness is the samadhi of suchness. Giving rise to the thought of compassion for all sentient beings who have not realized this nature is the all-illuminating samadhi. Since emptiness and compassion take the form of a seed syllable, in this case the white letter *hrih*, it is known as the samadhi of the seed syllable.

The whole mandala with its deities unfolds and manifests from this seed syllable. First, the different letters representing the five elements of space, wind, water, fire, and earth are emanated, one after another, to create Mount Sumeru. On the summit of Mount Sumeru, we visualize the celestial palace and the deities within it. In this mandala, the seed syllable first turns into a golden vajra, which then transforms into Guru Rinpoche. This is a self-visualization, meaning you visualize yourself in the form of the deity, in this case Guru Rinpoche.

What is more, in this practice, *The Ocean of Amrita*, the guru is inseparable from the peaceful and wrathful ones. Inside of your skull, "the bone mansion," is the mandala of the fifty-eight blazing wrathful deities. In your throat-center are the five pure knowledge-holders, *vidyadharas*, with their consorts. In your heart are the forty-two peaceful deities. In your navel-center is black Vajra Yogini, who is known as *Tröma Nagmo* in Tibetan. In your secret-center is Vajra Kilaya.

While maintaining this visualization of your body as a pure mandala of deities, you emanate offering goddesses who bow down and present offerings to you. They also render praises and so forth before dissolving back into you. All of this, up until the rendering of praises, is known as the development stage.

Next is the recitation stage. As mentioned, there are four aspects to this, called approach, close approach, accomplishment, and great accomplishment. Here, we are mainly practicing the great accomplishment aspect. Symbolically, this is like a beehive breaking open, meaning there is a constant buzzing everywhere. This represents the idea that all over the world, beings, sounds, thoughts, and so forth are actually the continuity of the pure wisdom that goes on uninterruptedly; hence the practice itself will continue without interruption for nine days.

In connection with the practice of the peaceful and wrathful ones, there is the four-part apology—the four parts being body, speech, mind, and their combination—and the four elements of mending, whereby we mend the samayas by means of the four elements that we already possess within us. We already have blood, which came from our mother, embodying attachment; the white bindu, which came from our father, embodying aggression; their combination, flesh, which embodies the darkness of delusion; and finally pure awareness. Hence, we make several offerings in which attachment is symbolized by the rakta, aggression by amrita, ignorance by the torma, and our pure awareness is symbolized by the flame of the butter lamp. In short, the purpose of offering amrita, rakta, and torma is to purify the three poisons; offering the flame of the lamp signifies the recognition of self-existing wisdom.

Included in this ritual is something called *sojong,* which is the mending and purification of the Hinayana, Mahayana, and Vajrayana vows. One after the other, we mend the *pratimoksha* precepts, the vows of individual liberation in accordance with the Hinayana system; the bodhisattva trainings in accordance with the Mahayana system; and the samaya commitments in accordance with the Vajrayana system. By doing so, these commitments are restored.

Next, a torma offering is presented to the Dharma protectors, followed by a feast offering, known in Sanskrit as a *ganachakra,* during which we present a feast to all the deities, buddhas, and bodhisattvas. When we eat something ourselves, it is not just to please ourselves; it is actually an offering to the dakas, dakinis, and male and female deities in the mandala of our own body. Therefore, food is offered in the manner of a fire puja.

Finally, we receive the Vajrayana empowerments. In Vajrayana, there are three general categories of empowerments corresponding to ground, path, and fruition. In this ceremony, the vajra master bestows the ground empowerment, and we bestow the path empowerment upon ourselves. The fruition empowerment, on the other hand, is not received until one reaches the end of the bodhisattva path. At that time, you receive blessings in the form of light rays from the protuberance called the *ushnika,* on top of the heads of all the tathagatas in all the ten directions. When that happens, the last trace of conceptual obscuration vanishes, and you obtain complete enlightenment.

During the drubchen ceremony itself, we receive four specific empowerments, the first of which is the vase empowerment. This empowerment is received by visualizing the deities in their celestial palace within the vase, and then drinking the water from the vase. Drinking a small amount of the infused alcohol from the skull cup confers both the secret empowerment and the wisdom-knowledge empowerment; this empowerment refers to the nondual bliss and emptiness of the union of the deity and the consort. The fourth empowerment is the word empowerment, which introduces the actual practice of self-existing wisdom.

Since we already possess the enlightened essence, if we practice, then we should be able to obtain complete enlightenment; however, obstacles do manifest while on the path. The main obstacles are breaches that damage our commitments; therefore, a practice that purifies them is very important within the short path of Vajrayana. If we can practice freely and unobstructed, purifying our habitual patterns and mending any breaches of samaya, then we will quickly progress on the path of development, recitation, and completion and attain the fruition of dharmadhatu, the self-existing wisdom from which we have actually never been separated for even an instant. For this reason, a drubchen is an extremely important practice and bestows great blessings.

In general, the Buddha gave two kinds of teachings: extensive and profound. The extensive are characterized as Mahayana teachings and the profound teachings as Vajrayana. However, this doesn't mean that some teachings are superior and others inferior. It means that because there are different kinds of people, the Buddha gave different teachings depending on peoples' varying capacities. Nevertheless, the Mahayana path is said to take longer to traverse, while the Vajrayana path is shorter and more profound. In Vajrayana practice, in order to obtain enlightenment, means and knowledge are practiced as a unity. That is why we must always practice combining both the development stage, which is the skillful means aspect, with the completion stage, which is the knowledge aspect.

Many people insist that deities are just our mind, and because the mind is empty there are no deities; but the mind is not just an empty void—it also has a lucid knowing quality. The empty aspect of mind is dharmakaya, but this empty aspect is naturally luminous. This luminosity is sambhogakaya, and these two kayas are never apart, just like the sun and moon are never apart from the sky. Another way to put it is that dharmakaya is self-existing wisdom and sambhogakaya is its natural expression. The dharmakaya is like a crystal, while the sambhogakaya is like the spectrum shining from the crystal.

This is what we call "the great mandala of appearance and existence abiding as ground nature." In this way, the nature of the ground is the empty aspect, dharmakaya, and the luminous or manifest aspect is sambhogakaya, the deities. Because these are always a unity, this is the real deity. So how can one say that deities don't exist?

There is a lot of discussion about what happens after death in the intermediate state called the bardo. At that time, the deities are said to manifest in different ways and forms. These are not physical deities because they do not have flesh and blood. They are actually the manifest aspect of the enlightened essence. Since emptiness is naturally manifesting, we cannot say that they don't exist—they are spontaneously present.

Right now, we are embodied within the structure of a physical body composed of aggregates, elements, and so forth. Our physical body, conditioned speech, and conceptual thoughts conceal our vajra body, speech, and mind. Just like when a house is dismantled or falls apart, its contents are unveiled and become evident; when the body, speech, and mind fall apart and separate from each other at the moment of death, then the so-called deities manifest. But they are not coming from outside to frighten us or to help us; rather that which is already naturally present within our own selves is simply revealed. These deities have been there all the time and simply become evident.

At the time of death, first there is the misery of having to acknowledge that we have died. Feeling completely lost, and in a state of great despair, we wonder, "What can I do? Now I'm dead. What should I do?" This experience is very overwhelming and almost unbearable. Then, as the obscurations of the conditioned body fall away, we see the forms of these innate deities and hear their sounds. At the same time, the naked self-existing wisdom will also arise. Like one hundred thousand suns shining simultaneously, the deities who manifest after death are endowed with tremendous splendor and radiance. They are quite overwhelming. Their forms range in size from the immensity of Mount Sumeru down to the minuteness of a mustard seed. The sounds are like one thousand simultaneous claps of thunder. Right now, someone shouting does not frighten us, but a huge thunderclap terrifies us. What would it be like if one-thousand claps of thunder occurred simultaneously? Moreover, the rays of light, the colors, and so on are like the rays emanating from one hundred thousand suns. If we are totally unprepared, we will suffer tremendously from our fear. Therefore, it is extremely important that we practice now, so that when the time comes we can recognize these things to be what they naturally are.

It is best if you have already had the view pointed out, recognized it, and gained some stability in the recognition through your practice. Next best is if, at the time of death, you can remember that all these colors, light rays, and sounds are your own manifestation. You think, "These are my own deities, they are none other than me. These are my own sounds, and these are my own light rays." Then you will not be afraid of your own true self, and the panic and misery will simultaneously dissolve. This is the crucial point to remember: the deities, their colors, lights, and sounds truly are you, yourself. If you can remember that, then the fear and panic will diminish. They are empty forms, empty sounds, and empty light rays.

In the drubchen ritual itself, there are different sections of the recitation, the presentation of offerings and praises, and the seven branches of prostrating, making offerings, reciting praises and prayers, rendering apology, and so forth. Each of these is pregnant with meaning. If you are attending a drubchen, of course it is best if you can follow the text and chant along, but if you can't, it is sufficient just to chant the mantras of the peaceful and wrathful ones: OM BODHI CHITTA MAHA SUKHA JNANA DHATU AH OM RULU RULU HUNG BHYO HUNG. Or if you are familiar with it, there is also a longer mantra, in which you first chant the Guru Rinpoche mantra, and then the mandala of the three kayas is recited.[2] But if you feel that both of those are too elaborate, then it is sufficient if you just recite the short Vajrasattva mantra: OM VAJRA SATVA AH.

When we come to the mantra recitation, people take turns reciting it so that it goes on day and night continuously for eight days without any break. You will also notice that the lama will sit with the dharani cord, a five-colored string tied to a vajra, held at his heart-center. The cord is attached to the vase at the center of the mandala. The five colors of the dharani cord represent the five colored lights of the five wisdoms. Through this dharani cord, the lama imagines the emanation of light rays that make offerings, carry back blessings, and so forth, incessantly. Finally, while chanting the mantra, the rays of light radiating from your own heart-center make offerings to the body, speech, and mind of all the buddhas in the ten directions and gather back the blessing of body, speech, and mind into the vase and you. Again, rays of light emanate to purify all the six kinds of sentient beings, relieving them from all their sufferings, evil deeds, obscurations, habitual patterns, and so on and gathering back the blessing of this purification. In between, you radiate light that subdues and tames all the negative and demonic forces. If you chant correctly, the purity of the recitation is said to increase the merit one thousand times, while maintaining purity of concentration—keeping the correct frame of mind—multiplies the merit one hundred thousand times.

In short, the main focus of the practice is to recognize that the world around us, whatever appears and exists, is a celestial palace; while the male and female sentient beings are all dakas and dakinis. All sounds are mantra, and all thoughts and emotions are pure wisdom. Whatever we see with our eyes is the pure form of the deity; whatever we hear with our ears is the sound of mantra; and whatever we think, all thoughts and mental activity, is actually the enlightened vajra mind, self-existing wisdom.

The Light of Wisdom

PART III

THE ROOT TEXT
Lamrim Yeshe Nyingpo
by Padmasambhava

as recorded by Yeshe Tsogyal *and revealed*
and decoded by Jamyang Khyentse Wangpo
and Chokgyur Lingpa

THE COMMENTARY
The Light of Wisdom
by Jamgön Kongtrül the Great

The Path of Accomplishing

The stages of the path that contain all the authentic
    practices⁚
To accomplish the supreme and common siddhis are as
    follows:⁚
The approach is great emptiness and compassionate magic,⁚
While the stable vivid presence of the subtle and coarse
    aspects of the single mudra,⁚
Together with the elaborate mudra, is the full approach.⁚
They can also be approach, full approach, and
    accomplishment.⁚
Through their practice you achieve the heat, signs, and
    indications.⁚

By means of the group assembly practice and the great
    accomplishment,⁚
In order to reach to the end of the vidyadhara levels,⁚
At a perfect location, remote and endowed with the
    splendor of blessings,⁚
At an auspicious time, when the planets and stars are
    suitably aligned,⁚
Possessing the articles of perfection,⁚
The group of the qualified teacher and disciples⁚
Should have clear concentration and correct rituals.⁚

Request the site, take possession, cleanse, and guard it.⁚
Purify your being and draw the boundary in the outer,
    inner, and innermost ways.⁚
Deliver, suppress, and imbue Matram with the splendor of
    being the vajra realm.⁚

Perform the appropriate preparatory consecrations.⁑

Erect the mandala, arrange the articles, and seat the
practitioners.⁑
With the ritual of approach, purify the world and clear
obscurations.⁑
With the full approach, purify the inhabitants and gather
the siddhis.⁑
With the accomplishment, purify the mind and take
possession of the siddhis.⁑

During the six periods, make feast offerings to please and
mend.⁑
Subjugate the spying nyuley spirits, shower down the great
resplendence.⁑
Do not break the continuity of deity, mantra, or the
samadhi of emanation and absorption.⁑

As a result of giving up distraction and practicing one-
pointedly,⁑
The painted image smiles or the amrita boils with sound,⁑
The butter lamp lights by itself or the practice articles
sparkle,⁑
The power of realization blazes forth, and there is mastery
of wakefulness.⁑

After certain signs have occurred, for the great
accomplishment,⁑
Receive from the deity at dusk, perform liberation at
midnight,⁑
Union at dawn, and obtain the siddhis.⁑

Commentary

Tukdrub Barchey Künsel Guru

25

The Path of Accomplishing

The explanation of how the path is accomplished has two parts: an overview of the manner of linking with the previous and a detailed explanation of the meaning

BRIEF STATEMENT IN THE MANNER OF CONNECTING

The *Lamrim Yeshe Nyingpo* root text says:

> The stages of the path that contain all the authentic
>   practices.⁸
> To accomplish the supreme and common siddhis are as
>   follows:⁸

In order to attain complete accomplishment in accordance with the profound meaning of the tantras, statements, and instructions, all that has been explained so far about the two siddhis in connection with the development stage, headed by the supreme sadhana and the common activities, one must follow a path that has a complete "body." Such a path has the following stages.

DETAILED EXPLANATION OF THE MEANING

This has two parts: The short explanation of the first four yogas, such as great emptiness and so forth, and a detailed explanation of the group assembly practice.³

Short Explanation of the First Four Yogas such as "Great Emptiness" and so Forth

The *Lamrim Yeshe Nyingpo* root text says:

> The approach is great emptiness and compassionate magic,§
> While the stable vivid presence of the subtle and coarse
>   aspects of the single mudra,§
> Together with the elaborate mudra is the full approach.§
> They can also be approach, full approach, and
>   accomplishment.§
> Through their practice you achieve the heat, signs, and
>   indications.§

First, the approach is to cultivate the suchness samadhi of great emptiness and the illuminating samadhi of compassionate magic. Next, the full approach is to attain the stable vivid presence of the subtle—the syllable—and the coarse—the single-mudra form of the deity—followed by visualizing the mandala of the elaborate mudra.

An alternative is to practice with the samadhi of suchness as approach, the samadhi of illumination as full approach, while the seed samadhi, along with the single and elaborate mudra, is accomplishment. Through that, you achieve a variety of temporary results that include outer, inner, and innermost degrees of heat from completing the above-mentioned five experiences,[4] a sequence of signs, and indications of siddhi. After this, you embrace the practice of great accomplishment.

According to the *Magical Stages of the Path,* "heat" means as follows:

> When continuing like that, free from doer and deed,
> The heat will occur in body, speech, and mind.

Thus, the outer heat is that the body feels light; the inner heat is that the movement of breath is barely discernible; and the innermost heat is to fully arrive at the nature itself. In this way, the threefold heat is blissful body, clear voice, and thought-free mind.

As for the signs, according to the *Commentary on the Lamp for the Eye:*

> Having definitely experienced the threefold heat,
> The signs will manifest in various ways.

Accordingly, the signs of having attained the heat are as follows: The outer signs are to see everything in the field of vision as filled with tiny attributes of the deity's enlightened body, speech, and mind. Also included is to see the "smoke-like," and so forth; to see the exhaustion of the five elements—earth, water, fire, wind, and space—into the five colors that arise and develop; or to see in the sky the light of huge lotus flowers, particles, stars, crescents, and the like.[5] Among the inner signs, you will attain acceptance in body and speech[6] and the mental stream of the five disturbing emotions naturally decreases so that the eight worldly concerns are evened out. The innermost signs are to attain a slight degree of control over the energies; to have minor superknowledges; and in dreams to repeatedly have omens of purifying misdeeds and obscurations, of attaining the bhumis or achieving the supreme and common siddhis.[7]

The indications of siddhi are the common activities and the great achievements, or, as mentioned in the *Root Tantra of Magical Illusion,* the six siddhis that are the source of qualities,[8] the five siddhis of the five elements,[9] and the eight siddhis of minor activities.[10] Furthermore, the *Exposition Tantras* describe numerous types, and, thus, they are countless. This is as the *Ratnakuta* mentions: "Inconceivable are the domains and the miraculous powers of the mind that has accomplished samadhi. Inconceivable also are the qualities of substances, medicines, mantras, and gemstones."

Detailed Explanation of the Practice of Group Assembly

This second part has two sections: an overview and a detailed explanation.

Overview

The *Lamrim Yeshe Nyingpo* root text says:

> By means of the group assembly practice and the great
>   accomplishment,
> In order to reach to the end of the vidyadhara levels,

For the first, after you have attained the heat, signs, and indications through the three aspects of approach, full approach, and accomplishment as just explained, you should next embrace the following—namely, you should take the group assembly practice as the main part and the great accomplishment as the activity applications—in order to reach to the end of the four vidyadhara levels that are the fruition of the path.

The meaning of "group assembly practice" is described in the *Framework Scripture*:

> "Assembly" is the threefold gathering.
> "Group" is of one, three, or five.

In the case of a smaller gathering, the group—with one, three, or five chief figures together with their consorts—makes a total assembly of two, six, or ten. A medium-sized gathering is one that has the same number of deities as in the mandala. A great gathering is one of any number larger than that. Each of these has three instances, described like this:

> With fortunate people, joyful deities,
> And with the fivefold articles of wealth.

Thus, in addition to these three aspects,[11] you add the "great gathering." In short, it means to practice after gathering the special shrine objects, the people, and the articles.

Detailed Explanation

This second point has two phases: taking the five perfections as the basis of the sadhana practice and following the sadhana structure with the specific four aspects of approach and accomplishment.

TAKING THE FIVE PERFECTIONS AS THE BASIS OF THE SADHANA PRACTICE

The *Lamrim Yeshe Nyingpo* root text says:

> At a perfect location, remote and endowed with the
>   splendor of blessings,
> At an auspicious time, when the planets and stars are
>   suitably aligned,
> Possessing the articles of perfection,

> The group of the qualified teacher and disciples.⁘
> Should have clear concentration and correct rituals.⁘

Regarding this first phase, for commencing a great accomplishment practice, or *drubchen,* you must bring together the five perfections. According to the *Activity Manual* they are:

> Of these, the first are place and time,
> Articles, teacher, and retinue of practitioners.
> Complete the practice text by using as the basis
> These perfections for the sadhana.

The place for performing the practice should be remote—without circumstances that distract concentration in general and, in particular, completely free from physical enemies, thieves, or vicious carnivores, and also not in areas frequented by vicious spirits. It should be a place that is pleasant—with the complete characteristics for accomplishing the siddhis of the four activities. Especially, it should be endowed with the splendor of blessings, having been personally visited by the conquerors and vidyadharas of the past. Thus, it should be in a perfect and auspicious location.

The time for performing the practice should be on the "divine day," when the sun moves to the north; during the waxing part of the moon of the four initial months of the four seasons; on one of the special days blessed by the teachers of Sutrayana and Mantrayana; on an exceptional day, such as when three factors converge to yield siddhis—the planet Jupiter, the Naksatraraja constellation, and the eighth day of the waxing moon; or on another time of perfection that the tantras and astrological scriptures praise as being most marvelous.

The articles based on which one practices include the general and specific types, such as sadhana shrine objects, offering articles, food for sustenance, medicine to avert sickness, special methods to keep adversity at bay, and so forth. They are the perfect articles.[12]

The practitioners who perform the practice should include the vajra master—a teacher endowed with the eight qualities, such as being a bearer of the sublime triple treasury of development and completion.[13] The designated vajra consort and four classes of regents down to the cook and sweeper should be appointed to their respective functions.[14] These, the perfect retinue, should be competent, free from the three defects of the vessel, and endowed with the five good qualities. In other words, it is this assemblage of qualified practitioners—the group that is great, medium, or small in size—that should carry out the practice.[15]

The method of practice is the following. The practitioners with the clear and stable concentration of both stages should engage in the rituals endowed with the four aspects of approach and accomplishment exactly as they are explained in the text. They should practice correctly in the sense of being free from the four causes of transgression, from duplicating the easier parts, or omitting the difficult ones. Thus, they embrace the practice by means of this perfect sadhana method.[16]

FOLLOWING THE SADHANA STRUCTURE WITH THE SPECIFIC FOUR ASPECTS OF APPROACH AND ACCOMPLISHMENT

The *Lamrim Yeshe Nyingpo* root text says:

> Request the site, take possession, cleanse, and guard it.
> Purify your being and draw the boundary in the outer,
>   inner, and innermost ways.
> Deliver, suppress, and imbue Matram with the splendor of
>   being the vajra realm.
> Perform the appropriate preparatory consecrations.
>
> Erect the mandala, arrange the articles, and seat the
>   practitioners.
> With the ritual of approach, purify the world and clear
>   obscurations.
> With the full approach, purify the inhabitants and gather
>   the siddhis.
> With the accomplishment, purify the mind and take
>   possession of the siddhis.
>
> During the six periods, make feast offerings to please and
>   mend.
> Subjugate the spying nyuley spirits, shower down the great
>   resplendence.
> Do not break the continuity of deity, mantra, or the
>   samadhi of emanation and absorption.

As a result of giving up distraction and practicing one-
 pointedly,§
The painted image smiles or the amrita boils with sound,§
The butter lamp lights by itself or the practice articles
 sparkle,§
The power of realization blazes forth, and there is mastery
 of wakefulness.§

After certain signs have occurred, for the great
 accomplishment,§
Receive from the deity at dusk, perform liberation at
 midnight,§
Union at dawn, and obtain the siddhis.§

For the second, the preparations for the sadhana include carefully ex-
amining the site, and when it is found to be suitable, asking for it with
payment and words of truth in case of an owner that is visible and has
material form. In the case of an invisible owner—the local gods who rule
the locality and region—you should ask for the site after satisfying them
with torma and oblation-drink (*serkyem*). Next, take possession of the site
by means of substances and visualization; cleanse it with mantra, mudra,
and samadhi; and guard it with the ten wrathful ones by planting their
daggers and performing their dance.

Purify your being in the outer way by the general procedures for purifying obscurations and gathering accumulations that include making
apologies, offering and giving, reciting scriptures, and so forth; in the inner way by the four great aspects of apology;[17] and in the innermost way
by performing the ritual of *Overturning the Depths of Narak*.

To draw the boundary line, the outer boundary is drawn by entrusting
it to the care of the four great kings. The intermediate boundary is drawn
by suppressing, with powerful force, those who have taken rebirth as destructive *damsi* demons due to violating the samayas of the Mantrayana.[18]
The *Galpo* describes the inner boundary in these words:

Put up the outer- and inner-gate placards
Of Dharma King and Amrita.[19]

Accordingly, assign the action *yama* and Kundali as guardians of the
outer and inner gates.[20] The secret boundary should be drawn with the

protection circle consisting of fivefold weaponry, Crazy Wrath, and so forth, and with the view of suchness.

To render minor obstructors incapable of causing disruption, you must deliver and elevate Matram Rudra, the king of obstructors, with forceful measures and suppress him with the imposing dance. Then, imbue his limbs, and so forth, with the splendor of being the eight charnel grounds and his torso with being the celestial palace, so that he turns into the vajra realm.[21]

Perform the appropriate sequence of preparatory consecrations of the deity in order to request the permission to draw the mandala, and perform those of the vase and disciples in order to confer empowerment.

Next, for preparing the shrine mandala, begin with sprinkling perfumed water, the five nectars, and so forth. Draw the action and wisdom lines with the ritual of blessings, and erect the authentic mandala consisting of the higher, medium, or lesser types of colored powder.

Then carefully arrange the various implements for the sadhana, the shrine, empowerment attire, siddhis and offering articles, and the ornaments. The male and female practitioners capable of performing the activities should be given their respective seats, invested with the peaceful or wrathful attire, and marked with the three glorious signs, so the *mamo* dakinis can recognize them to be on their side. Those who are beginners should be made suitable vessels with the ritual for inclusion.

Next, with the four aspects of approach and accomplishment, follow the set structure that belongs to the main practice. That is to say, having laid the basis with the three samadhis,[22] visualize the male and female yogis as being the corresponding number of deities with consort. Or, in the case of an aspirational training, visualize the practitioners as a whole to be the general mandala. Perform the emanation and reabsorption related to oneself as the samaya being and the deity as the wisdom being. Thus, carry out the activities correctly by means of possessing the threefold vividness.[23]

For the first third of however long the practice lasts, you should, by means of the ritual of approach, purify the world into being the celestial palace, so as to clear the obscuration of conceptual thoughts. During the second third, you should, by means of the full approach, purify the inhabitants into being the visible yet empty circle of deities, and thus gather the wealth of siddhis. During the last third, you should, by the intent of accomplishment, purify the mindstream into being the great self-existing wakefulness and thereby take possession of the two siddhis. For the duration of these phases, you should, during the six periods of day and night, make feast offerings to delight the deities and the vow-holders, to mend violations and breaches.

During the twelve intervals, apply the magic kilaya substance to subdue all the nyuley spirits who spy and seek to interrupt the practice, and invoke the twelve emissaries of the Glorious One to subjugate them.[24] At these occasions, since each of the devas who bestow siddhi also appear, you should bring forth majestic brilliance with ornaments and dresses, and shower down the great splendor upon yourself, the place, and the sadhana shrine objects.[25]

From the moment of commencing the sadhana until it has been brought to completion, do not depart from the continuity in which sights are the mandala of the deity, whatever you hear is the natural sounds of mantra, and thoughts are the continuity of dharmata. Do not interrupt the recitation and do not break the continuity of the samadhi of emanation and absorption. Instead, give up every type of mental distraction, including sleepiness, torpor and laziness, attachment and aversion, and, in this way, go about the practice one-pointedly.

When you have done that, among the general signs of accomplishment are—at best, in actuality, next best, in a meditative experience, or at least in a dream—that the painted samaya image on the sadhana shrine smiles, that the inner offering amrita boils with a bubbling sound and rising vapors, that the butter lamp lights by itself, that nectar flows from the torma, that the other practice articles sparkle, and, moreover, that you have a vision of the deity, receive predictions from the dakinis, or that lights, sounds, and sweet fragrance appear. The special signs are that the great power of experience and realization blazes forth without limitation, and that you attain mastery over the true state of original wakefulness through which you are able to transform things at will.

After these certain signs have occurred in full, for the concluding deeds, you should engage on the last night in the activities of great accomplishment. That is to say, at dusk, use the auspicious articles that include mamsa, *dagye, tsegal, madana,* and so forth, and invoke the key point of the heart-samaya in order to receive siddhis from the deity.[26]

At midnight, in the inner shrine of the temple,[27] perform deliverance involving the supreme and secondary objects to be delivered, the release of clinging by the proffering kingkaras as the deliverers, and the ritual of the seven marvels as the method. After that, receive the siddhis.[28]

At the break of dawn, a yogi who has the capacity should take a consort—a goddess, female naga, or a human woman of one of the five classes. She should be bathed and cleansed; she should don ornaments and be made a suitable vessel. As the approach, generate bliss with the arts of passion in the inner shrine. As the full approach, invoke the symbolic union while keeping in mind the three notions. As the accomplishment, enter the union by means of the four mudras and thereby recognize the four joys of descent. As the great accomplishment, draw the bodhichitta from the space with the vajra tongue, and bring the four joys of ascent to completion by applying reversal and distribution. In this way, by possessing the four aspects of approach and accomplishment belonging to the context of union, utilize union as the path and receive the siddhis.[29] Those whose training is merely an aspiration should receive the siddhis from the deity. In other cases, this can be accomplished by means of samadhi, and so forth, and having completed this, one should give the empowerment of the practice to others.

Perform the ritual for the residual and send the torma outside. In connection with special needs, invoke the subjugating torma as a *zor*. Request forgiveness and dissolve the mandala. Embark on the samadhi for daily activities, and seal with dedication and aspirations.

The way to undo the outer boundaries, the guarding of the site, and so forth, should be known from the framework scriptures for drubchen practice.

The Notes

PART III

Entering the Path of Wisdom

A SUPPLEMENTAL ORNAMENT TO THE LIGHT OF WISDOM

THE COMMENTARY ON THE LAMRIM YESHE NYINGPO,
THE ORAL INSTRUCTIONS OF PADMA—

A BACKGROUND TEACHING FOR THE
UNEXCELLED INNER THREE TANTRAS,
COMPILED AS MNEMONIC NOTES FROM
THE ORAL TEACHINGS OF THE LINEAGE MASTERS,
ENTITLED ENTERING THE PATH OF WISDOM
by Jamyang Drakpa *as recorded by* Jokyab Rinpoche

Supplemented with clarifying remarks by
Kyabje Tulku Urgyen Rinpoche,
and other lineage masters

Notes to Section 1

1. Padmasambhava and Jamgön Kongtrül, *The Light of Wisdom, the Conclusion* (Rangjung Yeshe Publications, 2013).

2. OM AMARANI DZIWANTIYÉ SOHA
   OM MANI PEMÉ HUNG HRIH
   OM AH HUNG BENZA GURU PEMA SIDDHI HUNG
   OM AH HUNG BENZA GURU PEMA TÖTRENGTSAL BENZA SAMAYA DZA
   SIDDHI PHALA HUNG ah

3. The four yogas are great emptiness, compassionate magic, single mudra, and elaborate mudra, which are followed by group assembly. [tr.]

4. *The Light of Wisdom,* v. 2, p. 111. [tr.]

5. The ten signs are the four daytime signs, including smoke, a mirage, a firefly, and clear space. The sun, moon, an eclipse (or blackness), a comet (with a tail of lightning and flames), and the sky image are manifestations of empty *dharmata,* which, together with (a five-colored sphere of) light, are experienced mainly at night. Moreover, you may see empty forms such as the light of a huge lotus flower, particles, stars, crescents, and the like. Jamdrak said that these signs principally resemble the above-mentioned attainment of proficiency in the three fields—the form of the deity appearing as either a perceptual object, in the experience of the senses by someone else, or as a mental object. But, he added, they are different from having a vision of the deity. He then told a story about a lama who, when experiencing empty forms, saw the *sambhogakaya* deity with brilliant ornaments, the eyes looking heavenward, and so forth. [JR]

   For the discussion of the attainment of proficiency in the three fields, see *The Light of Wisdom,* v. 2, p. 117. [tr.]

6. The inner signs are that body and voice are both free of discomfort and fretfulness. [JR]

7. In his *Commentary on Sangtik Yumkha,* Jamgön Kongtrül writes the following: "Through perfecting the vivid presence of the great development stage that is appearance and existence as the manifest ground, the extraordinary signs are that the ordinary clinging to perceptions is purified into being the deity's mandala, you attain the eyes and superknowledges, gain mastery over miracles, and, in the same life, accomplish the vidyadhara level of maturation." [tr.]

8. The *Essence of Secrets: The Root Tantra of the Magical Net* mentions the six *siddhis* that are the source of qualities as follows:

> This becomes nectar
> And serves to cure the 404 types of illness;
> Enjoyments are obtained, and the lower realms are purified.
> All things can be transformed into something else.

On the basis of transformation, like poisonous food that is marked with a syllable A, and through the actions of dissolution and stifling, it is transformed into the nectar of supreme medicine. By eating a little of it, all your wishes will be fulfilled. Emanating and reabsorbing rays of light from the letter, other's wishes can be fulfilled in accordance with the way practice is directed. By placing the letter that emanates and reabsorbs on the body of a sick person, the diseases involving wind, bile, or phlegm will be expelled. Alternatively, there are diseases of imaginary demonic forces, of momentary circumstances, of the aggregation of elements, and diseases naturally arising from previous actions. These four types of disease can each be divided into one hundred and one subtypes. This adds up to 404 diseases, which are all eliminated through this method, and well-being secured.

By imagining a syllable TRAM made of precious substances that emanates and reabsorbs rays of light to make offerings, all desirable enjoyments can be received. The letters of the three elements purify the obscurations related to birth in the lower realms. Also, each and every aspect of phenomena that appears can be turned into its opposite, like dryness into water, charcoal into a tree, or sand into gold. [JR]

"Dissolution and stifling" refers to the visualization of dissolving seed syllables (like the RAM, YAM, KHAM, OM, AH, and HUNG in the *tsok* practice) into the real substances, which are impure and might be poisonous. Mixing with the substances, the syllables literally "tame" or "stifle" them. In other words, this eliminates poison and impurity. [tr.]

9. Concerning "the five *siddhis* of the five elements," the same tantra says:

> Space becomes solid *vajras*;
> Even fire is burnt;
> Everything becomes like the flow of water.
> The elements of the world are disintegrated;
> It is totally emptied, [sun and moon] will fall [from the sky].

The commentary explains that in space the practitioner visualizes a syllable HUNG, and imagines there are stairs of *vajras*. The stairs become extremely hard. The practitioner places a syllable RAM in his palm. It transforms into the blazing fire of wisdom that burns even the ordinary fire. Likewise, he arranges a KHAM syllable that becomes the water of wisdom and purifies everything in its flow. The syllable YAM becomes the wind of wisdom that sweeps the world away and disintegrates it. Placing a syllable A that emanates and reabsorbs rays of light, all the realms of the world are emptied, and the zenith is sent to the nadir, for example. [JR]

10. The eight siddhis of minor activities: Again the root tantra says,

> Summoning, expelling, binding, releasing,
> Curing, killing, defeating, and bringing victory
> Can be accomplished through this *samadhi*.

The commentary explains that through *samadhi* the practitioners can summon the different objects of accomplishment, like consorts, enemies, and obstacle makers, and so on; they can expel beings and drive them away to another land; bind enemies, thieves, and so on; release the bonds of curses of harmful influences, and so on; cure the sick and make [sick] infants well, and so on; completely destroy enemies and obstacle makers; defeat other factions; bring victory to their own side—these different activities are accomplished in accordance with the way practice is directed. These are as given by the Zurpa tradition. There are also some slightly different explanations by Longchenpa that you should learn about. [JR]

For the instructions by Longchenpa, see Lama Chönam and Sangye Khandro. *The Guhyagarbha Tantra: Secret Essence Definitive Nature Just as It Is* (Ithaca, N.Y.: Snow Lion Publications, 2011), p. 315. [tr.]

11. These are the practice of the single warrior, the union practice of means and knowledge, and the practice of group assembly. [JR]

12. The five articles that have been presented above in the *ganachakra* section are also the articles mentioned for great accomplishment. Furthermore, Buddhaguhya explains that the *Magical Net* mentions the five path articles as follows:

> Samaya, view, samadhi,
> Bodhichitta, and compassion
> Are the five supreme substances to bring to the full.

The practice-support shrine articles, and so on, are presented clearly in the commentary. [JR]

For the *ganachakra* section cited, see *The Light of Wisdom*, v. 2, p. 130 and p. 201, n. 194. [tr.]

13. "Endowed with the eight qualities": As it is said,

> (1–3) He is a teacher who holds the treasury of the teachings, (4) has perfected the stream of empowerment,

(5) Has a sense of responsibility, is versed in the (6) tantras and (7) rituals;

(8) Holding the pith instructions, he has attained warmth in the practice: These are the eight qualities he holds. [JR]

14. "Regents down to the cook and sweeper": The consorts are Samantabhadri and so forth. The powerful yogis, the timekeepers, the observer, caretakers, cooks, sweepers, and male and female servants form the general *vajra* assembly, from a hundred to a hundred thousand or more. [JR]

The powerful yogis eliminate obstacles, the timekeepers indicate the time when obstructing forces are coming and the time for practice in general, and the observer knows the obstacles that are coming. [KYG]

15. The three defects of the vessel: (1) Not paying attention is to be like a container turned upside down; (2) not remembering is to be like a container with a hole in it; (3) mixing what you hear with mental afflictions is to be like a container with poison inside.

The five good qualities are (1–3) the three qualities that are the opposite of the defects of the vessel, together with (4) great faith, discipline, and wisdom, and (5) little hypocrisy, pride, or doubt. The list in the *Magical Net* is different:

Entrust this to (1) suitable vessels, who are (2) noble, (3) kindhearted, and (4) reliable;
This should be given to those (5) who abandon their body and possessions in generosity,

Also, followers endowed with the six qualities are presented as follows in this tantra,

Diligently make offerings to the one who reveals [the path]; by achieving clear realization,
All *samayas,* mantras, and mudras
are known without degeneration. Being endowed with the necessities . . . [JR]

For the quotations from the *Magical Net,* see Lama Chönam and Sangye Khandro. *The Guhyagarbha Tantra: Secret Essence Definitive Nature Just as It Is* (Ithaca, N.Y.: Snow Lion Publications, 2011), pp. 89 and 53, respectively. [tr.]

16. Jamdrak said that the "four causes of transgression" are the four doorways of downfall. [JR]

17. The four great aspects of apology are of body, speech, mind, and their combination. [tr.]

18. Downfall committed after having trained in the three *pitakas* of sutra teachings are the cause of birth as a demon. The four kings protect against them at the outer border. At the intermediate border, they suppress the *damsi* demons born from *samaya*-breakers who have impaired their precepts after having entered the vehicles of the three outer tantras of Mantrayana. [JR]

19. These are Yamaraja, the Dharma King, and Amrita Kundali. [tr.]

20. The karmic activities of the action *yama* subdue the world; the wisdom activities are accomplished by the deity Amrita Kundali. So you recite the mantras of both. [JR]

21. The way to deliver those who, after having entered the door of the three inner tantras of Mantrayana, break *samayas* and give birth to *rudras,* is the following. There are three types of *rudras* corresponding respectively to eternalist views, nihilist views, and wrong views; or in connection to grasping at the self in body, in speech, and in mind. Delivering them has three purposes: Delivering symbolic *rudras* leads to the realization of identity-lessness; as their stomachs are transformed into charnel-ground fields, they are naturally counted among *dakas* and *dakinis*; taming the greater obstructing forces naturally results in the taming of the lesser obstructing forces. [JR]

22. The three *samadhis* are the *samadhi* of suchness and so on—this is easy. [JR]

23. "Possessing the threefold vividness" refers to vividness of self as the *samaya* being, vividness of the deity as the wisdom being, and vividness of emanation and reabsorption of rays. When visualizing vividly the emanation and reabsorption of rays, continuously make offerings to the victorious ones, do not interrupt the purification of sentient beings' obscurations, and maintain the reception of the *siddhis* for yourself—these are the three things that shouldn't be interrupted. [JR]

24. In general, *nyuley* spirits are presented very clearly in the *Kagye* and in the *Lama Gongdü,* as well as in Ratna Lingpa's *Secret Gathering of the Compassionate One.* Yet, the specific approach of the Chokling Tersar is as follows. The twelve *nyuleys* who create obstacles to the practice and wander about meddling at the twelve times of day are given in the original terma in the *Practice Arrangement that Gathers the Entire Intent of the Root Heart Practice*: (1) The obstructing *nyuleys* who create obstacles at sunset are the Shatring daughters cawing like crows; (2) likewise, those who create obstacles in the evening are the black female robbers; (3) at nighttime, the ignorance-maintainers; (4) at midnight, the *ranus* of desire; (5) in the

middle of the night, the *duntses* of aversion; (6) at the break of dawn, the Hedö daughter of the sun; (7) at sunrise, White Space Dust; (8) in the morning, the black female *nagas* and *rakshasas*; (9) at midday, the four families of seals of the *nagas*; 10) in the late afternoon, the border *terang* demons; (11) in the early afternoon, the female owners of the land who spread epidemics; (12) in the early evening, the *maras* and *damsi* demons of *samaya*-breakers. They are tamed by the twelve messengers who are their antidotes: Ekadzati, Seyijadra, the Great Red One, Dragon-Faced Dakini, the Great Blazing One, Hundred-Headed She-Wolf, Great She-Crow, Blazing-Mouth Crocodile, Great White One, Rakshasi Form, Tsangpa Lingpamo. There are also twelve oppressing substances and mantras. [JR]

25. "The devas who bestow siddhi": (1) At sunrise, from the east, appear the deity Korisidha who brings blessing after the sun has risen and Brahma, Indra, and so on; (2) in the morning, from the southeast, Pulkakrangta and Rishi Lord of Medicine; (3) at midday, from the south, Chorivyakri and Yami, and so on; (4) in the late afternoon, from the southwest, Ghasmakangka, and all the *vidyadharas, dakas,* and *dakinis*; (5) in the early evening, from the west, Pramosrila and *yidams* and *sugatas*; (6) in the evening, from the northwest, Smeshakha, and the dharma protector Magön; (7) at nighttime, from the north, Baithashvana and the eight classes of gods of wealth; (8) at midnight, from the northeast, Tsendahulu and Ganchen Shugdro; (9) in the middle of the night, from the zenith, the seven of the twenty-eight *ishvaris* who separate to perform the seven pacifying activities, and the Three Jewels; (10) at the break of dawn, from intermediate space, the seven *ishvaris* who accomplish the enriching activities, and Tsangri Palgön who accomplishes the two purposes; (11) at sunrise, from Ling, the seven *ishvaris* who accomplish the magnetizing activities, the *naga* king, and all the bodhisattvas; (12) in the morning, from all sides, the seven *ishvaris* accomplishing subjugating activities, bodhisattvas, offering goddesses, and *vidyadharas* by the millions. Each of them grants *siddhis* at their specific time. [JR]

26. *Mamsa* is meat; *dagye,* yogurt; *tsegal,* food; *madana,* alcoholic beverage; and *khurwa,* fruits. Together, with the three whites and three sweets, cooked rice, and so on, they form the offerings of "various grains" and "various food." In the twenty-second topic of the *Heruka Galpo,* they are given as follows:

> *Vajra* substance (food) and *galche* (yogurt and *chemar*),
> *Jamdé* (butter) and *tü,* [buttery hard cheese] with sweet substances
> and *datrom* (bread),
> *Tsetri* (acidic substance), *dzage* (alcoholic beverage), and *dzakshi*
> (meat),

Drenmo (vegetables), *shawamo* (light food), and *kuntugyuk* (salt),
Amrigün (human flesh), *drooma* (elephant meat), *agaru* (horse
  meat),
Naling (cow meat), *gigye* (dog meat), and so on—all these you
  should offer. [JR]

27. Traditionally, the temples where *ganachakra* feasts were practiced had three shrines, one inside the other: the outer, inner, and secret shrine. [KYG]

28. This endnote has been moved to *Light of Wisdom, Volume III,* restricted book.

29. The *Secret Essence Tantra* says,

Regarding goddesses, female *nagas,* and low-caste women—
By making distinctions or without making these distinctions,
Through the approach, full approach,
Accomplishment and great accomplishment . . . [JR]

Drubchen Arrangement and Overview

ORGYEN TOPGYAL RINPOCHE

It is incredibly good fortune to receive teachings and empowerments from qualified masters, and to ripen the fruit of receiving such empowerments by joining in a drubchen, such as this one,[1] even if it is only for seven days. To get such an opportunity doesn't come easily; if it were easy, everybody would already avail themselves of such, but the fact is that there are only a few people who ever acquire such merit. So you really should make all the necessary efforts to receive the teachings and be able to fully practice them. Now those of you who are here, rejoice that you have made the commitment to practice in a drubchen and realize the preciousness of this occasion.

Yeshe Tsogyal said that to receive terma teachings, and to be able to practice them, is a sign of incredibly good karma and the result of the aspirations that individuals have made in the presence of Guru Rinpoche himself, while Guru Rinpoche said that to practice for seven days in a drubchen is equal to staying in retreat for seven years.

During the practice, in order to assure that everything is auspicious, the drubchen text states that each day we should bathe, wear fine clothing, recite the Hundred-Syllable mantra, and pay homage to the deities. This is important when practicing Vajrayana, particularly during the invocation and the descent of blessings, when it is said that we should dress in the very best clothing we have in order to emphasize the magnificence. It is also important to be wide awake so as to be able to bring forth the clarity of rigpa. Everything originates interdependently, and especially during the practice, we need to make sure that we carry out all our actions in the best possible way.

On the afternoon of the first day, we begin with the practices for securing the land. This is done in order to request permission to use the

---

1. Tukdrub Barchey Künsel Drubchen at Lerab Ling, France, August 2010.

27

particular property on which the drubchen is taking place. Hence this needs to be done genuinely and sincerely at the place where the mandala is going to be established. First, one requests permission to use the property from the owner, and next, one makes a similar request to the female spirits who reside there; in Tibetan these are known as *tenmas*. First, one offers them torma and serkyem, and then makes the request to use their land for the practice. Once we've requested the land and obtained permission to use it, we ourselves must take care of the land and make sure we treat it properly. To do this, we plant a ritual dagger, known as a *phurba*, in the ground. While doing this, we visualize the phurba as Hayagriva, asserting that he is the one responsible for taking care of and protecting the property.

Then comes a purification practice to cleanse the land. The vajra master holds another phurba that he will place; this phurba represents the buddhas of the five families, and on the basis of that, there will be a cleansing practice. Next, in order to erect the mandala and be able to practice without obstacles, we need to expel all the negative forces. To do this, we offer the *gektor,* the torma used to lead the obstructing forces away. Then, after all negativity has been expelled, we need to erect the protection sphere or dome. This is done by planting ten phurbas, which are by nature the ten wrathful ones. That concludes the practice of securing the land.

The second section is establishing the boundaries within which the drubchen will actually take place. This step is found in all practices. However, it isn't found only in dharma practice, but in worldly activities as well; for example, just as there are borders between countries, there is also a dividing line between the great peace of nirvana and the suffering of samsara.

Specifically, there are three boundaries that need to be established: the outer, inner, and secret boundaries. To set the outer boundaries, we go around the temple in the four directions, and we request the four guardian kings to prevent any obstacles from entering and any blessings from leaving the designated area during the seven days of practice. We do this by going to where they reside, making offerings, requesting their assistance, reminding them of their obligations to protect the Dharma, and erecting the four poles. In terms of the obstacles, there are some untamable negative forces that cannot be brought to the teachings, so with great compassion we request that these hostile beings be suppressed until the time that they themselves are actually able to bring forth some compassion.

Two protectors are placed at the entrance: the one facing outward is Yamantaka, and the other, facing inward, is Amrita Kundali. After this, all the practitioners enter through that door while being purified with water and smoke. This completes establishing the outer boundaries.

In order to establish the inner boundaries, we recite the Matram mantra[31] to dispel ego clinging.[2] Matram Rudra is "delivered and elevated," and within that space we'll be visualizing the palace.[3] Once we've expelled the king of all the obstructing forces, the lesser obstructing forces won't be able to create trouble.

To establish the secret boundary, the vajra master will enter into the Samadhi in which one realizes that all obstacles come from the mind, and the mind itself is utterly empty; therefore, there are no obstructing forces. By doing so, he establishes the secret boundary.

After the boundaries have been established, we begin the three preliminary practices: drawing the mandala, preparing the vase, and preparing the students. The preliminary practices in connection with the deity entail drawing two kinds of lines: karmic lines and wisdom lines. First, one establishes the wisdom lines in space, then the karmic lines representing the mandala are drawn on the ground, and finally these two sets of lines are merged. Within the Nyingma tradition, there are three ways to draw the mandala on the ground: with colored sand, with paint on cloth, or with heaps of grains. Here we will use a mandala painted on cloth. This concludes the first preliminary practice that is related to the deity.

The next preliminary practice is for preparing the vase, or *bumpa* in Tibetan. Water is poured into the vase and mixed with blessed substances. One then visualizes that the water in the bumpa is the deity. There are different ways of doing this practice; the best and most elaborate is to have as many vases as there are deities in the mandala. The second, middling approach is to have two vases, the activity vase and the main vase.

After that comes the preliminary practice for preparing the student. If there are people who have not received the empowerment, this is the time when the empowerment is bestowed. If the empowerment cannot

---

2. This is a mantra to suppress Matram Rudra, the original ego demon.
3. According to the *Lamrim*, "with forceful measures deliver and elevate Matram Rudra, the king of obstructors, and suppress him with the imposing dance. Then imbue his limbs and so forth with the splendor of being the eight charnel grounds and the torso with being the celestial palace so that he turns into the vajra realm."

be given, there is a practice for giving blessings. Through the blessings, the students are introduced to the actuality that all the components of body, speech, and mind, the elements, the aggregates [skandhas], and the sense faculties [ayatanas] are actually the vajra body, speech, and mind. This section also contains a teaching that explains the different samayas that must be kept. That then completes the stages of the preliminary practices.

Next is the request, in which there are two phases. In the first phase, people who have done the practice are separated from those who haven't, and then everybody is brought together again. If the participants are essentially equal, as is often the case in the West, then everyone can just sit wherever they want.

Next, having established the mandala, one must arrange the ornaments for it. There are many different ornaments that need to be placed on the mandala, and each ornament has a particular significance. These include representations of the enlightened body, speech, mind, qualities, and activities; all the substances of long life, such as the pills, the vase, the arrow, and the *chang* (beer). There are also the vases, the skull cups, and the different silken ornaments around the mandala, such as pendants, victory banners, and the tiger skin. Furthermore, if the sacred medicine known as *mendrub* is being made during the drubchen, the palace of mendrub is also required.

The following list, from this drubchen, will give you an idea of the kind of objects that were used and placed within the mandala: To represent the enlightened body of the deity, a small statue known as a *kutsab*, from *Kunsang Tuktig*, which is a terma revelation of Chokgyur Dechen Lingpa; to represent the enlightened speech, a copy of the *Sheldam Nyingjang*, which is the most important text among the revelations of Chokgyur Lingpa; to represent enlightened mind, the vajra and bell of King Trisong Deutsen, which was revealed by Chokgyur Dechen Lingpa in Yeshe Namkhey Dzod's terma place; for the qualities, a skull cup that has been used in over a hundred drubchens, and which contains all the blessed substances; to represent the enlightened activity, a terma of Nyang Ra'i Nyima Ozer. To make the mendrub,[33] we mixed together thirty different *pabta*, which is a portion of mendrub that you mix with the old genuine mendrub, some of which have been revealed as termas.

Next comes the second part of the request. The ideal is to have the vajra king sit on a lion throne, and next to him his consort on a throne of flowers. Then, there is a throne for the vajra regent, as well as thrones in the four directions for the deities of the four families—karma, ratna, padma, and vajra. And finally, thirteen lower thrones and vajra seats. In brief, there is the vajra throne, the lion throne of the Vajra King in the middle, then the female practitioners to the left, and the male practitioners to the right. At that point, you sprinkle a little beer, although, because they represent the deities, formally one should sprinkle it for each participant, individually requesting each one to take a seat. Each person should then really practice assuming the vajra confidence of being that particular deity. Later in the practice, there is also an extra section that is added in as offerings to the wrathful deities.

All the deities residing in the space above also need to be actualized, so we bless everything—the place, the people, the outer environment, the inner environment, the substances—into the nature of the wisdom deities. And with that, the preliminary phases are concluded.

The main part of the practice will last for seven days. During this time, the actual sadhanas are repeated three times during the day and three times at night. During each of these sessions, you also expel the negative forces and request the blessings to descend. The most important thing when we engage in a drubchen is that the actual life-force of the practice, the mantra recitation, continues uninterrupted during the entire practice.

Throughout the practice, it is crucial to understand the three statements that all appearances are deities; all sounds are mantra; and all thoughts are samadhi. The first, "all appearances are the deity," means that throughout the drubchen, you need to maintain the recognition that you are the deity. You do not just do it once when reciting the lines of the visualization; you need to continually recognize this fact. If you get distracted and forget, you must recall it again. To say that all appearances, including your own body, are the deity means that the three aspects of visualization, the clear visualization, remembering purity, and vajra confidence need to be practiced as one.

"All sounds are mantra" simply means that whenever you hear a sound, it is mantra. While reciting the mantra, you also emanate rays of light, purifying and making offerings, and then you draw them back in where they dissolve, granting us the siddhis and accumulating merit. There are also four phases of recitation: the moon with the garland of stars, the whirling firebrand, the king's emissaries, and the beehive that has broken open. During the drubchen, the most important is the last one. Just like when a beehive has been broken open, all the bees swarm around it buzzing, all the syllables of the mantra are buzzing with their own sounds. For example, each of the twelve syllables of the mantra OM AH HUNG BENDZA GURU PEMA SIDDHI HUNG resound over and over again, creating a droning buzz of all twelve together.

The third point, "all thoughts are samadhi," means that you shouldn't let ordinary thoughts that relate to past, present, and future invade your mind; instead remain concentrated in samadhi and focus on the practice you are doing.

To put it simply, these three can be summed up by saying: do not let your body, speech, and mind fall under the influence of delusion. Of course, it is impossible for beginners to be completely free of delusion, but you should do your best to diminish deluded appearances and to increase pure appearances. Maintain the continuity of the mantra and samadhi throughout the drubchen, and do not allow the ritual activities to dissipate into ordinary behavior. Relate to all that you do in an extraordinary way, for example, regard your clothing as the ornaments of the deities, and when eating, view your meal as a ganachakra feast offering.

It is said that if everyone from the vajra king down to the vajra sweeper—the person who cleans up the temple—maintains the continuity of actualizing the deity, an incredible power is generated.

After seven days of practice, we receive the siddhis. There are many ways of receiving the siddhis and many things to say about it, but that will have to wait for another time. Once we've received the siddhis, each of the mandalas, one after the other, are dissolved. The placards for the four kings that we used to set up will be removed, the boundaries will be taken down, and the phurbas will be raised. Some milk is poured on the tip of the phurbas, and the mandala itself is dismantled. The ceremony concludes with the dedication and aspiration prayers, including the aspiration associated with the offering of lamps in connection with this mandala. Finally, we dedicate any benefits for the sake of all sentient beings, and also make prayers to ensure that everything will be auspicious.

It is a truly incredible opportunity to participate in such a profound practice as this, and you should rejoice when you have such an opportunity. The Dharma is not just a bunch of theory to discuss and ponder; you need to actually practice it. Spending your entire life receiving teachings but not really practicing them, and instead continuing with your ordinary worldly tasks, will not result in much benefit. Yet, if you take just seven days to be diligent and joyful while engaging in a drubchen, great benefit can be attained, not only for you, but for all beings everywhere.

DRUBCHEN[1]

LAMA PUTSE PEMA TASHI

[1]. This section of *Great Accomplishment* is a commentary on the *Ngakso* Drubchen, the *Ocean Of Amrita,* A Tantric Mending Purification Practice. We have tried to make the text as general as possible but have opted to use certain parts of the translation for clarifying the explanation. All quoted texts, either in verse form or enclosed in parentheses, are reproduced with permission of Rangjung Yeshe Translations.

Tukdrub Barchey Künsel Mandala

Introduction

Please study this commentary while maintaining the thought, "For the sake of all sentient beings as innumerable as the sky is vast, I will attain true and complete enlightenment. In order to achieve this goal, I will carefully study these teachings and put them into practice with pure motivation and the proper behavior."

When giving teachings, it is standard practice for Buddhist teachers to begin by encouraging their students to assume the proper motivation. Motivation has to do with attitude, how we think, and how we regard the teachings. For instance, a toxic attitude of improper motivation is to greedily desire the teachings for your own profit. That approach is like a musk hunter who wants to chase the musk deer just for the musk that he can sell, while he abandons the rest of the deer. The right motivation is to acknowledge that you have faults that need to be corrected—in other words, regarding yourself as a sick person, the Dharma as a healing medicine, and the teacher as a skilled doctor. In that way, when you receive the teachings and apply them as instructed, you are sure to recover the state of buddhahood.

In this way, there is a motivation to avoid and a motivation to adopt. Similarly, some behaviors should be avoided and other behaviors adopted. Some things to avoid are basic etiquette. For example, traditionally, unless one is sick, one should not attend teachings wearing a hat or carrying an umbrella, walking stick, or other paraphernalia simply for show. If someone is sick, it's fine for them to wear a warm hat, or if you have to sit outside, then to sit in the shade of an umbrella. Of course, one should not bring weapons to a Dharma gathering. The behavior to adopt is to embrace the act of listening with all six *paramitas:* generosity, discipline, patience, diligence, concentration, and knowledge. Sometimes people think that the paramitas can only be practiced one at a time, but this is not true. In any situation, one can practice all six paramitas. In the context of receiving teachings, to provide a seat for the teacher, to put flowers out, and so forth are acts of generosity. To make the place nice and tidy without harming any insects, to make sure the dust settles, and the room looks pleasant takes discipline. To bear the hardship of heat or cold, sitting through long teachings, and so forth, develops patience. To exert oneself in being fully present and listening to the teachings is training in diligence. Refraining from letting one's attention stray is training in concentration. And last, to clear up any doubts or uncertainty and become clear about the meaning of the teachings is to achieve discriminating knowledge (Sanskrit *prajna*, Tibetan *sherab*). Thus, it isn't so difficult to embrace receiving teachings with all six paramitas.

When it comes to the context of the Vajrayana teachings, including this one on drubchen, the great accomplishment ritual titled *Ocean of Amrita*, those receiving teachings should have already received the ripening empowerment. Once you have received the ripening empowerment, then you can receive the liberating instructions. We should understand that.

The Dharma deals with improving oneself, with finding one's way out of the suffering of samsara. After all, becoming liberated and free of suffering is what Dharma practice is all about. It is not all fun and games: often it is difficult and plain hard work—that is why, when we look around we don't find that many Dharma practitioners. It is not so easy to change one's habits and pursue a life in accord with Dharma. Pursuing aims of temporary happiness and pleasure, which most people spend their lives on, is usually more fun—at least in the short term, anyway. A Dharma practitioner, on the other hand, must be willing to undertake the hardship of changing their habits and not succumbing to disturbing emotions. Milarepa's life is a perfect example of the dedication that one must have. Of course, many others have also achieved complete awakening in a single lifetime, but Milarepa exemplifies what is required to undertake the difficulties that this usually demands.

If you just give in to the ordinary way of dualistic mind, you will just continue on the same old track of negative habitual tendencies. Instead, it is important to become more mindful. Continually question yourself: "What exactly is happening in my stream of being? Is it positive? Is it negative? What am I doing? Why am I reacting like this?"

Early Kadampa meditators would put two equal-sized heaps of pebbles, one black and one white, in front of where they were sitting. When they noticed that they were getting involved in a negative thought or emotion, they would take a black pebble and put it in a separate pile. If they noticed they were involved in a positive frame of mind, like love, compassion, or renunciation, they would take a white pebble and put that in another pile. When they checked at the end of the day, in the beginning they would see a large black pile sitting in front of them. But over time, training more and more, there would be a few more white pebbles. Applying themselves day in and day out to the mind-trainings, eventually the pile would be all white.

On the other hand, you can practice in a way that does not require hardship, where you do not have to do anything physically taxing like prostrations or circumambulations. You can just sit, and this great magician called "mind" can conjure up some wonderful magic. For example, you can form a beautiful positive attitude and combine it with your natural breathing. When you breathe out, form an attitude of loving-kindness and compassion: "May all beings have happiness. May all beings be free of suffering." Imagine that all your pleasure, merit, and enjoyments are carried by your breath to all beings in all directions. Then, when inhaling, imagine that all beings' suffering, misery, pain, sickness, negative karma, disturbing emotions, and so forth are drawn into you. Pray that it will land right on top of the hard lump of ego-clinging that you carry around, dissolving and melting it. That is an excellent form of Dharma practice and creating merit.

Dharma practice means moving forward on the path, because, unless you actually apply yourself to the path, you will never become any nearer to enlightenment. In this regard, there are basically two kinds of practice: the long road, Sutra, and the short road of Tantra. But always remember that even if you follow the Tantric path of Vajrayana, the Hinayana and the Mahayana teachings are automatically included. You should never regard yourself as being a Vajrayana practitioner exclusively.

At times, there may appear to be conflicts. For example, the Hinayana teachings prohibits many things that Vajrayana teaches are fine, so it is easy to get confused and wonder which is right. The rule of thumb is that you should always follow the higher vehicle, but in the proper way. For instance, the *shravaka* teachings say that one should not eat meat or drink wine, while in the Vajrayana teachings this is required in certain ritual contexts, such as feast offerings in which consecrated meat and wine are consumed while regarding them as nectar.

The main focus of the *Ocean of Amrita* is mending and purifying the vows that one has taken. If one decides to refrain from doing something and vows not to, it can accumulate considerable merit. It all depends on attitude. For example, a hunter can vow not to kill any animals, and he will gain a lot of merit by keeping his vow. On the other hand, if he goes hunting but merely fails to kill anything, he doesn't gain any merit—it just wasn't a good hunt.

The main hindrance to progress along the path to enlightenment is actually the breaches of one's vows and commitments (*samayas*). Usually we tell ourselves that we are fine: "I haven't spoken badly about my guru, let alone physically harmed him. I do my best to get along with my Dharma brothers and sisters, and I practice and make offerings almost every day. So I haven't really broken any of my samayas." However the moment you take your first real empowerment, you commit yourself to the intent of the four empowerments of original wakefulness—and can you honestly say that you have upheld these without a break? Just the first of these, the vase empowerment, affirms that whatever appears and exists from the beginning is utterly pure, which means that the universe is a buddha field, all beings are male and female deities, and so on. The very moment we form any concept based on clinging to the notion of a concrete reality—such as, "This is a rock. That is a man. That is a dog"—we have broken the samaya of the first empowerment. Therefore, as we are constantly breaking our samayas, it is necessary to continually apologize for our failings and mend our commitments, which is done by the mending and purification practice known in Tibetan as *sojong*.

Just as it is important to wash our clothes regularly to keep them clean, and mend them when they are in need of repair, no matter what level of Buddhist practice you might be involved in, it is also important to regularly mend and purify your commitments. It is practically impossible for ordinary people, like ourselves, to keep any of the three levels of precepts, whether those of individual liberation (*pratimoksha*), the bodhisattva trainings, or the samayas of Vajrayana. The tendency to go against the precepts constantly increases due to strengthening the habit of breaking promises and not sticking to what we have committed ourselves to.

Therefore, it is absolutely necessary to atone for our failings by regularly doing a mending and purification practice.

As Buddhists, our aim is to attain complete true enlightenment. Just like when travelling on a journey there are different vehicles (*yana*) that we can take. The Hinayana teachings are comparable to going by foot; the Mahayana path is similar to taking a bus or train; and the Vajrayana is like taking an airplane. From this, you can see that there is a big difference in the speed and effectiveness of each vehicle, but the inherent risks increase as well. Going by foot is quite safe and little harm can come of it, yet if something on an airplane isn't properly repaired, a crash can easily occur, killing all on board. In the same way, in Vajrayana, if you can keep your commitments, all will go well, and you can achieve enlightenment within this very lifetime. However, there is also a great risk, because if you break your commitments and don't mend them, at the moment of death there is a strong likelihood that you will go straight to Vajra Hell without even passing through the bardo. On the other hand, if you keep all your commitments pure, upon death you will achieve complete awakening and immediately merge with the vastness of the innate nature of all things.

Many people think that being a monk or a nun is the most difficult, being a bodhisattva is easier, and practicing Vajrayana is the easiest because you can do anything you want: drink alcohol, have sex, and so on, but this is not the case. The vows of individual liberation that monks and nuns must take are primarily concerned with what one says and does. The Vajrayana commitments, on the other hand, deal with one's mental attitude and viewpoint. For example, if you have an enemy and you think, "That guy destroyed my father's business; he deserves to suffer. I must take revenge," but you don't act on it and decide, "I might as well just forget about it. It's a negative attitude to have." By refraining from actually committing an evil act, you haven't broken your vows according to pratimoksha; however, according to the Vajrayana, the very moment you harbor a negative attitude you totally break your root samayas.

When asked about the three sets of precepts, the great master, Lord Atisha, replied, "I took the pratimoksha vows when I was young and I have never broken any of them. I have kept all 253 monks' vows pure. I also took the bodhisattva vows though I didn't keep them perfectly and some got damaged. However, I always restored the bodhisattva vow on the same day that I broke it. But I cannot count the number of times that

I have violated my samayas in regard to the Vajrayana." That's how diffi-cult it is to keep the Vajrayana commitments. So if someone as noble and enlightened as Lord Atisha could not keep them, then certainly there is little hope that the likes of us will be able to.

Even though we have had the good fortune to connect with the teach-ings and practices of Vajrayana, we are still ordinary people who still get attached, dull, angry, conceited, jealous—in short, we still get caught up in all the disturbing emotions. You can't just pretend that this doesn't happen to you, and you must recognize that because of this, we further perpetuate the suffering of samsara.

Negative karma is created in various ways. One way is through ig-norance: simply not knowing what is right and what is wrong. But just because we don't know doesn't mean that we are not responsible for our actions. You may inadvertently step on an insect, but it is still killed. So out of ignorance you have crushed a sentient being. The next cause of negative karma is lack of respect, especially when you lack appreciation for the qualities of the yidam deities that are always present, as well as denigrating your own and others' intrinsic qualities. The third cause is carelessness. Not maintaining vigilance and presence of mind, we slip into negative patterns. The fourth cause is the tendency to get caught up in selfish emotions. And last is forgetfulness: we don't keep our practice in mind. Because we forget what we have been taught or what we have been introduced to, we fall into old habits and remain involved in all sorts of unconducive behavior.

We might as well admit to ourselves that our minds are continuously ruled by these negative karmic patterns. As this is the case, it is impera-tive that we restore our commitments and purify the negative karma that we constantly accumulate. There is an old proverb that there is only one thing good about karmic wrongdoing; it can be cleared up. That is the main purpose of great accomplishment rituals (*drubchen*).

Within the collection of Chokgyur Lingpa's termas is a cycle known as *Tukdrub Barchey Künsel* that contains great accomplishment practices (drubchen). The one I am going to discuss here is titled *Ocean of Amrita* (*Ngakso Drubchen*), the main purpose of which is the mending and purifi-cation of one's Vajrayana commitments. The text for this ritual is includ-ed in the seventeenth chapter of *The Essence Manual of Oral Instructions* (*Sheldam Nyingjang*). During this nine-day ritual, one visualizes oneself as Padmasambhava with the wrathful deities inside one's skull and the peaceful deities within one's heart. There are an incredible number of details to visualize in a great accomplishment practice, but the completion stage is woven into the practice too. However, it is important to keep in mind that the main principle of the ritual is to fully mend and purify our vows and commitments, especially those of Vajrayana. That is the bottom line. Padmasambhava very kindly designed this practice with people like us in mind, for just by doing this practice we can totally purify and restore all of our Vajrayana commitments.

The Excellent Preparation of Bodhichitta

No matter what level of practice we are at, whether according to the sutra system or the tantric teachings, we should always remember to embrace our practice with the three excellences: the excellent preparation of bodhichitta, the excellent main part beyond concepts, and the excellent conclusion of dedication. For example, when practicing a sadhana such as *Ocean of Amrita*, the preparation is to take refuge and the bodhichitta vow, followed by gathering the accumulations by means of the seven-branch prayer. After that comes the main part, which includes the development, completion, and recitation stages. At the end, we conclude the sadhana with dedication and the verses of auspiciousness.

REFUGE

Here I will describe Dharma practice from the perspective of applying the teachings. The very first step is to take refuge in the Three Jewels. If we haven't heard the names of the Three Jewels—Buddha, Dharma, and sangha—and don't know what they are, there is no basis for enlightenment, which is the whole purpose of Dharma practice. Therfore, first step on the path to enlightenment is to take refuge in the Three Jewels. We do so with the commitment that, at the cost of oulives, we will never forsake or turn our back on them.

You may already know many details about the Three Jewels, but to put it very simply, the one we call the Buddha is the supreme nirmanakaya, someone human beings can meet and can connect with, namely Buddha Shakyamuni. A lot can be said about Dharma; in fact the word *dharma* has many meanings, but here it basically refers to the Buddhist teachings that have been passed on orally, or written down and collected in volumes of scriptures. Just as the Buddha can be described as having abandoned whatever needs to be abandoned and having realized whatever needs to be realized, or in other words, as possessing completely the qualities of abandonment and realization, the same can be said for the precious sangha. However, for ordinary human beings like us, any gathering of just four pure ordained monks suffices to represent the noble sangha.

Taking refuge in the Buddha means acknowledging that now we are trapped in samsaric existence, like a criminal who is in prison, and we need help to get out. Ultimately, our rescuer is a fully enlightened one, a buddha, because no one else is really able to help one escape samsaric existence. There is no one else to turn to, and this is why we take refuge in the Buddha. The fact is that, until we ourselves become buddhas and don't need to take refuge any longer, we are still imprisoned in samsara; there we say, "From this moment until arriving at the essence of supreme enlightenment, I take refuge in the Buddha, Dharma, and Sangha."

Actually, taking refuge means deeply fearing the prospect of carrying on suffering in the same way that one has been for countless lives and continuing endlessly in samsaric existence. Self-concern, however, will never lead to complete enlightenment. Therefore, unlike a shravaka, whose main aim is to just escape samsara and be free, a bodhisattva strives not just for himself or herself, but for the welfare of all sentient beings.

A bodhisattva still holds such concepts as "I" and "other," thinking things like, "I need to exchange myself for others. I need to treat others as more important than me." A Vajrayana practitioner, on the other hand, fears clinging to attributes or fixating on characteristics. From the very beginning, a Vajrayana practitioner is someone who totally suspends these concepts into the great purity and equality of whatever appears and exists. Furthermore, from the Vajrayana perspective one takes refuge not only in the Buddha, Dharma, and Sangha, but also in the guru, yidam, and dakinis, as well as the dakas and Dharma protectors.

The attitude of refuge requires some steadiness. It is the foundation, the basis for all other practice. Whether we pursue the further training of a bodhisattva or practice the more profound stages of development and completion, we need this profound foundation of taking refuge, and it must be stable. Lacking such steadiness, one cannot really practice Vajrayana. One could pretend to go through the practices of profound development and completion stages, but it will not lead very far without stability in refuge. An analogy is building on ice in the winter. In some places the ice freezes so hard that you could build a house on it, but when spring comes the foundation will crack and the whole house will sink to the bottom of the lake. In the same way, going through the more profound practices without taking refuge will lack a firm base, and eventually one's apparent progress will collapse.

Without sincerely taking to heart the attitude of refuge, we may repeat the words "I take refuge in the Buddha, the Dharma, and the Sangha" again and again, but it won't really change anything. So how do we know if we really are stable or not? It is said that if you keep the commitment when bribed or threatened to give it up, then you are stable. For example, if somebody says, "Give up the Three Jewels or I'll kill you," or "I'll give you great wealth if you just forsake the Three Jewels," if, in our heart, we then refuse to forsake the Three Jewels, we have attained a certain stability.

Upon sincerely and genuinely taking refuge, we can practice the profound main part of a yidam practice, beginning with unfolding the structure of the three samadhis and so forth. The essential practice is the actual jewel, and the setting for this gem is taking refuge. All the other details—the celestial palace, offerings, development and completion, and so on—are the fine handiwork used to highlight and draw attention to the jewel itself.

THE THREE PROHIBITIONS

The difference between being a Buddhist or a non-Buddhist lies in whether or not one observes the precepts to be observed in taking refuge: the three prohibitions and the three things to adopt. The prohibitions are things to avoid.

Having taken refuge in the Buddha, the first prohibition is to not seek help from non-human spirits of various types, such as mountain gods, among others. It was not out of envy that Buddha said that one should not take refuge in such spirits, but rather because ultimately they can't really help, as they too are caught in samsara, and it would be like the blind leading the blind.

Having taken refuge in the Dharma, one should avoid harming other beings, no matter how small or insignificant. For instance, if a dog is lying comfortably inside the monastery hallway to stay warm, you should not kick it out into the cold. To do no harm is a fundamental principle in Buddhism and is the essence of the bodhisattva vow.

The precept to avoid, when taking refuge in the precious Sangha, is that one must no longer live with people who hold non-Buddhist views. This refers to anyone who has an opinion that is contrary to what the

Buddha taught—even if it is a member of one's own immediate family. For example, we should avoid people who maintain that there is no future life, and, therefore, no point in practicing the Dharma, and those who say things like, "We don't see any other realms; they don't exist, so there is no point in trying to avoid rebirth." Being around such people can be detrimental to our own progress because their beliefs will adversely affect us by making us timid or creating doubt.

To reiterate, the three precepts for what to avoid after taking refuge in the precious Buddha, Dharma, and Sangha are: not to place one's trust in mundane spirits, not to harm other beings and not to live with people who hold non-Buddhist views.

THE THREE OBLIGATIONS

Having taken refuge in the Buddha, we should pay respect to any form that represents the enlightened ones—buddhas, bodhisattvas, and so on. Of course, this includes pictures, *thangka* paintings, and statues, but even a fragment of a stupa, and the small molded sculptures known as *tsa-tsa*, should not be carelessly handled but put in a high place and respected. This isn't as easy as it might first sound, for we should respect every single character of every alphabet. Writing is extremely important because it is through language that we understand meaning, including the enlightened meaning that the Buddha sought to convey. The Buddha himself said, "In the future, for those who have not met me, I will appear in the form of writing. Written language will be my emanation, my substitute. The writing of the scriptures will be my representative." This refers not just to Tibetan or Sanskrit but all languages. Of course, Tibetans think that Tibetan books are the only ones that are sacred and holy, and therefore worthy of respect; but that is a mistaken view. If the Buddha's words are written in another language, why wouldn't someone be able to understand them? As the Tripitaka is slowly being translated into English, people can, of course, read it and understand it. Therefore, books in all languages should be considered as something very precious and treated accordingly.

But, because of that, this stricture is actually somewhat of a dilemma because books are now readily available. Many people who buy them have not taken Buddhist vows, and many who have taken vows still don't keep the precepts, so sacred books and texts are often just tossed here and there. Considering that we can't stop and pick up every scrap of paper lying around, what we should do is imagine that we have a volume of Buddhist scriptures on the top of our heads. That way, even if we happen to inadvertently step on some writing, we are simultaneously paying respect, and our transgression is automatically canceled out; otherwise it is an impossible situation.

Lastly, having taken refuge in the sangha, we should pay respect to anything that represents it, even down to a scrap of clothing. In Tibet that was pretty easy because the monks and nuns wore maroon and ocher garments. But it actually depends on the country and the time. For example, there were times in India when the sangha wore blue, in some countries they wore gray, and in others brown and black. Those are the three precepts to observe.

BODHICHITTA: THE BODHISATTVA RESOLVE

After chanting the lines of refuge, we come to bodhichitta, which is forming the resolve of a bodhisattva. This bodhisattva resolve is the dividing line between Hinayana and Mahayana. Hinayana practitioners are called shravakas or *pratyekabuddhas*, who seek enlightenment for themselves alone. This is limited though, and, no matter what kind of practice we do, we should seek enlightenment for all sentient beings. Whether it is a single circumambulation of a stupa or chanting one rosary of OM MANI PADMA HUNG, we should do it not just for our own benefit but for the benefit of all beings.

What does this really mean? When we chant the four lines for bodhichitta, such as these from the *Ocean of Amrita*:

HOH
As all the victorious ones and their sons of the past
Aroused their minds toward the unexcelled supreme
enlightenment,
I will also accomplish buddhahood
In order to benefit my mothers, all beings as numerous as
space is vast.

We are saying that we will imitate the example of the awakened ones, the buddhas and bodhisattvas of the past, who undertook to achieve enlightenment to benefit all sentient beings. We promise to practice in the same way, to complete the training, and attain enlightenment for all beings.

We say "all my mothers" as we have had countless lifetimes and parents in each, so all sentient beings are actually our own mothers. Although we can remember just how much our present parents have done for us in this lifetime, right now our memory is not good enough to remember all those parents from our past lives. We don't recognize them when we meet them. We feel some are friends, some are enemies, some are strangers, but, in fact, they are all our own parents from the past. None of them want to suffer; they all want to be happy. But beings don't create the causes for happiness, or the circumstances to avoid creating further suffering. We should become acutely aware that something needs to be done for all beings. We can't just wait for someone else to do it, but must assume the responsibility ourselves. The thought, "I myself will work to liberate all sentient beings," is the bodhisattva resolve.

To formally become a bodhisattva, first one takes refuge in the presence of a Buddhist master. Doing this, one must then choose one of the seven sets of precepts for individual liberation, the highest degree of which are those of a fully ordained monk or nun. Then, after understanding the precepts, traditionally one would ask to take the bodhisattva vow, which is done in a ceremony similar to the one for refuge. Informally, if there is no master around, one can simply imagine the Three Jewels as witness and form the resolve, "I want to attain enlightenment in order to benefit all beings." In so doing, one becomes a bodhisattva at that moment.

We should keep one point in mind here. All Vajrayana practices include refuge and the bodhisattva vow. In this way, the qualities of the lower vehicles are present in the higher ones, which is called "the principle of upward containment." We should not frown on, or belittle, the lower vehicles, thinking, "I am a Vajrayana practitioner, I am not following the Hinayana or the Mahayana," for this is simply not true as Vajrayana contains the qualities of the lower vehicles. That said however, the lower vehicles do not contain the qualities of Vajrayana.

In Vajrayana, the authentic method of introduction is the four empowerments. When we authentically receive these four empowerments, we become a *vidyadhara*, a knowledge holder, or in other words a true Vajrayana practitioner. The ceremony for receiving the four empowerments always includes taking refuge and forming the bodhisattva resolve. Furthermore, in the Tibetan tradition, Vajrayana practitioners still adhere to the Vinaya, for example by wearing robes. The foremost Vajrayana practitioner is called a *bhikshu vidyadhara*, which means a fully ordained monk, who is at the same time a vajra practitioner. The medium type of Vajrayana practitioner is a *geshe*,[1] a novice vajra practitioner, and the lowest type of Vajrayana practitioner is a layperson. So please understand a monk vidyadhara is the highest type of Vajrayana practitioner.

In Tibetan, lay Buddhists, are called *genyen*, which is a contraction of *gewa la nyenpa*. This literally means "approaching goodness," or "growing closer to what is virtuous." There are five different types of genyen based on what precepts one vows to uphold. The precepts deal with the four root downfalls as well as an additional fifth one. These are: not to kill, in this case of basic Vinaya, meaning not to kill any sentient being; not to steal, also defined as not to steal something really valuable; not to indulge in sexual misconduct; not to lie, meaning special lies about having superhuman virtues, such as "I saw such-and-such a god and he told me this-and-that," or "I subdued such-and-such a demon, gave it a present, and now it's on my side," or making up spectacular lies like this. The additional fifth one is giving up intoxicating substances or drinks. If one chooses to give up just one of these, then one is a one-precept genyen. Giving up two, also according to one's choice, one is a two-precept genyen; if one gives up three or four, one is a most-precepts genyen, and if it's all five of them, one is a complete-precept genyen. In addition to that, if one gives up sexual involvement altogether, one is called a celibate genyen, and the outer behavior is exactly like that of a monk or nun. Those are the different types of lay Buddhist precepts.

APPLYING THE PRACTICES IN DAILY LIFE

I am explaining this because most of you readers are from countries other than Tibet and you want to learn how to practice. These are not just rules to follow blindly. What we need to learn is how to use the Dharma in

---

1 Tibetan terms are in italics; Sanskrit terms, as they are in more common usage, are not particularly noted in the text.

our own lives, how to really put it to use so that it might be effective. You don't learn the key points of Buddhist practice by merely study alone. What it really comes down to is learning how to use the Dharma within our own experience, during all of our daily activities. There are certain instructions on how to do this at all levels of practice.

There is even a way to combine going to sleep with Dharma practice, in which you cultivate the attitude that "now as I fall asleep, may I dissolve into dharmakaya." Then on waking in the morning you think, "May I and all sentient beings rise above the three realms of samsara." When you walk up a staircase, form the attitude, "May we proceed up the staircase to liberation." When you walk down, think, "I am going down to the lowest hell and all other lower realms in order to help other sentient beings." Even when you put a piece of food in your mouth or take a drink, you could form the attitude, "I am now making offerings to the peaceful and wrathful deities, who are present in this body." This is not just something we imagine, for the Vajrayana perspective maintains that the body itself is the palace of the hundred peaceful and wrathful deities who are not in some other place, but are actually part of us. Therefore, any food and drink that we enjoy is actually making a feast offering. Whether we are aware of it or not, that's how it is.

You should train yourself to use every moment in your life, each and every activity, to apply the teachings. As they say: you must walk the walk, not just talk the talk.

Accumulation of Merit:
The Seven Branches

After taking refuge and bodhichitta, we perfect the accumulations. As a bodhisattva, after taking refuge and bodhichitta, we undertake to perfect the two accumulations: the accumulation of merit, with something held in mind, and the accumulation of wisdom, without holding anything in mind. This is why we recite the seven branches, which are said to actually include all the different ways a bodhisattva can perfect the accumulation of merit for the benefit of sentient beings.

THE FIRST BRANCH: BOWING

To begin, we imagine all the objects of refuge in the ten directions. For example, this is what the first two lines of *the Ngakso* refer to:

OM AH HUNG HRIH
I prostrate to Vidyadhara Padmakara
And to all objects of refuge in the ten directions.
I present you with a Samantabhadra offering cloud, filling
the sky
Of actual and mentally created offerings.

"Vidyadhara Padmakara" and so forth refers to all the objects of refuge. Many Westerners are not familiar with the ten directions, which are the four cardinal directions (north, south, east, and west), the four intermediate directions (northeast, southeast, southwest, and northwest), and above and below. The objects of refuge themselves include all buddhas of past and future, for example, the seven buddhas who came before Shakyamuni, and the thousands of buddhas of this aeon, and so forth; all bodhisattvas, lineage holders, and so on. We visualize them assembled before us, and then pay homage with body, voice, and mind. Physically, we prostrate or bow; verbally, we pronounce the words in the text; and mentally, we surrender, placing complete trust and confidence in the objects of refuge.

Bowing down is the antidote against conceit. No matter how consumed we are by the five disturbing emotions of stupidity, pride, jealously, anger, and attachment, we all still think that we are special. Prostrating helps us develop humility to counteract our conceit.

There are different ways of prostrating. According to the sutras, one bows down while touching five points of the body to the ground—the two hands, the two knees, and the forehead. First we join our palms, touch our forehead, throat and heart, and then we bow down in a kneeling position. The Vajrayana begins the same way, but then one stretches right out flat on the ground. Specifically, you should join the palms of your hands together, not pressed flat or with the fingers stretched apart, but forming a hollow with the two longest fingers just touching, like a lotus bud about to open. Raise your hands up and lightly touch the base of the palms to the crown of your head, then lower them to the throat, and lastly to the heart, and then bow down. Stretch out flat on the ground with your arms extended in complete surrender. Stand up straight again bringing your palms together in front of your chest. Don't just rush through it absentmindedly, but do it in a dignified way.

When bowing down, you should not imagine that it is only you. Imagine instead that you emanate hundreds of replicas of yourself, each replicating into hundreds more, until you are as many as there are atoms in a universe, an immense gathering. All other sentient beings are also there, all bowing together. That may be hard to imagine in the beginning, but at least you can start by thinking that there are two of you, then three, ten and so on to infinity. By doing so, we increase the effect of bowing down. Also, being accompanied by all other sentient beings makes it even more effective.

In addition, the Buddha has said that, when bowing down with our body stretched out, we cover a large number of atoms with our body, going all the way down to the center of the earth. It is said that the karmic effect of making just a single prostration is to have the enjoyment of a universal monarch for each atom that our body covers.

THE SECOND BRANCH: MAKING OFFERINGS

That was the first of the seven branches, the branch of bowing down. The second branch is to make offerings, as in these lines from the *Ngakso*:

I present you with a Samantabhadra offering cloud,
Filling the sky with offerings both actually present and mentally
created.

There are various types of offerings: outer, inner, innermost, and more. For now, we will discuss two types: "actually present" and "mentally created."

The seven general offerings to arrange on one's shrine are rinsing water, flowers, incense, perfume, drinking water, light, and music. Of course, it is excellent if we can display all these on our shrine, but sometimes, when traveling for instance, it can be too complicated, or one may simply not know how to do it according to Tibetan tradition. So, to be an "actually present" offering, it just has to be something. We must be careful not to form any attachment to the thought of making offerings. For example, if we impressively make a lavish display, such as setting up thousands of butter lamps every day, offering expensive substances and so on, we may start to develop pride or conceit, thinking our offerings are better than others. Such thoughts destroy any merit we might accrue by making offerings in the first place. On the other hand, seeing others make lavish offerings or with engraved bowls made from silver and gold we might think, "I'm too poor; I can't afford those things. Enlightenment is the luxury of rich people." But such thoughts are absolutely pointless. We can certainly accumulate merit by using just a simple cup of water, something that we are not attached to. It is very easy to pour water into a cup, put it on our altar or shrine, and afterwards just toss the water out the window. It's not at all difficult. This is much better than getting all caught up in needing a whole set of fancy offering bowls and filling them with an array of things we might find difficult to acquire. For this reason, often it is better just to make simple offerings without much attachment; for example, using just a single bowl of water to represent all the offerings together. It's hard to be stingy about water, and we are not very attached to it either; hence, a simple bowl of water can be a very nice offering. What you physically offer is really up to you, but whatever it is, the important thing is to offer it without attachment or stinginess. Imagine making thousands or millions more offerings at the same time. This then includes both what is actually present and what we can mentally create.

Another type of offering is light, which is commonly done by offering a butter lamp or candle. However, we can use anything that creates light, such as the sun, the moon, the stars, and so on, which are readily available to everyone. Very few people are envious of the sun's or moon's light. When you go to town at night and see all the lights shining you haven't paid for that beauty and don't feel stingy about it, so even streetlights can represent a beautiful clean offering. What you are really offering is light and awareness, so you can choose anything that represents this to you, and then just imagine it while multiplying it a million times and offering it to all the buddhas and bodhisattvas. In this way, we can make offerings throughout daily life, offering up whatever we come across during our day.

This is what is called a pith instruction, a *men-ngak*. A *men-ngak* must not only be very effective but also very easy; then it will have the potential to accumulate lots of merit without any hassle. It's just the kind of instruction one needs when living a hectic modern life.

THE THIRD BRANCH: APOLOGIZING

Next comes the lines of apology:

> *I apologize for transgressing and violating the pratimoksha vows,*
> *The bodhisattva trainings, and the tantric samayas of the vidyadharas.*

These three phrases—the pratimoksha vows, the bodhisattva trainings, and the tantric samayas—refer to the three levels of practice. The pratimoksha are the Hinayana vows as outlined in the collection known as the Vinaya; the bodhisattva trainings cover the sutra teachings of the Mahayana; and tantric samayas, of course, belong to Vajrayana. To be honest, if we were to cover this as it should be covered, it would be so detailed that it would fill numerous volumes, so for now one should receive some teachings on the main points of the three levels of precepts. A good place to start is the book by Ngari Panchen that has been translated into English as *Perfect Conduct*.[1]

The pratimoksha vows refer to the vows of individual liberation, which any practitioner can take. A fully ordained monk has 253 precepts to observe; a novice monk has fewer, and, if one is a layperson, there are only a few vows to keep. Some of these I mentioned previously. Regarding the bodhisattva trainings, it is possible to break the bodhisattva vow, and there are also certain infractions by which you damage the vow. You can learn the specifics elsewhere.[2]

For Vajrayana, the precepts are called commitments or *samayas*. Each level of teachings—outer tantra, kriya, upa, yoga, and so on—has different sets of commitments and lists of what to observe. For example, the *Ngakso* comes within the three inner tantras, mainly Mahayoga, and so certain relevant samayas are mentioned within the text.

All vows and precepts are simply commitments that one has made. Violating these vows by doing what one has vowed not to do is known as "pledge wrongdoing." There is also "natural wrongdoing," which includes actions that everyone should avoid without specifically having vowed to refrain from them, such as the ten unvirtuous actions, the four heinous crimes with immediate repercussion at the moment of death, the five associated ones, and so forth. We combine all of these together and apologize for transgressing and violating them all. We can commit such acts with our body or voice and also mentally. Physically we can kill others, steal their possessions, and commit sexual misconduct; with our voice we can lie or utter harsh words, divisive talk, and pointless gossip; and mentally we can harbor ill-will, covetousness, and wrong views. This is what we bring to mind here while saying or thinking something like, "Standing here before all of you buddhas and bodhisattvas, I am sorry for all that I have done wrong, and I promise not to do it again, buddhas and bodhisattvas."

THE FOURTH BRANCH: REJOICING

Next comes the practice of rejoicing. Rejoicing means that we think of the victorious ones:

> *I rejoice in all the noble and ordinary beings*
> *Who engage in the conduct of the sons and daughters of the*
> *victorious ones.*

"Noble" beings are those who have attained the path of seeing and above. "Ordinary beings" are those who have entered the path of accumulation. By simply rejoicing, thinking, "How wonderful!" you can partake in another's virtue. Likewise, if we rejoice in someone's negative actions, we receive negative karma equal to having done it ourselves. So it goes both ways, with both good and negative actions. So if you rejoice in whatever sublime or ordinary virtue is being created, without any envy or competitiveness, you gain merit equal to having done it yourself.

THE FIFTH BRANCH: REQUESTING

The next branch is requesting to turn the wheel of Dharma:

Please turn the appropriate wheels of Dharma
To benefit the infinite number of suffering beings.

"Infinite" means that just as space is endless, the number of beings is endless, and all of them have an endless number of disturbing emotions. In order to cure, help, and guide all these beings, the buddhas and great masters teach the Dharma, however, it is most beneficial to different beings' capacities, inclinations, aspirations, interests, and so on. Giving these different sets of teachings is what is called "turning the wheel of Dharma."

When making this request we should imagine that we are in the presence of all the different buddhas and masters in all directions, then respectfully ask each and every one of them to teach and help all sentient beings. Otherwise it is like the Buddha after he attained complete enlightenment and said, "I have discovered a nectar-like truth that is profound, tranquil, unconstructed luminous wakefulness. Whomever I would teach this to would not understand, so I will just remain here, silent in the jungle." He then did so, until Indra and Brahma appeared before him, offered him a thousand-spoked golden wheel and a conch turning clockwise, while requesting him to turn the wheel of Dharma for all beings. Because of this, the Buddha proceeded to Varanasi, where he taught his first disciples the four noble truths, and so on.

So, just like those gods, we should sincerely ask all the buddhas and other masters in the ten directions and three times to teach. Since enlightened beings, buddhas, and bodhisattvas all possess clairvoyant powers, they know whenever someone is addressing them, and they will respond.

THE SIXTH BRANCH: BESEECHING

The next is beseeching the noble ones not to pass away:

> *Without passing away, remain for the sake of beings*
> *throughout countless millions of aeons.*

When Lord Buddha reached old age, he said, "I am about to pass away." At that point, one of his disciples pleaded, "Please don't—please stay!" So Lord Buddha blessed his own physical presence in order that he might remain a few years more. Thus, he lived longer than he otherwise would have if he had not been asked to remain. In the same way, we can request enlightened beings to stick around and teach. We don't need to make an especially complicated ceremony repeating long-life prayers and doing a special ritual. We can simply request all buddhas and enlightened beings, "Please don't leave, remain for countless aeons." Being clairvoyant, they will know and will respond.

THE SEVENTH BRANCH: DEDICATION

Finally, comes the branch of dedication:

> *I dedicate all the virtue gathered in the three times*
> *so that all beings may attain the essence of enlightenment.*

This means dedicating all the virtuous karma that you have created throughout the past and present, together with what you will create in the future, as well as what has been and will be created by others, to the essence of supreme enlightenment for all beings. That is the dedication and aspiration. Usually it is said that an ordinary person cannot truly dedicate the merit, so we should wish to dedicate the merit in the exact same way as all the buddhas have done.

The Bodhichitta of Application:
The Four Immeasurables

Now we come to the four immeasurables. The bodhisattva vow is the bodhichitta of aspiration, and training in the four immeasurables is called "the bodhichitta of application" or "the applied bodhichitta." If we want to go to Bodhgaya, first we aspire to make the trip, and then we decide to go in a certain direction. But just wanting to go to Bodhgaya isn't enough; we actually have to work to save money for the trip, pack our bags, and then actually make the journey. So, if we want to attain complete enlightenment, we must first arouse the bodhichitta of aspiration: forming the resolve that all beings may be free of suffering and obtain true happiness. Then, we must apply ourselves to achieving this goal for both ourselves and for others, which is the bodhichitta of application. As expressed in *the Ngakso,* the four immeasurables are:

> *By this merit may all beings possess happiness.*
> *Freed from their suffering, may it ripen upon me instead.*
> *May they never part from the happiness devoid of misery,*
> *And may they abide in impartiality, the equal nature of all*
>   *things.*

The first line expresses boundless love: "By the merit that I have created in the past, created just now, and am about to create in the future, may all the infinite number of beings, my own parents from all lives, possess not just happiness, but the causes of happiness—the ten virtuous actions—and thereby be fully endowed with happiness."

The second line expresses the compassionate attitude of a bodhisattva: not wanting any being to suffer. This includes all sentient beings; those in the hell realms who suffer from heat and cold; hungry ghosts who suffer from hunger and thirst; animals who suffer from being eaten by others, being enslaved, and being killed; human beings who suffer from birth, old age, sickness, and death; demigods with their fighting and strife; and the gods themselves who suffer from carelessness, frivolity, and inattentiveness.

What does "me" mean in the phrase "may it ripen upon me instead"? It refers to this hard lump of ego-clinging that we all carry around. What is that hard lump made of? It is made out of our thoughts. Even when we are asleep and dreaming, we cling to thoughts of me and mine. We lie comfortably in our beds and imagine that others are chasing us, talking badly about us, that our possessions are being carried away, and other such things, and it makes us suffer, all because of this ugly lump of ego-clinging.

Next comes immeasurable joy, here phrased as, "May they never part from the happiness devoid of misery." Immeasurable joy is thinking, "How nice it would be if all sentient beings, not just my friends and relatives, but countless sentient beings, could be totally free of misery." And last is impartiality: not differentiating between close and distant so that love, compassion, and joy embrace everyone.

These are but words, however; to actually put them into practice, you mingle them with your breath. To do this, when exhaling, make the wish that all the roots of virtue created throughout the three times may stream out into all directions to all sentient beings, and may all beings actually receive these virtues and benefits. Then, when you inhale, you inhale all the pain and suffering of sentient beings that dissolve into yourself.

This practice is called "mind training," and it is necessary for ordinary beings like us. "Ordinary beings" are those whose minds are untamed, wild, and incorrigible; those who lack compassion for those who suffer and lack faith in enlightened beings, even when meeting one. Ordinary beings are selfish, hardened in egotism, like land that hasn't been cultivated for years with dirt so hard that no seed can take root in it. Mind training, especially training in the four immeasurables, is a way of changing those attitudes, softening up one's frame of mind, and becoming less rigid. When the soil has been tilled and cultivated, you will then have a fertile field in which the seed of enlightenment can grow. But before any of the accomplishments can sprout, first one must till the field with the mind trainings.

The four immeasurables are called "immeasurable" because they express boundless love and compassion. Sentient beings are infinite in number, just like space is infinite in dimension. Therefore, it is not enough to just be nice to your friends and care for your family—even vicious beasts actually care for their own offspring. We must open up our hearts and minds with a positive attitude, wanting all beings to be full of joy and free from suffering.

To conclude this first part, we dissolve the field of accumulation, meaning the objects of refuge: the buddhas, bodhisattvas, and so forth, the three roots who have been present as witnesses to our practice. By saying JAH HUNG BAM HO, the whole field of accumulation dissolves into the three syllables OM AH HUNG that mark the crown, throat, and heart of ourselves and all the other beings that we have imagined surrounding us. With this, we should feel confident that our two obscurations have been purified and we have received the blessings and accomplishments.

CLEARING AWAY OBSTACLES

All Vajrayana practice involves two main principles: clearing away unfavorable circumstances and providing conducive circumstances. We are already familiar with these two principles because they also apply to many other aspects of life. For example, when building a house, first one must remove all the undesired stones, trees, and so forth until the lot is ready for building. Then, the necessary building supplies must be acquired: bricks, cement, iron bars, and so forth. Only then can the house be built. Vajrayana practice follows the same principle.

Clearing away unfavorable circumstances cannot be done as an ordinary person; one must have the vajra pride of being a deity. In the case of *the Ngakso*, you first acknowledge that you are the lotus heruka, holding a lotus and skull cup. Then, you proclaim the mantra OM SVABHAVA SHUDDHO SARVA DHARMA SVABHAVA SHUDDHOH HANG, in order to suspend your attention's normal fixation on concrete attributes; in other words, to allow for all phenomena to be the vast state of emptiness. Then,

> *From within the state of emptiness,* BHRUNG *becomes a vast, open jeweled-vessel. Inside of which is the torma with perfect color, fragrance, taste, and potency.*

This refers to the basic principle in Vajrayana, namely the unity of emptiness and of what is perceived, which are indivisible. While our basic state is emptiness, everything is still perceived, and we still experience various phenomena. However, whatever is experienced is still empty by nature. In this way, everything takes place as the unity of experience and emptiness. It is from within the state of emptiness that the syllable BHRUNG becomes a vast open vessel inside of which sits the torma for the obstructors.

We purify and multiply the torma while saying OM AH HUNG, consecrate it with HA HO HRIH, and then, by performing the hook mudra and saying OM SARVA BHUTA AKARSHAYA JAH, we invite the obstructors to partake of the torma. You should imagine that the torma becomes an immense quantity of whatever they desire. If they desire the three whites (milk, butter, and curd) and the three sweets (molasses, sugar, and honey), then it will appear to them as that. If what they want is flesh and blood, then they see the torma in that way. Whatever they desire, the torma will be. Actually, this is no different than what we do in normal life when we invite guests to dinner: we prepare a nice meal, put out clean dishes, and then, we call them to table. In this case, however, we do invite them confident that we are the heruka. In regard to the mantra, OM SARVA BHUTA AKARSHAYA JAH means "all spirits are summoned here, right now!" Then, just like Christians say grace before a meal, you dedicate the meal by repeating the sky treasury mantra[3] three times:

BHAYO VISHVA MUKHEBHE SARVA TAKHAM UTGATE SAPARANA IMAM GAGANA KHAM GRIHANA DAM BALING THAYE SVAHA.

What we do next is express our wish,

All demons, obstructors, and evil spirits of deluded dualistic perception,[g]

Enjoy this torma and disperse to your own places.[g]

Essentially this means, "I have an aim to achieve, so now please listen. All of us are yogis who aim to progress on the path to complete enlightenment by means of the profound stages of development and completion, and we are doing so for the benefit of all beings. So, you spirits, obstructors, and so forth, don't make obstacles for us. Instead, take this torma and leave us alone." If they do not want to go willingly, then we let them know that they will be destroyed if they stay.

The evil spirits are called *"demons and obstructors of deluded dualistic perception."* "Dualistic" refers to concepts of duality, such as self and other, good and bad, pure and impure, and so on. Being habituated to a dualistic view and desiring things based upon this delusion appears in the form of different types of demons and obstructors, such as *tsen, gyalpo,* and *mamo* who cause obstacles for practitioners. This is the outer way of understanding what is going on here.

The inner way to understand it is that the demon obstructors and evil spirits of deluded dualistic fixation are actually me. I myself am that evil spirit because it is out of my own habituated deluded fixation on duality that I have such ordinary concepts as self and other, here and there, good and bad, and so on. The fact is that our own concept of self, our ego is the evil spirit. However, when we simply let be into the state of equanimity, this deluded notion of a self simply dissolves into our basic nature. That is called "dispersing into its own place."

Up till now, we have asked nicely and given a torma. But, if there are some obstructors that won't listen and won't leave, we make a more insistent threat such as:

If you don't leave, a rain of vajra weapons will completely reduce your body, speech, and mind to dust, all the way down to the seventh generation. Therefore, be gone this very moment.

In other words, with the pride of being Hayagriva, the lotus heruka, we imagine that all negative forces are exorcised or expelled by wrathful means, especially when chanting the wrathful mantra, HUNG HUNG HUNG VISHVA VAJRA KRODHA JVALA MANDALA PHAT PHAT HALA HALA HUNG

You "cast the torma outside, throw mustard seeds, burn *gugul*,[2] brandish the vajra, and expel the obstructors with awesome music."

DRAWING THE BOUNDARY LINE

Next comes drawing the boundary line. After you discover a thief in your house, you chase him out and then lock the door so he can't come back in. Similarly, having expelled the obstructors we now draw a boundary line to ensure that they don't return.

We start out by assuming "the great and glorious form of the lotus king," Hayagriva. Then, we acknowledge that all of samsara and nirvana is complete as the mudras, our body, speech, and mind. Within this basic space, we imagine the protection circle starting with an immense vajra cross on the ground. In between its spokes and filling up the ground are

---

2 A strong smelling resin, which is burned and whose smoke is believed to dispel obstructors.

smaller vajra crosses. The circumference has a fence also made out of vajra crosses, and all this is covered with a huge dome, also made of vajras. This dome is plastered with very tiny vajras so that it is totally impenetrable, and not even the cosmic wind at the end of the kalpa can penetrate it. On top of that is a vajra canopy filled with smaller and smaller vajras. There is also a dome made of the weapons carried by the wrathful deities of the five buddha families, namely vajra crosses, swords, wheels, hooks, spears, chains, and shackles. This dome is then engulfed in blazing tongues of fire, with countless tiny herukas flying, like sparks, into all directions.

The ultimate protection circle is actually summarized by the following lines from the *Ngakso*,

> In the nondual wisdom state of deity, mantra, and
> dharmakaya,⁸
> The boundary mandala is naturally self-perfected.⁸

This is the ultimate type of protection circle; instead of holding on to dualistic notions of self and other, we should simply let be in the state of nondual wakefulness. In this state, everything is deity, mantra, and dharmakaya. In other words, what we usually call "I" or "me" naturally has no true existence, so there is nothing to be harmed in the first place. Furthermore, anyone or anything that might appear as a threat or negative force also naturally lacks any true existence; hence, there is nothing that can cause any harm. In this nondual wisdom state, all that is seen is the form of the deity; all that is heard is the sound of mantra, and all movement of mind is dharmakaya. This is the ultimate protection circle, which is naturally and spontaneously perfect.

Recognizing this fact, we say the mantra HUNG HUNG HUNG VAJRA RAKSHA RAKSHA BHRUNG. Each word and syllable has a meaning, but it is not necessary to go into every single little detail; even if you don't know the precise meaning, a mantra will still work.

The ultimate protection circle is nothing other than thought-free wakefulness that holds no duality. Embracing our visualization with the experience of emptiness makes it perfect. It's the sovereign approach that perfects any aspect of the practice. Even normal practices, like generosity, never become perfect, unless embraced with the genuine experience of emptiness.

Buddha Nature

The Buddha taught that the true nature of each and every sentient being is identical with that of a fully enlightened buddha. This is known as the sugata essence, the buddha nature, which is the focus of the third turning of the wheel of Dharma, which is known as "the final dharma wheel of the complete uncovering." The unformed buddha nature is every sentient being's natural state. This basic state lies beyond confusion and liberation, and does not grow closer nor more distant whether one's experience belongs to samsara or nirvana.

This basic buddha nature is not unique to the third turning, for it is also mentioned in the first turning, when it is said that everyone belongs to the family of potentially enlightened ones—everyone has the potential to awaken.

The second turning of the wheel of dharma describes it as the suchness that is totally free of any mental construct, the basic nature of emptiness of all phenomena. Furthermore, it is said that without the basic material, the potential for enlightenment, one would never weary of suffering nor want to pursue the state of peace. The Mahayana teachings state that being moved to tears when hearing teachings on emptiness, the qualities of the enlightened state, or simply the sufferings of those beings in the lower realms is proof of having the potential for enlightenment. So, just like when you see smoke on the mountainside, you can infer that there is a fire burning. When you see someone so moved by the teachings, you can infer that they are already prepared for receiving the Mahayana teachings.

In the third turning of the wheel of dharma, to which both the outer and inner tantras belong, buddha nature is given different names, according to the different levels of tantra. What is common throughout all these teachings is that we have a basic nature in which the qualities of a fully awakened state, the fourfold fearlessness, the ten powers of a buddha, the eighteen unique qualities, the thirty-two major and eighty minor marks of an excellent one, and the sixty-four qualities of abandonment and realization are already fully present in our original buddha nature.

How is it possible that the basic nature of any sentient being and that of a buddha are no different whatsoever, when the quality of a buddha, on one hand, is the ability to perceive past, present, and future simultaneously in one instant, as well the ability to lead countless sentient beings out of samsara each moment, and the quality of a sentient being, on the other, is so limited? Take for instance beings like ourselves; if we were born in the hell of incessant torment, we couldn't even get ourselves out of samsara, much less countless sentient beings. It seems like all these qualities that one possesses are kind of useless, doesn't it? The term *nyingpo*, which is translated as "essence," refers to something invisible, something that is present but that cannot be seen directly. It is covered at present by other veils so its actual nature is not directly evident. It can also be translated as "kernel" or "seed." Whether covered by a skin, peel, or not, a seed still remains a seed. Similarly, what happens to us, sentient beings, is that, due to not recognizing or acknowledging our nature as it is, we experience coemergent ignorance,[4] which becomes like an enveloping veil that covers up the buddha nature itself. In that way, whatever qualities this buddha nature does possess are not evident, and we don't fully manifest our potential. Fortunately, as we already possess the purity of the original essence, the buddha nature itself is the basis for purifying and removing the veil of obscuration. According to the sutras, that which purifies are the two accumulations, the accumulation of merit with concepts and the accumulation of wisdom without concepts; according to Vajrayana, it is the two stages of development and completion.

The outcome of purifying is the absence of temporary obscurations. Buddhahood is when, in addition to the original purity of our true nature, we are also free from temporary obscurations. That is why buddhahood is defined as the twofold purity.

When we speak of a buddha, it does not mean the physical form of Buddha Shakyamuni, which is just a body, but rather the truly and completely awakened state. The real buddha that possesses the true qualities of abandonment and realization is the dharmakaya buddha. This truly and completely awakened state can be explained with the analogy of the sun in the sky. The sun shines with brilliant rays of light; however, if a thick layer of clouds fills the sky, it will appear that the sun is no longer shining, even though it actually is. This is simply due to the clouds. Even though clouds cover the whole sky and we can't see the sun, the sun itself is not affected in any way. Nor, when the clouds dissipate, is the sun improved—it's still shining away exactly as it has always been. Likewise, while one is a sentient being and the buddha nature is obscured by the veils of ignorance and delusion, is it worsened in any way? No, it isn't; its qualities are simply not apparent. When we practice the dharma in order to remove the veils of obscurations, our buddha nature is not improved upon or changed in any way; it is just that the very qualities it had all the while become apparent.

Therefore, unless our own nature is the awakened state of dharmakaya that is unformed like space, no amount of practice would enable us to create it. The unconditioned can never be achieved through conditioned practice, nor can the unformed be formed. On the other hand, you may begin to think, "Well, since we are already buddhas, why bother to practice at all?" However, such notions will also not help, because as our buddha nature is obscured by temporary obscurations, it is necessary to apply the methods that remove them in order to reveal what already exists. So, it is important to remember that the state of enlightenment and all its qualities are not the product of the path nor produced by practice.

Sentient beings can become buddhas because they have that pure basic nature already, just as gold ore already contains pure gold. Nevertheless, in order for the qualities of the gold to become fully apparent, the ore must be refined in order to remove the dross. Similarly, someone who wants to pursue the awakened state needs to gather the accumulations and remove their obscurations, so that they too can shine forth as a fully awakened buddha for the benefit of all.

APOLOGIZING

The text continues to explain that, although we all possess this buddha nature—naturally luminous wakefulness—we tend not to appreciate it for what it is. For that reason, we must confess to our erring ways:

> Out of confusion, I have exaggerated it or denigrated⠠
> The naturally luminous sugata essence.⠠
> In the nondual state beyond concepts,⠠
> I apologize for all the faults of straying into unwholesome
>   ways.⠠
> SAMAYA SHUDDHE AH⠠

We exaggerate when we attach values to the buddha nature that do not actually exist. We do this all the time by believing that things and phenomena, such as forms and sounds, actually exist. At the same time, through the power of innate or conceptualizing ignorance, we label things, and hence, due to our ignorance we denigrate the real qualities that the buddha nature actually does possess. This is all due to confusion, and by deluding ourselves in this way, we obscure the buddha nature. Therefore, we should *"rest evenly in the state in which the one who apologizes and the object of apology are not conceptualized."* In other words, by simply composing ourselves in equanimity within the state of thought-free wakefulness, we apologize for all the faults of straying into such unwholesome ways. This is the ultimate kind of apology.

SAMAYA is "commitment" or "vow"; SHUDDHE means "utterly pure." Hence, the mantra is an acknowledgment that we have restored our commitment not to stray from the nonarising nature of all phenomena by resting in the equanimity of this basic state. Then, while resting in that state, we should recite an apology chant such as the one that begins *"Om yeshe kuchok...."*[5]

TAKING THE VAJRA PLEDGE

Next, we should reaffirm our commitment to not stray from the natural state; to do this we take the vajra pledge, for example:

HUNG:
Through the pledge of practicing one-pointedly, without
    breaking:
The chain of brothers and sisters of great bliss,:
I will keep the supreme vajra samaya of the difficult to
    transgress,:
By the profound samadhi of approaching and
    accomplishing:
The yidam deity beyond beginning and end,:
And the vidyadhara guru, Ever-Excellent Padmakara,:
Right now without separation, though diverse is of one
    taste,:
Within the original state that is inherent to me.:
BODHICHITTA VAJRA SAMAYA HUNG:

68

The "brothers and sisters" mentioned in the second line refer to the fact that those who have taken empowerment and pith instructions from the same master are like close family members, as we have all taken the pledge to practice one-pointedly. In order to maintain this vow, we must "keep the supreme vajra samaya." As our basic nature is already dharmakaya, the essential samaya cannot actually be transcended.

"The profound samadhi of approaching and accomplishing" refers to the profound stages of development and completion—gaining confidence that you are the deity and resting in the natural state. While "the yidam deity beyond beginning and end" is the buddha nature itself. "The vidyadhara guru, ever-excellent Padmakara," is Guru Rinpoche, who is also sometimes referred to as Samantabhadra Padmakara.

"Right now without separation" means that Guru Rinpoche's own essence does not differ in the slightest from our own. Although diverse, they are of one taste, "Within the original state that is inherent to myself."

That is taking the vajra pledge. This is the indestructible commitment of awakened mind (bodhichitta).

SHOWERING DOWN THE GREAT RESPLENDENCE

At this point, there is music and dancing while streamers and banners are waved around, and the congregation sings a verse calling down the host of deities of the three kayas, as in this verse from the *Ngakso*:

HUNG HRIH:
Host of Trikaya Guru deities, manifest from dharmadhatu!:
Come to this place from your unmanifest space.:
Bring down the great vajra resplendence of Body, Speech, and Mind:
Into the samaya substance and the outer, inner, and secret mandala.:
Quickly display wonderful signs and indications.:
Empower all supreme practitioners and bestow your blessings.:
Let resplendence descend on this place, and bestow empowerments and siddhis!:

OM AH HUNG VAJRA GURU DHEVA DHAKINI JNANA
ABESHAYA A AH̥

The first two syllables, HUNG HRIH, are probably the seed syllables within the hearts of the deities and from which the deities arise. According to the *Barchey Künsel,* the "Trikaya Guru deities" are the following: dharmakaya is Buddha Amitayus; sambhogakaya is the great compassionate one, Avalokiteshvara; and the nirmanakaya is the lotus-born, Padmakara.[3] They are asked to "manifest from dharmadhatu," the invisible expanse of emptiness, and instill the blessings of their body, voice, and mind "into the samaya substance and the outer, inner, and secret mandalas." In other words, the practitioners, the articles on the shrine, and the surrounding environment all become a pure buddha field. We ourselves, the male and female practitioners, are the gods and goddesses. We request empowerment, blessings, and siddhis, and that the great resplendence might descend so that our practice place becomes identical with the Glorious Copper-Colored Mountain. When a practice like this is successful, various signs may occur such as seeing one's yidam deity face-to-face, a butter lamp igniting and burning all by itself, nectar flowing from the torma, and so on. In the mantra, OM AH HUNG, are the seed syllables for body, speech, and mind; VAJRA means indestructible, GURU DEVA DAKINI are the master, the yidam deity, and the dakini. JÑANA means wisdom, and ABESHAYA means to shower down.

CONSECRATING THE OFFERINGS

In the extensive guru sadhana from the *Barchey Künsel* cycle of teachings, it clarifies that one is still Hayagriva at this point, so like before, visualize yourself as the Lotus Heruka and then imagine that from the three syllables OM AH HUNG, the syllables RAM YAM KHAM are emanated. RAM is the essence of fire, and it burns away any concepts that we might have of the offering articles, the mandala, and the entire environment having a concrete reality. The YAM sends out vajra wind that blows away all concepts; and the KHAM, being the essence of vajra water, washes away any remnants.

---

3 Guru Rinpoche, "the Lotus-Born" (symbolizing his self-arising within primordial purity) is commonly referred to as either Padmasambhava or Padmakara.

The entire universe together with everything and everyone within it, is then blessed as the great offering mudra. Sometimes it is said that the world is the torma plate and the beings are the torma. That is the great natural torma offering. So, whatever appears and exists, the entire universe with all beings, is the offering of manifest ground. "Manifest ground" means that all existence and appearances represent the intrinsic qualities of buddha nature that are already originally present.

We then recite a couple of mantras in order to consecrate all of appearance and existence as an ocean-like display of Samantabhadra:

HUNG HUNG SARVA PUJA MEGHA AH HUNG꞉

OM VAJRA ARGHAM AH HUNG PADHAM AH HUNG PUSHPE AH HUNG DHUPE AH HUNG ALOKE AH HUNG GANDHE AH HUNG NAIVENTE AH HUNG SHABTA AH HUNG꞉

SARVA means all; PUJA is offerings; and MEGHA is cloud. Therefore, the first mantra means that everything is a great offering cloud.

The next mantra lists the eight traditional offering articles: ARGHAM is the rinsing water for the feet, PADHAM the rinsing water for the face, PUSHPE is flowers, DHUPE incense, ALOKE the lamp, GANDHE perfume, NAIVENTE food, and SHABTA is sound, represented by music. We append AH HUNG to the end of each of them.

We must also consecrate the amrita, rakta,[6] and torma. In the *Sarma* schools, this is often very extensive; in the *Nyingma* sadhanas, however, it is condensed because Nyingma practitioners cultivate this attitude from the very beginning throughout all of their practice, so it is not a specific new point that needs to be introduced. Therefore, as one only needs a quick reminder, all three can be together in a single set of verses, as in these from the *Ngakso*:

> HUNG HRIH꞉
> Empty and luminous, wind and fire, skull stand of the three
>   emancipations.꞉
> Within the great self-existing bhandha of dharmadhatu,꞉
> The elements and aggregates as the five meats and five
>   nectars,꞉
> Melt into bodhichitta through the action of fire and wind.꞉

The five-colored vapor streams out into the ten directions⁏
And the essences of the world and beings are gathered back
    as OM AH HUNG.⁏
Inviting the nectar of the sugatas,⁏
It becomes the nectar of binding the chakras in union.⁏
Amidst the palace of an excellent jewel-vessel arising from
    BHRUNG,⁏
Is the torma of the five sense pleasures appearing from the
    three syllables.⁏
Amidst the excellent rakta vessel, the nature of E,⁏
The Great Red showers, like rain, from the space of Girti.⁏

To begin with, we imagine a skull cup. Being the unity of appearance and emptiness, everything is "empty and luminous." The "skull stand" is composed of three skulls representing the three emancipations, namely those of the shravaka, pratyekabuddha, and bodhisattva. On top of these rests a skull cup that is used as an offering bowl. "Bhandha" refers to the great skull, dharmadhatu, which is the self-existing sphere which contains all the elements and aggregates that make up the universe and beings "as the five meats[7] and five nectars." When the wind fans the flames of the fire, everything heats up. All our concepts of things being concrete and real, all our notions of impurity, accepting and rejecting, and so on melt into the juice of the awakened state, which is the awakened mind known as bodhichitta. The steam rises curling upwards and spreading to fill the ten directions.

We then imagine putting a lid made from the Ali-Kali mantra,[4] and a top ornament, like the knob to lift the lid, which is the sphere containing OM AH HUNG, like that found on a vajra. All the essences are gathered back into the OM AH HUNG. The OM AH HUNG then dissolve into one another, inviting the nectar of all the sugatas. This becomes the nectar that binds all the chakras in union.

While repeating OM AH HUNG, from the seed syllable BHRUNG, the palace of dharmadhatu arises, containing the torma of beautiful forms, exquisite sounds, smells, tastes, and textures, etc. that continue to emanate from OM AH HUNG. While into a triangular vessel that has the nature

---

4 The vowels and consonants.

of E, representing the nonarising dharmadhatu, "the great red"—rakta—showers down, like rain, from the secret place of the goddess Girtima. This rakta also heats up and swells like waves, in which there are dismembered parts of sentient beings.

One stirs the amrita nectar and repeats OM AH HUNG SARVA PENTSA AMRITA KUNDALI HUNG HRIH THAH three times. SARVA means all; BENZA means five-fold, hence refers to the five nectars; AMRITA KUNDALI is a deity who helps eliminate negative influences.

One then sprinkles the torma with this amrita and recites OM AH HUNG MAHA BALINGTA TEJO BALINGTA BALA BATE GUHYA SAMAYA HUNG HRIH THAH three times. BALINGTA is the word for torma and means "that which produces strength." GUHYA means secret; MAHA means great.

Lastly, the vessel containing the rakta is raised while the mantra OM AH HUNG MAHA RAKTA JVALA MANDALA HUNG HRIH TA is also recited three times. JVALA means blazing like a fire; and MANDALA refers to the mandala circle.

CONFIRMING NATURAL AWARENESS

Now all that is left in the preliminaries for buddha nature is indeed present:

> HUNG:
> The three roots of the bodhichitta of natural awareness:
> Do not exist anywhere but in the state indivisible from
>   myself.:
> Within it, all the mandalas of victorious ones are complete.:
> I naturally confirm this in the primordially uncontrived
>   state.:

As previously explained, all beings, including ourselves, actually have this nature. So, here, we merely need to remind ourselves of our own buddha nature, which is natural awareness (*rang rig*). Natural awareness can also be understood as rigpa, which differs from dualistic mind (*sems*). Dualistic mind is clinging to notions of subject and object, self and other. *Rigpa* is free of all such attachment. *Rigpa* is bodhichitta, awakened mind, or in Tibetan, *byang chub kyi sems*. In the *Dharmadhatu Kosha*, Longchenpa explains the Tibetan word for *bodhi*, which is *byang chub*.

Byang means "purified" or "cleared of any obscuring veils" that might cover our original buddha nature. *Chub* means "perfected" or "complete" in the sense that all the qualities are originally complete and perfected. That is bodhi, while *chitta* means "mind." So all together the phrase refers to our pure and perfect mind.

Within the primordially uncontrived state, we acknowledge that the three roots—the gurus, yidams, and dakinis—are indivisible from our own nature, and do not exist anywhere other than the state of *rigpa*. All buddhas, all the victorious ones, are complete within my natural mind.

This is then sealed with the mantra OM AH HUNG GURU DEVA DAKINI SARVA SAMAYA SATVAM BODHICHITTA JNANA AH. OM AH HUNG refers to the enlightened body, speech, and mind of the masters, yidams, and dakinis. SARVA means all. SAMAYA is the bond or committment; SATVAM means with me; BODHICHITTA means awakened mind; JÑANA means wisdom, original wakefulness; and AH means is. So, you could translate the mantra as, "the original wakefulness of my awakened mind is, in fact, the bond with all the gurus, yidams, and dakinis."

The Main Part

We have covered the preliminaries, which provide favorable conditions and clear away unfavorable conditions. Now we begin the main part, which can be divided into four different sections: (1) erecting the framework—the three samadhis: (2) visualizing the base, i.e., the celestial palace; (3) visualizing the based, the deities; (4) consecration and empowerment.

ERECTING THE FRAMEWORK—
THE THREE SAMADHIS

Within Vajrayana, all practices begin by erecting the framework of the three samadhis: the samadhi of suchness, the samadhi of illumination, and the seed samadhi. Once you gain some familiarity with the basic structure of sadhanas, you will notice that no matter what practice it is, although the words may differ, the meaning remains the same.

Many great masters, including Paltrül Rinpoche, repeatedly stressed that whatever yidam practice one trains in, the three samadhis must be included in order to assure that development stage does not stray into an ordinary concept of concreteness. To conceive of the celestial palace, deities, and so forth as having a concrete reality is the very opposite of recognizing emptiness; instead it is just further strengthening one's habit of clinging to the illusion of a solid reality. There is the old story of a woman who visualized herself in the form of a tigress to such an extent that even other people started to see her as a tiger. Her belief that she was, in fact, a tiger resulted in mass delusion. It is said that one who is very skilled in development stage, but not in completion stage, usually takes rebirth as a powerful spirit such as a *mamo*, *tsen*, or *gyalpo*. Often it takes a highly realized master to eventually subdue these spirits. So, it is important to guard against and remedy such mistaken habits with an understanding of emptiness, and then one should be able to avoid suffering such an unfortunate rebirth. In order to avoid further clinging to ordinary concreteness, it is very important to begin any visualization with the samadhi of suchness, which is simply recognizing the unconstructed suchness, or emptiness, that is the nature of mind.

No matter what sort of yidam practice you might be doing, the three samadhis are indispensable; therefore, you should understand that their purpose is to bring an end to the recurring state of suffering known as samsara. Each of the three samadhis purifies one aspect of this cycle: (1) the samadhi of suchness purifies the concept of death; (2) the samadhi of illumination purifies the concept of the bardo, the state between dying and being reborn; (3) the seed samadhi purifies the concept of rebirth.

The *Liberation Through Hearing in the Bardo*, commonly known as *The Tibetan Book of the Dead*, describes the various stages that one experiences at death, during which the various elements—earth, water, fire, and wind—dissolve one after the other ending not only with the normal exhalation of breath, but also with the inner breath, as the subtle circulation of energy ceases. At that moment, one's state of mind is identical to the unfabricated state of dharmakaya. The difference lies in whether or not we recognize at the time that this state is not oblivion, but rather our true nature. This can only happen by thoroughly familiarizing ourselves with the nature of mind that we can be introduced to by our root guru. Simply catching a glimpse of it, however, will not suffice; hence it is necessary to train again and again during this very life, so that you will naturally recognize the basic unfabricated nature of dharmakaya at the moment of death.

Also, training in the development stage is not possible without the three samadhis. Here we have the following lines from the *Ngakso* in which the three samadhis are clearly formulated:

> AH
> Dharmakaya's space of suchness is the realm of luminous
>   wakefulness.§
> Sambhogakaya's unceasing illumination is compassionate
>   expression.§
> Nirmanakaya's seed samadhi is the white HRIH,§
> Radiating light that purifies clinging to a real universe with
>   beings.§

SAMADHI OF SUCHNESS

To begin, we utter the syllable AH to remind us that our very nature has never arisen nor come into existence—it is the nonarising dharmakaya nature of all things. This is expressed in the first line: "Dharmakaya's basic space of suchness is the realm of luminous wakefulness." This "luminous wakefulness" is emptiness. In other words, the identity of any given thing is not to be found in any way whatsoever; it cannot be formulated, and is totally impossible to manufacture with thoughts or constructs. The buddha nature actually is luminous wakefulness. So, when we recognize this luminous wakefulness, we reveal our buddha nature. And by simply acknowledging the nature of things as they already are, and remaining in equanimity, the more we refine our experience of death. By doing so, at the moment of death we will be able to naturally recognize dharmakaya.

When we are chanting this text together in a group, there doesn't seem to be much time to just let be. We chant one line and then go straight on to the next. But that is not the intent of this type of practice; rather the words are simply a reminder for someone who is already familiar with the three samadhis. For someone who is quite adept in recognizing and is able to let the expression of that recognition of the samadhi of suchness arise as compassion, reading these lines rejuvenates one's embrace of the fundamental practice. When you practice by yourself, you shouldn't rush through it. You should read the first line and then remain in the recognition of luminous wakefulness for a while. Then, when the expression of emptiness becomes compassion, read the next line, and so on.

SAMADHI OF ILLUMINATION

The samadhi of illumination purifies one's experience of the bardo. The bardo occurs when the original state of dharmakaya is not acknowledged at the moment of death. What happens then is that one faints, during which the consciousness seemingly dissolves within the white and red elements. This blackout can last for three and a half to four days, and the bardo begins upon reawakening from that blackout.

At first, you are disoriented. Not realizing that you have died, out of previous habit everything will appear the same as when you were alive, so you will seek out familiar places, friends, and family. However, when you talk to them, they won't respond at all, further disorienting you. Then the bardo experiences begin, one day after another, and everything becomes very ungrounded. At the longest, this can go on for forty-nine days. It is said that each week the circumstances of death reoccur so that one experiences death over and over, and all other kinds of experiences take place; you can learn the details of these from various other books.

The experiences of the bardo are purified by the samadhi of illumination, which is nothing other than the naturally arising compassion that is indivisible from emptiness. Just like wetness is inseparable from water and heat is inseparable from fire, compassion is an intrinsic quality of emptiness.

When the nature of mind is recognized as emptiness, an unceasing, unobstructed compassion automatically arises that is directed toward any being who does not recognize their own nature. Training in this samadhi of illumination, right now, during our lives, will purify our grasping and prepare us to be free during the experience of the bardo.

The instruction is that, right now. This is why we are taught, that once compassion arises from the samadhi of suchness, we should remain in the samadhi of illumination as long as possible. Then, upon emerging from the samadhi of illumination, let the first concept be the confidence that the bardo is pure sambhogakaya.

SAMADHI OF THE SEED SYLLABLE

Last of the three samadhis is the samadhi of the seed syllable. This samadhi purifies the process of seeking rebirth after going through the experience of the bardo.

The samadhi of suchness, emptiness totally free of mental constructs, is indivisible from the samadhi of illumination, great compassion. That unity of emptiness and compassion manifests as a seed syllable, just like the full moon rising on the fifteenth day, brilliant and clear, in the middle of space, shining in all directions. This syllable is the seed or the root cause for all the deities of the mandala, and to focus one's attention on it without distraction is the samadhi of the seed syllable.

You should train in this samadhi for quite a while, concentrating on the seed syllable illuminating the entire universe. The particular seed syllable depends on which deity you happen to be practicing with, whether it is a guru, yidam, or dakini. However, no matter which practice you might do, it is important to know that although the shape and color of the syllables may differ, the three samadhis themselves always remain the same. For example, when practicing a peaceful deity like Guru Rinpoche, the seed syllable could be a white HRIH and for a wrathful deity it could be HUNG. The syllable itself will be the same color as the chief figure of the mandala. In every case though, the seed syllable is self-luminous, radiantly shining like the moon.

Keep focused on the shape of the seed syllable in the beginning, and then you should place a drawing of the seed syllable in front of you. Concentrate on the drawing for a while, then close your eyes and allow the image to appear in the field of your mind. When it begins to fade and become indistinct, open your eyes and concentrate on the drawing again and repeat the cycle.

In order to purify the habitual notions that we have of a physical environment made of earth, water, trees, buildings, and so on, from the main seed syllable, light radiates in the form of the syllables for fire, wind, and water. This purifies our clinging to any misconceptions of there being a substantial universe. First, RAM, fire, reduces all matter to ashes, so that no substantial object remains. Then, the mighty wind of YAM scatters the ashes. Finally, KHAM, water, washes away any remains until even the slightest notion of a concrete universe is totally obliterated.

Finally, when emerging from the samadhi of the seed syllable, your first thought should be that the entire universe is a buddha field and the pure experience of rebirth is nirmanakaya.

VISUALIZING THE MANDALA OF THE SUPPORT

Although specific details might differ from one practice to another, the basic structure of the development stage remains essentially the same. Here we will continue to use the *Ngakso* as our example. The *Ngakso* has Guru Rinpoche as the central figure, surrounded by all his manifestations, as well as the one hundred peaceful and wrathful deities.

Now, we come to the second, visualizing the base, the celestial palace. First, we must visualize the support, beginning with the mandalas of the four elements, then Mount Sumeru, the celestial palace, and so on. Just like when a world is formed, the environment is created first and then the beings arise; once this foundation has been established, we then visualize the deities.

To visualize the creation of the universe, first imagine the gradually piled elements of space, wind, fire, water, and earth. From the letter

E, the mandala of space unfolds, stretching out into all directions. On top of this, from the syllable YAM, an immense vajra cross forms. From the syllable RAM arises a triangular diagram symbolizing the force of heat. Next comes the cohesiveness of water, symbolized by an immense ocean. All those forces interact, churning the ocean so that a creamy substance is formed on the surface, just like cream floating on milk. When this is churned further, just as solid butter forms from milk, the solid element of earth takes shape in the immense form of Mount Sumeru. Then, slowly, the four continents and the eight subcontinents all take shape.

On the summit of Mount Sumeru is another vajra cross surrounded by a perimeter of vajras all around, as well as above and below, so that it becomes a protection circle. In the middle of the vajra cross is a four-petaled lotus flower. The syllable BHRUNG is emanated from the initial seed syllable and descends into the middle of the lotus. This syllable then transforms into the celestial palace. In the *Ngakso*, it has four sides, four gates, three stories, and numerous other details. Words can't really describe it, so I would recommend that you look at a model or good rendering of it and have someone point out all the different details. Note, however, that the celestial palace is transparent and appears to be made out of rainbows. None of the different decorations have material, concrete existence; they are all insubstantial. In the center of the celestial palace are eight huge lions holding up a platform that supports a lotus flower with 100,000 petals. In its center is the disk of the sun and the moon.

DEVELOPMENT STAGE

There are three important principles to keep in mind while practicing the development stage. The first is vivid presence, in which all the details of the deities are complete and clear in our minds. Next is stable pride, not ordinary conceit or arrogance, but rather the unshakeable confidence that all the qualities of the enlightened state are intrinsic to the deity and to oneself. And, third is the recollection of the pure symbolism of the various features and accoutrements of the deity; for example, Padmasambhava's one face symbolizes the single sphere of Dharmakaya, his two arms the unity of means and knowledge, his white skin that he is utterly free from clinging to subject and object, and the red hue that shines through from within is his passionate love and affection for all beings. The six arms of the wrathful deities symbolize the six paramitas, and their three faces are the three kayas. The dakinis are from the four families of vajra, ratna (jewel), padma (lotus), and karma (activity). They are the lords of the four activities: pacifying, enriching, magnetizing, and subjugating. The dakinis are the essential nature of the eight emancipations: the emancipation of regarding what has form to be form, the emancipation of regarding the formless as having form, the emancipation of the repulsive and clearing away hindrances, the four emancipations of the four formless states, and the emancipation of cessation. It is important to study and learn what all these mean as each feature represents a very profound teaching.

The simplest visualization is to visualize oneself as the single unelaborate form of a deity. At your forehead, throat, and heart are the three buddhas of body, speech, and mind, which can be represented either by the three syllables (OM AH HUNG) or the three buddhas themselves—Vairochana, Amitabha, and Akshobhya. One is also crowned with either the five syllables (OM HUNG TRAM HRIH AH) or the five buddhas. You are the samaya being, and in the center of your heart is the wisdom being. Altogether that makes only ten deities that one must visualize. However, if you prefer more detailed, elaborate visualizations, then you can get really complicated. For this, the best approach would be to study *the Guhyagarbha* tantra and *the Secret Essence* tantra.

If you are confident in the teachings, particularly those of primordial purity, then by uniting the completion stage with the development stage, it is possible to practice the ultimate form of development stage in which all that is seen is a strand in the magical web of male and female deities, celestial palace, and buddha field; everything heard is mantra; and all mental activities are manifestations of the five wisdoms. In short, all phenomena are the compassionate influence of the awakened state assuming whatever form is necessary for the benefit of deluded beings.

VISUALIZING THE SUPPORTED MANDALA:
THE DIETIES

The third point is about the based, meaning the deities. In the center of the palace, the syllable HRIH appears as my awareness (rigpa), buddha nature itself, in the form of Padmasambhava. Padmasambhava is an expression of the qualities of all the awakened ones, so by visualizing yourself as him, you acknowledge that your basic identity is identical to that of all buddhas. Of course, our true buddha nature is already perfect and complete; however, we ourselves often lack confidence in this fact. Visualization practices are a means to develp this confidence and overcome our habitual attachments. This, however, requires training, developing the visualization of the mandala until the celestial palace, complete with the deities, is crisp and clear in one's mind in a single instant. This may sound difficult, but it is just a matter of familiarity. For example, if someone mentions the name of a good friend, then their face will instantly appear in your mind. Similarly, eventually, simply by saying OM AH HUNG VAJRA GURU PADMA SIDDHI HUNG, the whole visualization of Padmasambhava will appear without any effort on your part.

It may not be so easy to view yourself as Padmasambhava or whatever deity you are practicing right from the beginning, but that is why development stage is called development stage: it is slowly and gradually developed by training. You should focus more on any aspects or details of the visualization that are not clear until they are. It is useful to have a statue or painting in front of you for reference. You can also stare at it for a long time until you can see it clearly, even when you close your eyes. As a further aid to one's practice, it is also traditional to have a shrine mandala representing the celestial palace and deities. At best, this is made of colored sand, next best is a painted version, and third best is one comprised of heaps of grains. In our visualization, of course, the three kaya gurus are one above the other, like a three-story building, but when you put the three heaps of grain on the mandala plate, you first put one in the center, then one a little beyond that, and the last one a little further. Then, of course, you put the twelve manifestations at the appropriate places, as well as the four dakas and dakinis, and so on.

In brief, to begin, you imagine yourself as the nirmanakaya guru Padmasambhava. Your skin is white with a reddish glow. You are smiling, though with a wrathful expression, and you wear the lotus crown. You are wearing the secret white tunic over which is the blue dancing gown, the three dharma robes, and a brocade cloak of maroon. You raise a five-pronged golden vajra in your right hand, and in your left you hold a skull cup with a vase of longevity sitting within it. Your secret consort is hidden in the form of the *khatvanga* held in the crook of your left arm.

Your two feet are in the playful, or reveling, royal posture. You are poised majestically within a sphere of five-colored rainbow light.

Behind your back, a lotus tree reaches up into the sky. On the second story of the palace, a lotus flower unfolds upon which the sambhogakaya deity, the white lord Avalokiteshvara, sits. He has four arms, two of which have palms joined at his heart, holding a wish-fulfilling jewel. His other right arm holds a crystal rosary, and the other left arm a white lotus. There are many other details, including the thirteen adornments, eight jewel ornaments, and five silken garments, which you can learn about from elsewhere if you are so interested.

The lotus tree extends into the top story of the palace, where, on another lotus blossom, sits the dharmakaya buddha Amitabha. He is dark red in color, and his hands, in equanimity, hold the vase of longevity. He, too, possesses the complete sambhogakaya ornaments.

Next are the twelve manifestations of Padmasambhava, who are arranged in groups. The first group comprises the four inner manifestations, who surround Padmasambhava on the four petals of the lotus, namely Gyalwey Dungdzin, Mawey Senge, Kyechok Tsülsang, and Dukyi Shechen. Outside of them, on the facets of a jewel, are Dzamling Ghenchok, Pema Jungney, Kyepar Phakpey Rigdzin, Dzutrül Tuchen, Dorje Draktsal, Kalden Drendzey, Raksha Tötreng, and Dechen Gyalpo. Some of them embrace consorts, and all appear in various forms and attire. For those who need to be influenced by peaceful means, they adopt peaceful forms; and for those requiring wrathful means, they assume a wrathful form, each with the appropriate kinds of ornaments, accoutrements, and implements.[5]

If a god appears among human beings and tells them what to do in order be like him, people will say, "You're not one of us. You were born different from us, and we cannot be like you; you are a different species." We are more apt to believe that we can achieve enlightenment when we see that it has been attained by others who have had to study and practice themselves. This is why buddhas assume appearances that others can relate to, whether that is as a human being, an animal, or any of the other forms found throughout the six realms. Buddhas don't appear only as human beings; they come in all sizes and shapes; even in excrement there

---

5 Detailed explanation of the twelve manifestations has been moved to Appendix 1.

are all sorts of tiny bugs, and, there too, buddhas appear to guide them. Some people require peaceful means, others need to be enticed, and some incorrigible people need to be subdued, so buddhas take on a wrathful expression for them.

Now, the four gates in the four directions have portals that are like small rooms, where the four dakas reside, together with their consorts. In the east is the white daka, who possesses a pacifying air. He holds a curved knife with a vajra handle, signifying that he is from the vajra family. In the south is the yellow ratna daka with his consort; his curved knife has a handle that looks like a jewel. The ratna daka and dakini possess an air of increasing or enriching. In the west is the red lotus daka and his consort with a magnetic air. The handle of his knife is in the shape of a lotus. Lastly, in the north is the green karma daka embracing his consort and holding a curved knife with a vajra cross handle. Each of the dakas holds a skull cup in the left hand, and all of them are in dancing postures with one leg bent and one extended.

All the surrounding space and those in between are filled with countless enlightened beings, the three roots, gurus, and masters of the various lineages, yidam deities, dakas and dakinis, dharma protectors, and guardians. The chief guardian of the male class of protectors is Vajra Sadhu, or Dorje Lekden as he is known in Tibet. The chief protector of the female class is the guardian of mantra, Ekajati, and the chief of the neuter class is Maning. There are an incredible number of other deities, all of whom are "magical wisdom forms of united appearance and emptiness." They are all visible and distinct, just like the moon reflected in water, yet they are also insubstantial, like rainbows in the sky.

The peaceful and wrathful buddhas are not just figments of our imagination; we are actually composed of them. As a human being, we have the five sense faculties and experience the five sense objects. We have a physical body composed of the five elements, and possessing the five sense aggregates (skandhas). And, we have the different consciousnesses. The pure nature of each of these factors is one of the peaceful or wrathful buddhas. For example, the five aggregates are the five male buddhas; the five elements, the five female buddhas; and the eight consciousnesses are the eight male and female bodhisattvas. Everybody actually possesses all of these, so we visualize the deities in order to reacquaint ourselves with what we truly are.

CONSECRATION

At this point in the practice, you, as the central deity, visualize a white
OM at your forehead, a red AH at your throat, and a blue HUNG at your
heart. The white OM at the forehead is in the center of a white wheel. It
radiates rays of white light that turn into offerings pleasing to the countless buddhas and bodhisattvas in the ten directions. You then absorb the
qualities of their own enlightened bodies in the form of OM syllables,
which dissolve into the original OM on your forehead. Then, the red letter AH, in the center of a red lotus at your throat, sends out countless rays
of light that again turn into pleasing offerings to the infinite number of
buddhas and bodhisattvas in the ten directions. And the qualities of their
enlightened speech, in the form of the syllable AH, dissolve into the red
AH in your throat. Finally, the blue HUNG, which is in the center of a blue
vajra in the heart center, radiates blue light out in all directions, making
pleasing offerings, and then absorbing the blessings of enlightened mind
in the form of HUNG syllables.

Having received the blessings of enlightened body, speech, and mind
in this way, the white syllable OM transforms into the white buddha Vairochana with one face and two arms; the red syllable AH transforms into
the red buddha Amitabha with one face and two arms; and the blue
HUNG becomes the blue buddha Akshobhya. Imagining this, you should
utter the three syllables OM AH HUNG, while performing the three corresponding mudras.

EMPOWERMENT

Now, you perform the mudras that correspond to the empowerments of
the five wisdom families, while saying the related seed syllables OM HUNG
TRAM HRIH AH. All the deities send out rays of light calling upon the
buddha families in the ten directions to send wisdom nectar to empower
you. The nectar fills up your body and overflows from the top of your
head. This excess then becomes the five buddha families adorning your
head as a crown.

This symbolic act is an acknowledgement that our basic being is already identical with the five buddha families. The Abhidharma states
that the aggregates, elements, and sense sources are impure, but in the

Vajrayana context, they are all seen to be pure, and even the body is viewed as a mandala of the five families. For example, the five fingers of the right hand are the five male buddhas, and the five fingers of the left hand are the five female buddhas. Another viewpoint is that our head is the Buddha Vairochana, our right arm is the Buddha Akshobhya, our left arm is Ratnasambhava, our right leg is Amitabha, and our left leg is Amoghasiddhi. Generally speaking, the five aggregates (skandhas) are the five male buddhas; and the five elements (earth, water, fire, wind, and space) are the five female buddhas. So, you can see that the buddhas are not elsewhere, but part and parcel of your very being.

Corresponding to the five buddhas: OM is Vairochana, HUNG is Akshobhya, TRAM is Ratnasambhava, HRIH is Amitabha, and AH is Amoghasiddhi. When you form the five mudras at the corresponding places on your head, you should imagine that the related buddha is present there; either simply imagine the syllables alone or, if you prefer, imagine the five buddhas in their bodily forms. This is called "being crowned with the lord of the family." Doing so purifies one's habitual tendency to identify with belonging to a certain ancestry or any of the five castes: royalty, priests, nobility, merchants, or commoners.

The central lord of the mandala depends on the practice. In the *Ocean of Amrita* drubchen, it is white Vairochana. Therefore, you should hold your fingers in the mudra related to OM, symbolizing Buddha Vairochana, at the top of your head. Hung, at the front of your skull, is Buddha Akshobhya; TRAM, on the right, is Ratnasambhava; at the back of your neck is HRIH, Buddha Amitabha; and on the left side is Buddha Amoghasiddhi.

So, to briefly summarize, first there is the consecration in which light is emanated from the three syllables representing body, speech, and mind, which invokes the blessings of all the buddhas and bodhisattvas. The light from all the deities then invokes the lords of the five buddha families to come and bestow empowerment. The nectar overflows from the crown of your head and becomes the five buddhas, who are actually now seated as adornments around your head. As you are in the samaya being in the form of Padmasambhava, you are wearing the lotus crown inside of which is the sambhogakaya crown of the five buddhas. At the end of the five seed syllables, you say ABHIKENSA HUNG, which means that the empowerment has now been bestowed.

INVOKING AND DISSOLVING THE WISDOM BEINGS

These deities are called the samaya beings. When we visualize ourselves as the bodily forms of the deities, with ornaments, certain clothes, emblems, and so on, this is called the samaya beings as oneself. Now we invite the wisdom beings "from the buddha field of the three kayas, the Glorious Palace of Lotus Light," to arrive in the sky before us. To do this, rays of light—each of which has a hook at the tip—radiate not just from our own heart centers, but from each and every deity in the mandala. In the *Ocean of Amrita* the wisdom beings include the form of Padmasambhava known as Guru Padma Tötreng Tsal, who is the three inseparable kayas, together with his assembly of infinite deities of the three roots. With deep yearning and longing, we invite him to come to where we are practicing. Since all buddhas and bodhisattvas have taken a solemn vow, they must come to "dispel all obstacles and bestow the supreme and common siddhis." We then utter the mantra OM AH HUNG VAJRA GURU PADMA TÖTRENG TSAL VAJRA SAMAYA JAH SIDDHI PHALA HUNG AH, followed by the mantra of invocation JAH HUNG BAM HOH.

Once they arrive we request them to take a seat and stay "unwaveringly and permanently."

HOMAGE AND OFFERINGS

The next point has two parts, now that the buddhas and bodhisattvas have all joined us, we should pay homage to them and present them with offerings. Still being in the form of Padmasambhava, from your heart center you emanate countless male and female servants, as numerous as the particles of dust in a beam of sunlight. These servants pay homage and make outer, inner, and innermost offerings to all the deities in the mandala.

HOMAGE

First, for homage, we begin with the two syllables of enlightened mind, HUNG HRIH. Then, we acknowledge the pure nature of the deities, which does not arise nor cease. It never changes, and yet all its activities are perfect. This is the sugata essence in its awakened state, which is self-existent, in that it is not made by anyone or anything. Its compassionate activity liberates all beings. Like a wishfulfilling jewel, the assembly of knowledge-holders (*vidyadharas*) bestows a rain of siddhis and accomplishments. You then pay homage with the mantra ATIPU HO to which the deities reply PRATICCHA HO.

OUTER OFFERINGS

The outer offerings are the pleasant peaceful offerings, like the three sweets, three whites, and so on that are common to the outer tantras. You offer these, both actually present and mentally created, to the deities of the mandala. Traditionally, there are eight outer offerings: (1) pure water for drinking and rinsing the mouth; (2) water for cleansing the feet; (3) flowers; (4) incense; (5) a lamp; (6) refreshing perfumed water; (7) food; and (8) music. All of these fill space, like the clouds of offerings made by the bodhisattva Samantabhadra.

We make these offerings not because the wisdom beings themselves have such concepts as thirst or hunger. However, the purpose of making these outer offerings is to purify our own habitual concepts about eating, drinking, experiencing pleasant sensations, and so on.

INNER OFFERINGS

The inner offering is comprised of two parts: amrita and rakta together, and the torma offering. The first offering is described as:

> Self-existing substance, perfectly pure from the beginning,§
> Supreme medicine composed of eight major and a
>   thousand minor parts,§
> Great rakta offering of unexcelled bliss and emptiness,§
> Ocean of amrita and rakta, white and red bodhichitta,§
> Essential extract of samsara and nirvana,§
> Passionate rakta of the three realms,§
> Accept this as the undefiled great bliss.§
> GURU DHEVA DHAKINI SARVA PA CA AMRITA MAHA RAKTA
>   KHAHI§

"Self-existing" (*rangjung*) simply means natural, not manufactured. Unlike Western pharmaceuticals, Tibetan medicine is pure and contains only natural ingredients. In regard to the mantra, GURU DHEVA DHAKINI are the three roots, SARVA means whole, PA CA AMRITA means the five nectars, MAHA RAKTA is great rakta, KHAHI means "please enjoy"—so it roughly translates as "All of you, gurus, deities, and dakinis, please enjoy these five nectars of the great rakta." You then dip your ring finger in the amrita and sprinkle a bit of it around, while imagining that the amrita fills up the infinity of space and showers down a rain of great nectar that suffuses all the deities in the mandala, generating unconditioned great bliss. At the same time, we chant the nectar offering to each of the lineage masters. The last such line is "To the mouths of the deities who are the world and the beings manifest," which means that whatever we perceive, all that exists, the world and beings, possess a divine nature and are, in fact, deities.

It is not that we are here in Nepal, for example, doing the *Ngakso*. It is said that when someone practices development stage, yet still remains in his or her own house, the development stage will be ineffective. Instead, one should view one's surroundings as a pure land, where all that is seen is a buddha field, all sound is mantra, and all mental activity is the play of wisdom.

At this point, we ourselves partake of a little nectar. While saying OM AH HUNG, we pinch some nectar between our thumb and ring finger, imagining that they are two half spheres of the sun and moon. These join together containing a portion of the nectar, which is the *siddhi*, the accomplishment of all the deities. Then saying KAYA SIDDHI HUNG, you put a drop on your forehead, with VAKA SIDDHI AH you touch a drop to your throat, and with CHITTA SIDDHI HUNG to your heart. Then, you place the nectar on your tongue, which you imagine in the shape of a vajra, and swallowing it, the nectar completely fills up your body, suffusing it with great wisdom.

For the torma offering, though, we physically offer a torma on a tray; in reality, the entire universe is the tray and all sentient beings are the torma. You offer this self-existing, "magnificent and majestic, glorious torma to the assembly of gurus, yidams, and dakinis," while uttering the mantra OM AH HUNG GURU DEVA DAKINI MAHA BALINGTA KHAHI which simly means "Gurus, deities, and dakinis please enjoy this great torma."

A torma can be understood in four different ways: 1) when receiving empowerment, the torma is regarded as the deities; (2) when making offerings, as in this case, it is regarded as sense pleasures; (3) when receiving the siddhis, tormas are regarded as the accomplishment; and (4) when performing an exorcism, the torma is a kind of repelling force that is thrown into the face of the obstructors.

INNERMOST OFFERING

Now we come to the innermost or secret offering which is:

> The bodhichitta of indivisible means and knowledge,⸴
> The cloudbank of liberated confusion that produces the
>   delight of great bliss,⸴
> Primordially free from the reference points of offering and
>   object,⸴
> Is the self-existing great offering of spontaneous presence.⸴
> TANA GANA DHARMADHATU ATMA KOH HANG⸴

"Bodhichitta" means the awakened state of mind, while in this case, "means and knowledge" refers to subject and object which are indivisible. Although we talk about a sensory organ and an object perceived by that organ, in actuality they form a natural indivisible unity. These offerings are primordially free of any notion such as the act of offering, an object to be offered, anyone making an offering, and anyone to whom they are offered. Hence, they are the most profound offering possible—the "self-existing great offering of spontaneous presence." In regard to the mantra at the end, tana gana means union and liberation, DHARMADHATU ATMA KOH HANG means that's me, I am that.

GIVING PRAISE

We have come to the fifth branch that of offering praises. That means, having presented offerings, we now extol the qualities of enlightened body, speech, mind, qualities, and activities. To do this, the male and female vajra servants that were emanated from the heart center of Padmasambhava praise the intrinsic qualities of the awakened state, the non-dual state of awareness, which is Padmasambhava's true identity, as well as what manifests as the natural expression of this awareness: the gurus of the three kayas, the twelve manifestations, the male and female dakas and dakinis at the gates, and so on.

Padmasambhava appears not just in this world, but also manifests in all the infinite realms in the ten directions. At the same time, however, all the infinite buddha fields are contained within his own body. His speech is said to contain the modulations and tones of the sixteen modes of purity, the voice of Brahma, which resounds in all directions throughout space. His mind, or state of realization, is unimpeded, totally open, and uncompounded. His inconceivable qualities cannot be fully described, even by noble beings who possess the eye of wisdom, and his activities to tame and influence sentient beings are unceasing and effortless.

At the end of the praises, all the male and female servers who were emanated out, made offerings and praises, gather back into one's heart center.[6]

---

6 Section moved to Appendix 1

Combined Mantras of Tukdrub
and the Peaceful and Wrathful Deities

Mantra Recitation

You recite mantras properly. In order for the mantra to have the best effect, you must avoid the ten faults described in the tantras by chanting (1) too loudly, (2) too quietly, (3) too quickly, or (4) too slowly. Nor should you interrupt the recitation by (5) talking, (6) coughing, (7) yawning or sighing, (8) hiccupping, (9) dozing off, or (10) becoming mentally distracted. You shouldn't sip tea while reciting mantras either. You should do your best not to willfully interrupt your recitation in any of those ways, but as not much can be done to avoid them when they are involuntary, you can make up for any involuntary failings by adding one-tenth of the total number of recitations. If you avoid interrupting the mantra, the effect will be achieved without great difficulty. But leaning back, taking it easy, and letting our minds wander while reciting will have little more effect than providing you with a little rest. So, when you pick up the mala to start to count your recitations, you should set your mind to focus on the visualization and accomplish a set number of recitations.

Tibetans don't feel that they need to understand the meaning of each and every verse and mantra. They just chant them, knowing that they mean something. It's not necessary to understand every word and syllable from the beginning, and even if someone were to explain them, it is unlikely that you would understand or even remember what everything means. So please, put your minds at ease, and accept that it's fine not to understand every single word. Over time, with practice and study, new meanings will come to light, and even what you thought you already understood will be discovered to have further profound depths that had, until then, been hidden.

In Vajrayana, a mala is considered very special. When doing recitation in retreat, you need to be very particular about the rosary that you use. The tantras describe that it should be made of particular material according to the type of practice one is doing. For example, when focusing on a pacifying mantra, one should use a mala made of conch or crystal. If one is reciting an increasing mantra, one should use a mala made from a yellow-colored material such as sandalwood or amber. For magnetizing mantras, one uses red beads such as rubies, and for subjugating mantras, one uses a raksha-seed mala. For practices that include everything, the best type of bead is said to be seeds from the bodhi tree. The mala should be new, not previously used, and the string used to hold the beads together should also be the appropriate color for the particular activity that one seeks to accomplish. The guru bead, the larger one that keeps it all together, should have two additional parts so that the three together symbolize the three kayas. The knot should not only be tied tightly but neatly as well. After that, nobody else should see or touch it. Although in Tibet it is customary to walk around with a mala, doing so is not actually in accordance with the tantras. The mala we actually use for our practice should be treated as something very special, and should not be worn like jewelry or even carried in public, but kept discreetly in a little bag. You can use another mala to walk around with.

At the beginning of the retreat, the mala should be consecrated with special mantras and sprinkled with saffron water. During the first session of the retreat, you should visualize that each bead is actually a deity itself. Then, at the end of the mantra recitation, each day the mala should be reconsecrated.

OPENING THE RECITATION MANSION

In the *Ocean of Amrita,* the mantra recitation is divided up into three parts: approach, accomplishment, and activities. The approach is combined with the gurus of the three kayas; accomplishment is a combination of all the deities; and the activities are the application of the four activities, namely pacifying, increasing, magnetizing, and subjugating. But first, one must unfold the wisdom mandala.

Up until this point, the visualization of the deities has primarily been a self-visualization, but now the deities must also appear before you. The mantra for this is BHRUNG VISHVA VISHUDDHE HRIH HUNG PHAT JAH. The syllable BHRUNG is the nature of all five elements together. It emanates from your heart, and then, in the sky before you, it becomes an immense celestial palace. VISHVA VISHUDDHE means a variety of utterly pure forms. Among the twelve manifestations of Guru Rinpoche, some are peaceful and some are wrathful. The seed syllable of the peaceful ones is HRIH; and the seed syllable of Dorje Draktsal, and the other wrathful manifestations, is HUNG. Then, with PHAT JAH, they all become vividly present. With that, an identical replica of the root mandala, which you had already visualized your own self to be, appears in the sky before you. This is known as the wisdom mandala.

"From myself, the root mandala detaches a second wisdom mandala to be present in the sky before me." A replica, identical in form to what we visualized before as ourselves, is mirrored out and appears in the sky in front of ourselves.

INVOCATION

The invocation comes before starting to recite the mantras as we need to summon all the deities. If performing an extensive, detailed practice, you would invoke each deity individually, but it is also possible to combine them all into a single verse as it is done in the *Ocean of Amrita*:

HUNG HRIH§
Divinities of vidyadhara gurus, manifest from space.§
I invoke you from the core of your heart samaya, utter the
 sounds of recitation.§
With apparent and empty bodily forms, you fill the
 billionfold universe.§
With resounding and empty mantra tones of speech, you
 roar like thunder.§
With the aware and empty space of mind, you rest in the
 state of luminosity.§
All the deities, delighting in the dance of bliss,§
Invoke the mantras with effortless vajra songs.§
The liberating life-force of wisdom endows your minds.§
Until reaching clarity, I will endeavor in visualization and
 recitation.§
Until perfection, don't forsake your intentions!§
Do not forget me, the time for your great heart samaya has
 come!§
On this very seat, let me perfect the fourfold approach and
 accomplishment,§
And let me realize the lord of the mandala.§

GATHERING THE BLESSINGS FOR THE BENEFIT
OF ONESELF BY MEANS OF
DHARMAKAYA BUDDHA AMITAYUS

Next is the approach of the deities of the three kayas, namely Amitayus (also known as Amitabha), Avalokiteshvara, and Padmasambhava. We begin with gathering the blessings for the benefit of oneself by means of the Dharmakaya Buddha Amitayus.

Now for the approach of the three-kaya deities, the first one is gathering the blessings for the benefit of oneself by means of Dharmakaya Buddha Amitayus. What we imagine first, and what we say, while chanting the mantra OM AMARANI JIVANTIYE SVAHA, is a red HRIH within the heart center of Dharmakaya Buddha Amitayus that emanates light in all directions. This light summons all buddhas and bodhisattvas by making pleasing offerings and gathers up the essential extracts of all the qualities of their body, speech, and mind. These rays are reabsorbed together with the enlightened qualities. Then, more rays of light extend into all directions and gather back the essences of the five elements—earth, water, fire, wind, and space. Longevity and all the other qualities are gathered up and collected in the vase of longevity that Buddha Amitayus holds in his hands. There is so much that the vase overflows and the nectar streams down directly into the crown of your own head (remember you still have the form of Padmasambhava). It enters through the gate of Brahma at the crown of your head, and fills your entire body, totally purifying all sickness, harms, misdeeds, obscurations, and accomplishing the twofold benefit of self and others.[8]

The reason that one seeks to extend one's life in this way is not just to be free of the ordinary fear of death, but comes out of the appreciation that a life spent in dharma practice is very valuable not just for oneself, but more importantly, for what one can do for others. Therefore, the longer one's life is, the more help one can provide others. If one's life is cut short before achieving complete liberation, one may go astray in the bardo, and progress on the path is interrupted. To provide us with the best chance possible, Padmasambhava has given us various methods for ensuring longevity—including special medicinal concoctions, special mantras, special yoga exercises, and so on—so that we can continue our practice and attain accomplishment in this very lifetime.

FILLING SPACE WITH ACTIVITY FOR THE BENEFIT OF OTHERS BY MEANS OF THE SAMBHOGAKAYA AVALOKITESHVARA

Next, we benefit others by means of the sambhogakaya Avalokiteshvara. To accomplish this,

> Light radiates from the heart of the Noble Tamer of
>   Beings⣿
> And pervades all the realms of the six kinds of beings.⣿
> It purifies each of their six disturbing emotions⣿
> And turns them into forms of the Great Compassionate
>   One.⣿

OM MANI PADME HUNG HRIH⣿

Rays of light radiate from the seed syllable HRIH, this time within Avalokiteshvara's heart chakra. The light spreads in all directions illuminating the three higher realms of gods, demigods, and human beings; and the three lower realms of animals, hungry ghosts, and hell beings. The light purifies six disturbing emotions (*kleshas*)—anger, stinginess, ignorance, pride, jealousy, and attachment—which are the causes for the existence of the realms. Encircling the seed syllable HRIH are the six syllables of OM MANI PADME HUNG, in white, green, red, white, yellow, and dark indigo blue respectively. Just like light shining through tinted glass, when the pure light from the HRIH shines through these syllables, it becomes the colour of that specific syllable and removes the causes for rebirth in the related realm.

We can already benefit beings right now by a simple practice like this where we personally identify with the nature of the Great Compassionate One, and then imagine the colored rays of light, while visualizing the syllables and reciting the mantra. More specifically, the letter HRIH stands on a clear, shining moon disk, on top of which sits a six-petaled lotus blossom with one of the six syllables of OM MANI PADME HUNG on each petal. The white OM purifies the pride of the god realm. The green MA, the nature of all-accomplishing wisdom, purifies the asura realm. The red NI has the nature of discriminating wisdom, and purifies the attachment that leads to the human realm. The white PA has the nature of dharmadhatu wisdom, which purifies the ignorance or dullness that is the cause of the animal realm. Next is the yellow DME, the nature of the wisdom of equality, which purifies the miserliness of the hungry ghosts and makes them realize the same wisdom of equality. The deep blue syllable HUNG shines into the hell realms, purifying the anger and aggression of the beings there, so that instead of suffering from unbearable heat and cold, they all realize mirror-like wisdom. In this way, all are liberated from the realms of samsara in which they have been enmeshed. Finally, imagine multicolored light radiating from the letter HRIH into all directions and transforming all sentient beings without exception into different forms of the Great Compassionate One, forms that are luminous, clear, and empty, like reflections in a mirror.

RECITATION OF THE UNITY OF
DEVELOPMENT AND COMPLETION

The third recitation is in regard to the unity of development and completion. This is done for the nondual benefit of self and others by means of the nirmanakaya Padmasambhava.

Generally speaking, there are the three *sattvas* or beings: the *samaya sattva* or commitment being, the *jnana sattva* or wisdom being, and the *samadhi sattva* or samadhi being. Often we hear that the samaya sattva is adorned with jewels, silks, and so on, while the jnana sattva in the heart center looks exactly the same except that it is unadorned, and then, in the center of the heart of the jnana sattva, is the samadhi sattva in the form of the seed syllable. However, in some practices, such as *Ocean of Amrita*, the jnana sattva is symbolized by a vajra.

You imagine that you are Guru Rinpoche (Padmasambhava), who embodies all the buddha families. In your heart center is an eight-faceted jewel dome made of light. Inside this, a golden five-pronged vajra stands on a moon disk, and inside its central sphere is another little moon disk upon which the letter HRIH is encircled by the mantra OM AH HUNG VAJRA GURU PADMA SIDDHI HUNG in slightly smaller letters. At first, the seed syllable and the mantra are silent, but then each resounds, of its own accord, with the sound of its own syllable, clear and radiant, just like the full moon surrounded by a garland of stars on a clear night.

Until you are completely comfortable with all the details of the visualization when chanting the Vajra Guru mantra, you should first focus only on the seed syllable, nothing else. For example, if you are doing one thousand recitations, spend the first three hundred, the first three rosaries, concentrating on just the visualization for the seed syllable:

> Being the Guru embodying all families,⁝
> In my heart center⁝
> Is a five-pronged vajra on a moon disc.⁝
> In its center is HRIH, encircled by the mantra.⁝

Then for the next three hundred, visualize that:

> Light radiating from it makes offerings to the noble ones,⁝
> And gathers the blessings and siddhis into me.⁝

Continue to chant the mantra while visualizing that the light from the syllables spreads in all directions and becomes pleasing offerings to all the buddhas and bodhisattvas, and gathers back their blessings and accomplishments into you. Once you have completed three rounds of your mala, then move on to the visualization described in the remaining lines:

> By radiating again, the universe becomes a pure land⁝
> And the inner contents, all the beings contained in it, are
>   forms of deities.⁝
> Resounding sounds are the tones of Vajra mantras,⁝
> And thoughts the luminous state of wakefulness;⁝
> Everything is the single mandala of nonduality.⁝

Then, again light radiates and transforms the entire universe into the realm of Lotus Light, which is the pure buddha field of Padmasambhava. All beings are the forms of male and female deities, and all sounds are mantras, while everything is embraced within the luminous nondual state of wakefulness. Continue imagining this until you reach the total number of recitations you had decided upon, in this example one thousand.

THE RECITATION OF GREAT BLISS

After the approach comes the accomplishment recitation. This can be done in one of two ways. The more extensive way is to recite the mantras for each of the twelve manifestations of Guru Rinpoche, one by one. However, all these mantras can also be combined into one, the Tötreng Tsal mantra, also known as the great vase recitation.

In this case, then, the forms of oneself and the root mandala, both you, as the samaya being Guru Rinpoche, and the wisdom mandala composed of the deities in the sky before you, all emanate replicas; first one at a time, then hundreds, then thousands, multiplying exponentially until utterly countless. These emanations fly throughout the universe, filling up space in all directions, each one chanting their mantras that roar, like the sound of thunder, resounding to the ends of the universe. Our minds remain the changeless state of luminosity, the awakened state of the buddhas, while offerings are sent out to all the victorious ones, buddhas and bodhisattvas in all directions and all times, pleasing them and gathering back their blessings. In this way, again, the twofold benefit of beings—benefit both for oneself and for others throughout the three realms of samsara—is achieved. Everything is completely perfected as the inconceivable great mudra mandala, in which whatever is seen is the form of deities, all sounds are mantras, and all movements of mind are the great awakened state of original wakefulness. Keeping this in mind, we sing the mantra as a song with its own particular tune.

The analogy for the great accomplishment recitation is a beehive that has broken open. The bees are flying hither and thither, all over the place. They are all buzzing and there is no longer any difference between here and there. Everything is all-encompassing total purity. This state, like a beehive broken open, is the state of great accomplishment.

The song of hung combined with the key points of prana and the vajra recitation of great bliss and so forth are meant for the time of accomplishment, so there is no fault in omitting them during occasional practice. A special visualization accompanies these practices, but I do not want to spend too much time on it now. If someone is interested in doing the specific practice connected to these, they are found in detail in the *Dzapkyi Köljang*, the recitation manual. For now this will suffice.

APPLICATION OF THE ACTIVITIES

Among the three aspects of mantra recitation, we have completed the approach and accomplishment, we now move on to the application of the activities. For this, you visualize the following while reciting the Tötreng Tsal mantra with HARINISA RACHA HRIYA CHITTA HRING HRING DZAH

SARVA SIDDHI PHALA HUNG added to the end of it one-tenth the number of times that you had recited the accomplishment mantra.

For the visualization, you imagine that from your heart, still as the central deity of the mandala, the syllable HRIH radiates white light to the eastern gate touching the vajra daka and dakini. It invokes the vow of the vajra daka and dakini, causing them to multiply into endless numbers of white dakas and dakinis that fly out into all worlds in all directions, filling the universe up and carrying out their duties. They return back in the form of white light, and enter one's heart center. You then should be confident that you have accomplished the activity of pacifying evil influences, sickness, disease, various kinds of fear, and so on. Next, yellow light shines forth and touches the ratna daka and dakini at the southern gate, making them multiply into emanations and reemanations again and again, until the whole universe is full of yellow dakas and dakinis. This yellow light returns and you should feel confident that you have accomplished the activity of increasing all that needs increasing, such as life spans, merit, resplendence, prosperity and wealth, and so forth. After that, red light shines forth, and invokes the lotus dakas and dakinis at the western gate. They multiply and emanate in all directions, filling up countless worlds. The red light returns, having magnetized or attracted whatever needs to be influenced by such activity. Lastly, dark blue light shines out to the karma dakas and dakinis who again multiply into an inconceivable number, filling up the universe and obliterating whatever needs to be destroyed, such as the seven types of violators and the ten objects that need subjugation and so on. The deep blue light, and thus the subjugating activity, is accomplished.

The seed syllables of the dakas and dakinis are in the appended mantra: HA RI NI SA are the seed syllables of the four families of dakinis; and RA TSA HRIH YA, the four syllables of the four dakas. SIDDHA is the samaya of their heart. HRING HRING DZA means to perform all the activities, and SARVA SIDDHI PHALA HUNG means to fulfill all accomplishments.

OMISSIONS AND DUPLICATIONS

After completing however many recitations you have decided on, you amend for any omissions or duplications. Omissions occur when skipping, missing, or omitting something that was included within the text, either in the mantras or the verses themselves. Duplications are when you chant something that is not in the text, adding something extra such as an extra syllable to the mantra. This doesn't include saying a few extra mantras themselves, however. For example, you decide to recite a hundred but end up saying a hundred and two; that is not considered a duplication. To make up for any such mistakes we might have made, we chant the vowels and consonants which are called the *Ali-Kali* mantra.[9] Next we stabilize the effect of the mantra by chanting the *om ye dharma*.[10] We then repeat the offerings and praises; and lastly recite the one-hundred syllable mantra of Vajrasattva.[11] That completes the recitation.

THE RECITATION PRAISES

Offering, Praising and Requesting the Desired Aims

Next, it is traditional to recite some simple verses of offerings, praises, and requests. Since these have already been described above, there is no point in going into them again. If they have the time, some people include the entire *Barchey Lamsel*[12] chant.

Apologizing

Now you should apologize for any mistakes you might have made during the practice. You don't apologize to some deity on high, perpetuating your own sense of inferiority; instead, you are still the chief figure of the mandala, Guru Rinpoche. You then emanate a being who looks like you. This emanation joins his or her palms in front of his or her heart and utters the apology to you, the chief figure of the deity. You should apologize for any mistakes that have been made out of ignorance and confusion, for example, neglecting to properly visualize the forms of the deities, slipping into one of the ten faults or recitation as mentioned previously, or not maintaining the visualizations or intentions during the recitations. Other faults one should apologize for are being dull, agitated, feeling mixed up, unsure, hesitant, and so on. In short,

> Whatever mistakes we may have made
> We openly admit with sincere regret.

Please grant the blessings and accomplishments of
unobscured purity.

And then we chant the Hundred-Syllable mantra three times.

Up until now, some notions of subject, object, and their interaction
have been held in mind. Now, we should let be in a state of nonarising,
free of any notion of subject, object, or action; for example, the one to
whom we are apologizing, the thing that we are apologizing for, the act of
apologizing and even ourselves, the one who apologizes. All these notions
are totally suspended and, totally free from all mental constructs, we rest
in what is called the sphere of threefold purity, while saying A three times.

ENTERING THE WISDOM MANDALA
IN ORDER TO RECEIVE EMPOWERMENT

Now you perform a self-empowerment. Empowering yourself in this way
is not like in kriya yoga, in which there are dualistic concepts of self and
other in which someone higher grants powers to someone inferior. Instead, you simply acknowledge and affirm that you are the chief figure of
the mandala.

Endowed with the power of nondual awareness (*rigtsal*), since the
very beginning, the deities are intrinsic to, and indivisible from, you as
the four vajras of body, speech, mind, and wisdom. This is what is called
"the unity of samaya and original wakefulness," in that it has the same
taste as bodhichitta. The Tibetan term for *bodhi* is *changchub*, in which
chang means to be utterly purified of any kind of obscuration or defilement, and *chub* means that the qualities of the awakened state are already
present. So, "bodhichitta" refers to the original purity of the mind that
we already possess. In this way, the blessings are spontaneously present in
the form of the four kayas. The mantra itself, OM AH HUNG SVAHA VAJRA
SAMAYA KAYA VAKA CHITTA GUNA KARMA SVABHAVA ATMA KOH HANG,
clearly expresses this perspective in that it translates as "I have the indestructible samaya of being the nature of the body, speech, mind, qualities,
and activites of all the buddhas." The following verses then merely reaffirm this basic fact.

Being intrinsic to your true nature, the wisdom beings present in the
sky before you are always indivisible from you, but through the visualizations of the development stage, the recitation of mantra, and the comple-

tion stage, this reality is stabilized. So, by maintaining "the samadhi of perfecting the vivid presence," you rest in the equanimity of your already enlightened nature.

This completes the sadhana for the root mandala and we shall now proceed with the mandala of the peaceful and wrathful deities.

The Special Mandala of the Peaceful and Wrathful Ones

If you have trained in *tögal* practice and can rest in the nature of mind, then it is possible to recognize the deities during the bardo. Otherwise, it all happens too fast. Each deity will be just like a flash of lightning, and you won't realize what's actually happening. But, if you have done some practice and have become stable in the state of meditation, it is possible to not only recognize the deities, but also to recognize each deity as the natural radiance of buddha nature itself. If that happens, then complete liberation is definitely a possibility. Otherwise, you will believe the natural expression of your nature to be something that has come from elsewhere to haunt or torture you. And, when you try to get away from what is actually the natural expression of buddha nature, then the real trouble starts. It's just like in our dream state right now, where if we don't recognize that we are just dreaming, we feel that we are actually drowning, being crushed by rocks, chased by wild animals, and so on. However, if we can learn to recognize our true nature during the dream state, then it also becomes possible during the bardo. Fortunately, it is possible not only to recognize the nature of mind before you die, but also to become stable in that state. To this end, visualizing the one hundred peaceful and wrathful ones and training in the unity of development and completion stage is very beneficial.

The *Guhyagarbha* tantra describes three different ways of visualizing the mandala of the peaceful and wrathful ones: extensive, medium, and condensed. In the extensive version, not only do the five male and female buddhas in both their peaceful and wrathful forms have three faces and six arms, but so do the eight male and female bodhisattvas; all the other deities have only one face and two arms. In the medium version, only the male and female buddhas have three faces and six arms. In the condensed version, only the central figures— Samantabhadra and his consort in the peaceful mandala, and Chemchok Heruka and his consort in the wrathful mandala—have three faces and six arms. In the condensed version, each of the buddhas holds its individual symbolic attribute in their right hand and a bell with the emblem of their particular family on its handle in their left.

Therefore, there are many more details that you can study, such as the nine peaceful modes of a peaceful buddha, the thirteen silken and jewel ornaments, the six types of inconceivable light rays that radiate from the buddhas, and so on. The specific details can differ slightly from one tradition or text to another, however a detailed description of how they appear in the *Ocean of Amrita* can be found in Appendix 2. But don't worry if it seems too complex to visualize all the different faces, arms, and implements, for it's perfectly fine to just visualize the abbreviated form in which all the male and female buddhas just have two arms and one face. In that case, you don't need to know much more than where they are located, their proper colors, and the symbolic implements that they carry.

MANDALA OF THE PEACEFUL DEITIES

First one reveals the celestial palace by reciting the mantra DHRUNG BISHO BISHUDDHE. DHRUNG is the seed syllable for the celestial palace composed of the five elements. In the *Ocean of Amrita,* this seed syllable is described as being maroon-coloured and located within a swirling sphere of five-colored light in the heart of the chief figure of the mandala, Padmasambhava. The seed syllable melts into light and becomes the celestial palace which stands upon a wheel. VISHVA VISHUDDHE means pure of all conceptual thoughts.

Earlier a celestial palace was described. The Tibetan word for "square" refers not to the four sides; it means four corners. The celestial palace for the peaceful mandala is square, and on each side is a gate with a protruding entranceway. Just inside each gate are two pillars, and these eight pillars support eight interlaced beams that hold up the ceiling. At the top of the palace rises a golden spire. In the center of the main hall is a raised platform standing on eight lion-shaped supports and decorated with the design of a golden Dharma wheel with four spokes. At the hub of the wheel sit two thrones, each supported by eight lions, two lions on each side. Where each of four spokes intersect with the rim there is another throne, each of which has legs carved in the shape of different symbolic animals, giving us six thrones in total. Upon each of these six thrones, and in the places of all the other deities of the mandala, are the naturally resounding seed syllables, each in the color of its respective deity. In total, there are forty-two syllables that are collectively known as the root mantra of unmistaken seed syllables. Each of these seed syllables transforms into the form of the related deity.

In the *Ocean of Amrita*, the main buddhas in both their peaceful and wrathful forms have three faces. You should note that the central face is always the same color as the deity, and, in the text, the color of the right face is always mentioned first, and the color for the left face is always mentioned second. As noted earlier, each of the male buddhas has six arms symbolizing the six perfections (paramitas) of generosity, discipline, patience, diligence, concentration, and discriminating knowledge. They hold various implements, as well as emblems symbolic of their specific buddha family; namely a vajra, a wheel, a jewel, a lotus, and a sword. Their consorts have two arms symbolizing means and knowledge. Each of the consorts holds a bell in her right hand, and with their left hand they embrace their partner, while also holding the emblem symbolic of their particular buddha family.

On the central lion throne are the syllables OM and AH. The OM becomes dark blue Samantabhadra and the AH transforms into his consort, Samantabhadri, who is a slightly lighter shade of blue.

On the second lion throne, which is just in front of Samantabhadra and his consort, are a blue HUNG and MUM, which transform into Vajrasattva and his consort, Dhatvishvari. Being members of the vajra family, their symbol is, of course, the vajra. Farther to the east, in line with Vajrasattva, is an elephant throne on which rest a white OM and LAM, which transform into Vairochana and his consort, Buddha Lochana. Being of the Buddha family, their symbol is a Dharma wheel.

To the south, on a horse throne, are a yellow SVA and MUM which transform into Ratnasambhava and his consort, Mamaki. Being of the Ratna family, their symbol is a jewel.

To the west, on a peacock throne, a red AH and PAM become Amitabha and his consort, Pandaravasini. They each hold a lotus symbolizing the fact that they belong to the Padma family.

Finally, to the north on a *shangshang*[13]-throne, a green HA and TAM transform into Amoghasiddhi and his consort, Samaya Tara. They each hold a sword, which is the symbol of the karma family.

On the rim of the wheel between the buddhas of the five families are lotus flowers with sun and moon disks on them. Sitting on these are the eight syllables KSI HING TRAM TRAM HRIM HRIM JRIM AH, which become the first four pairs of male and female bodhisattvas. Then, at the corners of the platform, are the syllables MAI JAH THCHIM HUNG HUNG BAM MUM HOH, which transform into the remaining four pairs of bodhisattvas.

Inside the celestial palace now, occupying the intermediate space in the eastern and western directions, farther to the east, in the area surrounding the raised platform, is a jeweled throne comprised of a lotus, sun, and moon upon which rests the syllable HUNG. To the west is a similar throne on which rests the syllable AH. The HUNG transforms into another sky-blue Samantabhadra and the AH again turns into his consort, Samantabhadri.

Along the other two sides are the seed syllables KHRIM SRUM KSHAM BRAM HUNG TRUM YE from which arise the six munis, who are each responsible for benefiting beings in one of the six realms. At the four gates of the peaceful palace are the syllables for the gatekeepers. All four male gatekeepers have the same seed syllable, HUNG, while the syllables for the four female gatekeepers are DZA HUNG BAM HO. The gatekeepers all stand up in a striding stance and are enveloped in swirling flames. They wear the charnel ground attire of the wrathful ones, such as skull necklaces, garlands of severed heads, winding sheets, and so forth.

That accounts for all of the forty-two deities of the peaceful mandala.

MANDALA OF THE WRATHFUL DEITIES

Having completed visualizing the peaceful deities in the heart center, we now visualize the celestial palace containing the wrathful mandala inside our cranium. It is important to understand that the fifty-eight blood-drinking herukas are nothing more than the compassionate transformation of the peaceful deities, who have taken on these wrathful forms in response to those beings for whom peaceful methods were of no benefit.

The wrathful palace unfolds in much the same manner as the peaceful palace did. In the center of your skull is a flaming sphere of five-colored light. Inside this blazing sphere is a maroon syllable BHRUM which transforms into the celestial palace of the wrathful deities. The palace itself is a terrifying place comprising outer and inner walls within a blazing mass of fire, turbulently glowing with the swirling lights of the five wisdoms.

While the outer and inner walls of the peaceful palace are made of the pure lights of the five wisdoms, the walls of the wrathful palace are made of severed heads nailed together with bolts of Brahma's lightning. These severed heads spew flames from their nostrils, have blood dripping from their mouths, and streams of smoke billowing out of their ears. Blood and fat oozes down the walls. The whole wrathful palace actually has two sets of walls; it is like a double mansion, one within the other. The outer has five layers of skull walls; the inner has three layers of walls made of fresh, dry skulls. There are various kinds of wrathful accoutrements, such as skins and other corpses, hanging from, or draped over, the walls. The windows are made of severed hands and feet, leaving openings for the light to shine through. The beams and pillars are made out of corpses and decorated with various symbolic ornaments, such as tortoises. Above, numerous sun and moon ornaments shine, and the palace is protected by the vast dome of Mahadeva's skull cap, the top of which is adorned with a beating heart.

Here, the wheel on the raised platform is not round, but square, with the four spokes intersecting the corners in the cardinal directions. The wrathful deities are seated on thrones located in the same respective places as their peaceful counterparts. As in the peaceful palace, each throne is comprised of a lotus, sun, and moon, but the supporting animals differ and the cushions are crossed pairs of male and female *gandharvas*, yamas, rakshas, and *yakshas*. All the wrathful buddhas have three faces, six arms, and four legs in "the nine dance postures." In their six hands, they hold vajras, skull cups filled with blood, and various symbols particular to their families. Their consorts, except for Shvari, all hold a bell and proffer a skull cup filled with blood to the lips of the male. All male herukas wear tigerskin skirts and the females wear leopardskin skirts. And all are adorned with charnel-ground attire, such as vajra wings, big tongues of fire, skull necklaces, and so on. Their three faces symbolize the three deities of emancipation, their four legs represent the four legs of miraculous action, and their six arms illustrate the six perfections or paramitas. But most importantly, each consumes one of the five poisons.[14]

On the central throne, which is supported by carved bears, a pair of dark blue HUNG syllables transform into dark blue Ngöndzog Gyalpo, whose name means "Truly Perfected King of Herukas," together with his consort, Dhatvishvari, "The Sky-Faced One." He holds various kinds of vajras in his right hands and skull cups filled with blood in his left. She carries a vajra and another skull cup filled with blood. His body is adorned with "the complete attributes of samsara and nirvana."

Just in front of these, on another throne, another pair of blue HUNGS transform into Vajra Krodha and his consort, Krodhishvari. He holds two vajras and a corpse in his right hands, and a bell, a blood-filled skull cup, and the world in his left. " He shows passion by embracing his consort."

Directly in line with the first two, at the point where the spoke intersects the point of the wheel in the east, on a throne, a pair of maroon colored HUNGS transform into Buddha Khrodha and his consort, Buddha Khrodi. He holds a wheel, a vajra, and a corpse in his right hands and a bell, a blood-filled skull cup, and a trident in his left.

To the north, on a throne, a pair of yellow HUNGS transform into Ratna Krodha and his consort, Ratna Krodhi. In his right hands, he holds a jewel, vajra, and corpse; and in his left, a bell, a blood-filled skull cup, and a battle axe. He devours pride and arrogance.

To the west, on a throne, a pair of red HUNGS transform into the herukas of the Lotus family, Padma Krodha and his consort, Padma Krodhi. He holds a lotus, vajra, and corpse in his right hands, and a bell, a blood-filled skull cup, and a small drum in his left. "He devours attachment."

Finally, to the south, on a throne, a pair of green *hung* syllables transform into Karma Krodha and his consort, Karma Krodhi. He holds a swastika, a vajra, and a corpse in his right hands; and a bell, a blood-filled skull cup, and a ploughshare in his right. "He devours envy."

Surrounding the herukas is an octagonal wheel with eight spokes at the angles of which eight HA syllables in different colours transform into the eight goddesses of the sacred places called *mamos*. Along the surrounding sides, where the six munis stood in the peaceful palace, are eight HE syllables that become the eight goddesses of the sacred valleys known as *tramen*. They are called *tramen*, which means hybrid, because each of them has a human body with the head of an animal symbolizing their particular nature.

At the four inner gates are four PHAT syllables which become one set of gatekeepers. While between the inner and outer walls there is a moat of blood and human fat in which twenty-eight BHYOH syllables transform into the twenty-eight *ishvaris*—six along each side and four guarding the outer gates. The ishvaris are yoginis with animal heads, who are bound by oath to carry out one of the four activities in order to protect the Dharma.

All these wrathful deities are dancing on corpses or skeletons, and wear charnel ground attire, such as skirts made from human skin, bone jewelry, and garlands of severed heads.

Please remember that, although the one hundred peaceful and wrathful deities appear in distinct, individual forms in different colors, carrying various emblems, and so on, all are actually of one indivisible nature. All that appears and exists throughout the entire universe, including all beings, has the nature of the male and female deities; all sounds are mantra; and all movements of mind are original wakefulness.

Samantabhadra and Consort

Dissolving Duality

CONFERRING EMPOWERMENT

If you were to zoom in on the peaceful or wrathful deities, you would see that in each of their heart centers is a wisdom being (jnana sattva) who looks identical to it, in a simple unadorned form without ornaments, implements, or symbolic emblems. If you were then to look closely at these wisdom beings, you would discover that within their heart centers is the same symbolic emblem that the deity itself holds, and inside this emblem is the radiant seed syllable from which the deity was originally generated, surrounded by its shining mantra. The wisdom being within each deity is the same color as the deity itself, as is the seed syllable. The specific mantras that encircle the seed syllables can be found elsewhere. The seed syllables and the mantras shine into all directions and invoke the forms of the buddhas of the ten directions to approach.

The buddhas of the five families in union with their consorts appear at the crown of our heads. From the union of each pair appears a stream of nectar that purifies the tendencies for one of the five disturbing emotions.

You should now assume the confidence that the five male buddhas are the purity of the five aggregates (skandhas). The first one, Buddha Vairochana, is the natural purity of the aggregate of forms. Ratnasambhava is the natural purity of the aggregate of sensations. Amitabha is the natural purity of the aggregate of perceptions, and Amoghasiddhi is the natural purity of the aggregate of formations. Lastly, Akshobhya is the natural purity of the aggregate of cognition or consciousness.

But it is not only we who bear a crown, for each of the one hundred deities is similarly crowned with five buddhas; these are not in union, however, but solitary. The buddha related to whichever family the deity belongs is in the center on the top of the head, with the other four on the surrounding sides. For example, for male deities belonging to the lotus family, Amitabha will be in the center with the four other male buddhas surrounding him; the female deities of the lotus family are crowned with

Amitabha's consort, Pandaravasini, and the other four female buddhas.

Imagining each and every deity crowned with the five buddhas, we recite the mantra related to each of the five family buddhas while forming the corresponding mudra. Each mantra relates to one of the five wisdoms:

> OM MAHA SHUNYATA JNANA VAJRA SVABHAVA ATMA KOH
> HANG
>
> OM MAHA ADARSHA JNANA VAJRA SVABHAVA ATMA KOH
> HANG
>
> OM MAHA SAMATA JNANA VAJRA SVABHAVA ATMA KOH
> HANG
>
> OM MAHA PRATYA BEKSHANE JNANA VAJRA SVABHAVA ATMA
> KOH HANG
>
> OM MAHA KRITYA ANUSH THANA JNANA VAJRA SVABHAVA
> ATMA KOH HANG

The first mantra relates to Buddha Vairochana and the wisdom of emptiness. As I explained earlier, each of our fingers is one of the five male and female buddhas, so joining our two middle fingers, you make the mudra of Buddha Vairochana and his consort at the top of your head while saying the first mantra, which means, "I am the nature of the indestructible wisdom of great emptiness." Next, you join your two index fingers at your forehead in the mudra of Buddha Akshobhya and recite the mantra of the mirrorlike wisdom: OM MAHA ADARSHA JNANA VAJRA SVABHAVA ATMA KOH HANG. For Ratnasambhava, join your two ring fingers together at the right side of your head and say the mantra for the Wisdom of Equality, OM MAHA SAMATA JNANA VAJRA SVABHAVA ATMA KOH HANG. The mudra for Buddha Amitabha is made by joining your two thumbs at the back of your head, and the mantra for Discriminating Wisdom is OM MAHA PRATYA BEKSHANE JNANA VAJRA SVABHAVA ATMA KOH HANG. Finally, join your two little fingers at the left side of your head, forming the mudra for Buddha Amoghasiddhi, and recite the mantra for All-Accomplishing Wisdom.

CONSECRATION

Having conferred the empowerments, we now perform the consecration. To do this, you, still in the form of Padmasambhava, and all the other deities, have a white OM on a moon disk within your skull, a red AH on a lotus in your throat, and a blue HUNG on a sun disk in your heart center. As there is already a seed syllable in your heart center, this HUNG is just in front of it.

These three syllables radiate light in all directions and invoke the heart samaya of the victorious ones (*jinas*), meaning the buddhas of the ten directions, to send out countless copies of the three syllables from their own three places, which dissolve into our three places, as well as those of the forty-two peaceful deities within our hearts and the fifty-eight wrathful deities within our skulls. Upon their entering our three places, the three syllables melt into spheres of light, which then transform into the three buddhas in sambhogakaya attire—Vairochana, Amitabha, and Akshobhya. The OM in our head becomes white Buddha Vairochana holding a wheel; the AH in our throat becomes red Buddha Amitabha holding a lotus; and the HUNG AT OUR HEART BECOMES BLUE BUDDHA AKSHOBHYA HOLDING A VAJRA. YOU SHOULD VISUALIZE THIS WHILE FORMING THE CORRESPONDING MUDRAS AND SAYING THE RELATED MANTRAS:

> OM SARVA TATHAGATA MAHA KAYA VAJRA SVABHAVA ATMA
> KOH HANG
> OM SARVA TATHAGATA MAHA VAKA VAJRA SVABHAVA ATMA
> KOH HANG
> OM SARVA TATHAGATA MAHA CHITTA VAJRA SVABHAVA
> ATMA KOH HANG

AS FOR THE MEANING OF THE MANTRAS, SARVA means all; TATHAGATA refers to the buddhas; MAHA means great; KAYA is body, VAKA is speech, and CHITTA is mind. VAJRA means indestructible, SVABHAVA is nature, and ATMA KOH HANG MEANS, "I AM." SO RECITING THESE THREE MANTRAS SHOULD INSTILL WITHIN YOU THE CONFIDENCE THAT:

> I am the great vajra nature of the body of all buddhas.
> I am the great indestructible speech nature of all buddhas.
> I am the great indestructible nature of mind of all buddhas.

SUMMONING AND DISSOLVING THE WISDOM BEINGS

In order to loosen any dualistic concepts of self and others that we might have, once again we summon deities from the space around us and then dissolve them into ourselves.

First, we must ask them to come.

The light of my awareness, manifest in the form of a blue HUNG,⁞
    Pervades to the ends of dharmadhatu.⁞
    The dharmakaya becomes manifest in the form of
        rupakayas.⁞

    HUNG⁞
    Deities of space, with the samaya of having perfected the
        two great accumulations,⁞
    Forms of the great display, with completed enjoyments,⁞
    Vajrasattva, resplendent lord of the good aeon,⁞
    Manifest from the space of great bliss through the display
        of your mind.⁞
    VAJRA SAMAJAH.⁞

When we imagine the dharmakaya to assume the form of a radiant blue HUNG in the heart centers of all the deities' heart centers, its light extends into infinity in all directions, totally permeating the basic space of all things. Due to this, all unmanifest dharmakaya buddhas are requested to visibly reveal themselves as sambhogakaya forms.

When fully perfected, the two accumulations of merit and wisdom are the realization of rupakaya and dharmakaya. *Rupakaya* means "form body" and includes both sambhogakaya and nirmanakaya. Having perfected the two accumulations, and due to their related vow to help those in need, when we invite the deities, they reappear in sambhogakaya forms of the great display, namely the hundred peaceful and wrathful deities. The "resplendent lord," Vajrasattva, is none other than our own buddha nature. So, all these deities who were unmanifest as dharmakaya now appear.

Now that the deities have responded to our request to visibly manifest, we now invite them to approach.

    HUNG⁞
    Dharmakaya awareness self-manifest,⁞
    Assembly of vajradhatu deities,⁞
    All tamers of the three realms without exception,⁞
    Heruka mandalas with your retinues,⁞

Line of vajra-holders and vidyadharas;
Of the great yogas of the two stages,;
According to your perfect aspirations and samayas,;
All of you, come here!;
JAH HUNG BAM HOH
E HAYE HI RULU RULU HUNG BHYO JAH JAH

JAH HUNG BAM HO are the nature of the four immeasurables: immeasurable love, compassion, joy, and equanimity. These four immeasurables take the form of countless female gatekeepers who are sent out with hooks, lassos, shackles, and bells to entice the buddhas to remain indissolubly part of us. This is the purpose of the mantra, VAJRA HERUKA TISHTHA SAMAYA LHAN, for it means "Indestructible blood drinkers, please remember your oath and please be seated."

HOMAGE AND OFFERINGS TO THE MANDALA DEITIES

Just like one flame can light countless others, from the central figure in the mandala innumerable vajra servers appear, all looking like Amoghasiddhi. They then pay homage to all the deities. You say AH LA LA HO, which means "how wonderful; how amazing!" The vajra servers pay homage by saying "ATIPU HOH," to which the deities reply, "PRATICCHA HOH."

The purpose of this symbolic gesture is to bring to mind the qualities of the enlightened body and to purify our habitual tendency to become attached to our homes, our bodies, and pleasurable sensations. Keep in mind that wisdom beings (deities) honestly don't exist separate from you and your own experience. But, even if a separate wisdom being did exist, as they don't suffer hunger or thirst, they wouldn't particularly be moved whether anyone made offerings to them or not. If there were some kind of being that was pleased by receiving offerings and displeased if they don't get any, they would not be a wisdom being, but some sort of a mundane being, maybe even an evil spirit.

THE OUTER OFFERINGS

You now make outer and inner offerings, but first you should welcome your "guests":

HUNG OM⁞
Welcome, Bhagavans.⁞
Through the wisdom of an ocean of jinas,⁞
The entire infinite ocean of existence⁞
Is manifest as a supreme Samantabhadra offering-cloud.⁞
OM NAMAH SARVA TATHAGATA BHAYO VISHVA MUKHE
BHYAH SARVA TEKHAM UTGATE SAPHARANI MAM GAGANA
KHAM SVAHA.⁞

Here the Tibetan word for "welcome," *bde bar gshegs so*, has a double meaning, as it also refers to the path that leads to the ultimate state of bliss. In Sanskrit, *bde bar gshegs pa* is *sugata* and means "one who has reached bliss." So here we have both a greeting as well as the identity of the path to enlightenment, namely "the wisdom of an ocean of victorious ones." The ocean symbolizes infinity, so an infinite number of buddhas. You imagine that everything that appears or occurs is part of the infinite offerings as exemplified by the boundless offerings made by the bodhisattva Samantabhadra.

Then, you say the Sky Treasury mantra, the Namkhadzö mantra, while performing its related mudra. At the end of the mantra, you snap your fingers, signifying that you multiply and emanate an infinite cloud bank of offerings, extending to the farthest reaches of space. Performing the mudra and snapping the fingers a second time signifies that all the sense offerings are presented to the different deities: sights, smells, sounds, and so on. With the second snap of your fingers, these sense offering are accepted and enjoyed.

Although pure in the perfect meaning,⁞
For the sake of all beings,⁞
Having refreshed your hands and feet,⁞
Please be seated on the vajra thrones.⁞
OM AHARA AHARA SARVA VIDYADHARA PUJITE NAMAH
SAMANTA BUDDHA NAM GAGANA KHAM SAMAYE SVAHA

Say the next lines even though the deities are already utterly pure. You offer them water to clean their hands and feet. Then, you ask them to be seated on the vajra thrones. While saying the mantra, you perform the mudra for rinsing the hands and feet, which symbolizes two conches, as conches are often used to hold water during empowerment ceremonies.

Next are the general offerings. Even though this is from a terma, the offerings are identical in intent with those found in the *Nyingma Kahma*, the original tantric scriptures of the Nyingma schools. They are *dhupe, pushpe, aloke,* and *gandhe,* four lines for each. The first is for incense. We imagine that infinite numbers of goddesses holding scent and garlands emanate, spreading the fragrance everywhere in the mandala of the buddhas. "Out of the means and knowledge of love, enjoy the offering of Vajra Dhupe," and we say the mantra.

According to the old Nyingma tradition, one would perform the revolving lotus mudra five times while saying the mantra: at the heart, the right breast, the heart again, the left breast, and once more at the heart. These five probably refer to the five satisfactions; the mantra has five parts as well, so I assume that they are connected. The mantras for all the offerings are the same except for the last line, which refers to each particular offering. Here we make the mudra for the incense. It represents the censer, the incense container. The top finger and the lowest one are the top and the bottom, and the middle fingers are the container itself, so it is just like a cup. *Pushpe* means flower, and the mudra is like two flowers, the stamen and four petals.

The next one is *aloke,* which means "lamp." Part is for the lamp, for the feet of the butter lamp container; the top and our thumbs are the flames. The last is offering perfume. The mudra represents applying perfume to the body after having bathed, and also showering rain to cool down if anybody feels too hot. Applying perfume also has a cooling effect. When chanting the four lines before the mantra, we should press the bases of the two ring fingers, because that is exactly where the nadi, the channel of the disturbing emotions, touches. There is nothing to do with the fingers; we just press that point. Pressing like that, we hold the hands to our side, pressing down on the left thigh, while chanting those four lines. The channels of the disturbing emotions are being closed here. When we breathe, there is a circulation, and it is said that we have both the breath of disturbing emotions and the breath of wisdom circulating within us all the time. At the end of the four lines, we say the mantra with the particular offering mudra.

There are different traditions that vary slightly, but we should continue with whatever tradition we ourselves were taught. At the end of each offering, snap your fingers twice. The first finger snap is for emanating a boundless amount of that particular offering; the second is so that it may be enjoyed by each of the related senses into which the offerings dissolve.

THE INNER OFFERINGS: AMRITA, RAKTA, AND TORMA

The three inner offerings are amrita, rakta, and torma. The first of these is the nectar called amrita. Amrita is made from the sacred medicine known as mendrub. Mendrub is natural (rangjung) and pure, as the eight main and one thousand secondary ingredients that it is made from are all naturally occurring. The original recipe was shared by Padmasambhava himself. Mendrub has wonderful properties, such as being able to pacify the five disturbing emotions,[15] the five major diseases, and so on. In this way, mendrub is a very amazing form of amrita offering.

When making the amrita offering, even if it is just a few drops in the palm of your hand, imagine that it is as vast as an ocean, and when you dip your finger in and sprinkle it around, those drops become an immense cloud bank filling the sky and raining down amrita to the delight of all the gurus of the lineage, starting with dharmakaya Buddha Samantabhadra, sambhogakayas of Vajrasattva, and the peaceful and wrathful deities, and all the nirmanakaya gurus of the lineage, including your own root guru. The mantra accompanying each verse, MAHA SARVA PANCA AMRITA KHARAM KHAHI, simply means "Please enjoy all five of these great nectars."

At the end, you receive the siddhis while saying the mantra KAYA VAKA CHITTA SIDDHI OM AH HUNG. To do this, imagine that you receive the accomplishments (siddhis and blessings of the body, speech, and mind of all the deities and lineage masters), while you dip your finger in the remaining amrita and anoint your three places: your forehead for body (KAYA), your throat for speech (VAKA), your heart for mind (CHITTA). Then, you drink a few drops of the offering yourself.

Next is the rakta offering:

> HUNG:
> Unfixated great redness of nonattachment,:
> Free from the clinging attachment of the three realms,:
> In order to fully purify the three poisons,:
> I present this to the mandala deities.:
> maha rakta pratich cha kharam khahi:

Within the three realms of desire, form, and the formless, beings cling to the three poisons of desire, anger, and ignorance or delusion. The liberation of all such attachment is called the great redness (*mar chen po*), which is symbolized by the red-hued rakta. So, we offer the desire-free state of nonattachment to all the deities.

Now for the torma offering:

HUNG⁞
A great offering-cloud of the five wisdoms,⁞
Endowed with the five sense-pleasures,⁞
This offering-cloud of consecrated torma⁞
I offer to you, accept it joyfully!⁞
MAHA BALINGTA PRATICH CHA KHARAM KHAHI⁞

Sometimes it is said that the entire universe is the torma tray, while all sentient beings comprise the torma it carries; while here, in the *Ocean of Amrita*, the torma symbolizes the five wisdoms and five sense pleasures that we offer to all the deities. As for the mantra, MAHA BALINGTA means great torma, PRATICH CHA means I offer it, and KHARAM KAHI means please enjoy. So, altogether it means "I offer this great torma to you— please enjoy it!"

THE SECRET OFFERING: UNION AND LIBERATION

Now we come to the secret or innermost offering, which has two aspects: union and liberation. The lord is nondual, self-existing rigpa, while his consort is the basic space of all things, the dharmadhatu. These two are a natural unity. Recognizing this natural unity of rigpa and dharmadhatu is the union that is offered to all the buddhas and bodhisattvas. The mantra is OM SARVA TATHAGATA ANU RAGANA VAJRA SVABHAVA AMA KOH HANG, which means, "I am the indestructible nature that is the great passion of all buddhas."

Liberation, on the other hand, means that the deluded thoughts of samsara automatically dissolve when letting be in the unconstructed state of equality in which no concepts of offerant, recipient, or offering are held in mind. The mantra is BODHICHITTA SAPHARANA PHAT DHARMADHATU SHUDDHE AH. BODHICHITTA is awakened mind, SAPHARANA is to spread, DHARMADHATU is the basic space of all things, and SHUDDHE is pure.

Chanting

PRAISES

Having completed the offerings, we now praise the enlightened body, speech, mind, qualities, and activities of the peaceful and wrathful ones. These five aspects can each be further subdivided into five, giving us the twenty-five never-ending adornment wheels of enlightenment. There is a verse corresponding to each of the five family buddhas and a general praise of the peaceful deities. This is then followed by verses for each of the five wrathful herukas, and a general praise for all the wrathful ones. Each line of each verse is accompanied by a mudra that is performed while holding the vajra and bell. At the end of the offerings and praises, all the vajra servers dissolve back into the heart center of the central figure.

RECITATION FOR THE ONE HUNDRED PEACEFUL AND WRATHFUL ONES

Now we come to the recitations for the peaceful and wrathful deities that have five parts: (1) the recitation for the peaceful deities, (2) the recitation for the wrathful deities, (3) purification of breaches and conceptual obscurations, (4) application of the activities, and (5) the recitation of praises.

RECITATION FOR THE PEACEFUL ONES

To prepare for reciting the mantra there is an invocation:

> HUNG༔
> With the blessings of knowledge speech,༔
> Arranged on the tip of the tongue,༔
> Divided one by one into diversity,༔
> Within the great mandala of vajradhatu,༔
> Perfected within the nature of the aggregates, elements, and
> sense factors,༔

Is me, the yidam deity!༔
I present you offerings, grant your blessings!༔

There are three types of mantras: vidya mantras, dharani mantras, and guhya mantras. Vidya mantras are the essence of skillful means, dharani mantras are the essence of discriminative awareness, and guhya or secret mantras are the essence of nondual pristine cognition. "Knowledge speech" (*rig pa gsung*) refers to the vidya mantras[16] that are "arranged on the tip of the tongue," meaning uttered by you and all the deities. Within the heart center of each of the peaceful deities is the emblem unique to their family, inside of which is their seed syllable surrounded by their particular mantra. Though you should imagine each specific mantra for each deity, you only need to recite the general mantra for the peaceful deities: OM BODHICHITTA MAHASUKHA JNANADHATU AH. Not only is "the great mandala of vajradhatu [indestructible space] perfect within the aggregates, elements, and sense factors;" but you could also say that the aggregates, elements, and sense factors are perfected within the vajradhatu.

Just as described earlier, there are three beings or sattvas. You yourself as the central deity are the samaya sattva, or commitment being. Then, inside the heart center of each deity is the jnana sattva, or wisdom being, which is an unadorned replica of themselves. And then, within the jnana sattva's heart centers, is their hand emblem, containing their specific seed syllable, which is the samadhi sattva. Remember the seed syllable is surrounded by each deities' own particular mantra. This includes not just the main male buddhas of the five families, but also all the female buddhas, as well as all the other deities, including the bodhisattvas, six munis, the gatekeepers, and so on—they all have their own individual seed syllables surrounded by their own mantras.

There are other practices for the peaceful and wrathful deities, such as the *Karling Shitro* or Chokgyur Lingpa's terma entitled *Narak Dongtruk*, where you recite each deity's mantra a few times while focusing on that particular deity, and only after going through them all individually do you do the main recitation of the combined mantra. In the *Ocean of Amrita*, however, you just have two mantras: the Bodhichitta mantra for the peaceful deities and the Rulu mantra for the wrathful deities.

This all may seem rather detailed and complex, but instead of just letting your mind drift off while repeating the mantra, it provides you with something to focus your attention on. Still, even though you visualize all forty-two peaceful deities with their adornments, hand emblems, seed syllables, and so on, you only need to chant the Bodhichitta mantra, which is the general mantra combining the essence of all forty-two peaceful deities into one: OM BODHICHITTA MAHASUKHA JNANADHATU AH.

Generally, whenever doing a deity practice that involves chanting a mantra, you should divide the number of recitations that you have decided to do in a session into three equal portions. For the first third, imagine that the seed syllable is in the heart center of the deity, the mantra syllables are around it, each one shining and resounding with their own tone, but standing still. This is called the moon with a garland of stars, like on a calm summer night, when the sky is very quiet and radiant. For the second third, the mantra garland starts to rotate, and while it does so, sends out rays of light. This is called the firebrand, as it is similar to how a circle will appear when quickly twirling a burning stick in the dark. For the third, the messenger of the king, rays of light shine forth from the syllables and take the form of beautiful luscious offerings, which are presented to all the buddhas and bodhisattvas in all the different buddha realms. All the deities, buddhas, bodhisattvas, and so on then send back their blessings, siddhis, empowerments, and so on in the form of light so that you absorb the blessings of their body, speech, and mind. You then view everything that you perceive to be divine—all beings have the forms of deities, all sound are the nature of mantra, and all thoughts are the play of original wakefulness—which is called "the threefold practice of sight, sound, and samadhi."

Recitation for the Wrathful Ones

Next, you address the wrathful deities, the "manifest herukas," acknowledging that they are the transformed aspects of the peaceful deities, and asking them to remain:

> Unmoving, endowed with the body, speech, mind, qualities,
>   and activities,⁈
> Until you are vividly present, I shall visualize you and
>   engage in the recitation,⁈
> Until I am accomplished, do not forsake me!⁈

Again, there are the three sattvas and the mantra garlands, however the seed syllables for the wrathful deities are a little easier, as many are the same, with just the color changing. Chemchok Heruka and his consort as well as the five male herukas and their consorts all have the seed syllable HUNG in their heart centers. Still, they each do have their own specific mantra.

The eight goddesses of the sacred places have the seed syllable HA, and the eight goddesses of the sacred valleys have HE. The inner four female gatekeepers have the seed syllable PHAT, and, for the twenty-eight ishvaris, it is JO. Each of these then have their own mantra encircling their seed syllable. It is good to note that this threefold principle symbolizing body, speech, and mind is the same for any deity practice you might undertake. In the heart center, there is always the wisdom being (jnana sattva) representing body, a seed syllable symbolizing mind, and surrounding the seed syllable is a mantra symbolizing speech.

Just as for the recitation of the peaceful mantra, now you only need to chant the Rulu mantra, OM RULU RULU HUNG BHAYO HUNG, together with the various stages of the accompanying recitation visualization described earlier.

PURIFICATION OF BREACHES AND CONCEPTUAL OBSCURATIONS

We now come to the third part of the recitation, the purification of breaches and conceptual obscurations, for which we chant the Hundred-Syllable mantra of glorious Vajrasattva, the lord of all infinite mandalas. The first line of this section in the *Ocean of Amrita* is:

> In the wisdom being Vajrasattva,⊰
> the hundred syllables encircle the life letter.⊰

At this point, the wisdom beings in all the male deities, which look identical to the deity whose heart they are in, transform into Vajrasattva, and in all the female deities into Vajrasattva's consort, Vajratopa. In their heart centers is "the life letter" HUNG, around which is the Hundred-Syllable mantra with OM HUNG PHAT appended to it. The mantra is written counterclockwise in the male deities, while in the female deities it is written clockwise.

So, while chanting the mantra, the mantra garlands spin clockwise in the male deities and counterclockwise in the female deities, and they shine with infinite rays of light that extend into the ten directions, where all the buddhas and bodhisattvas of the ten directions and three times are pleased with amazing offerings. They send back blessings of their body, speech, and mind that dissolve not just into you, but also into all sentient beings. By doing so, all conceptual obscurations and breaches of samaya dissolve and are purified. Even the deepest hells become the buddha realm of knowledge-holders.

APPLICATION OF THE ACTIVITIES

Stirring the Depths of Hell

Then, "the sounds of mantras and the light rays of compassion streaming forth from the mouths of all the mandala deities illuminate the three realms, purify all the lower realms, and carry all sentient beings, headed by the person concerned, over to the enlightened realms." The person concerned could be someone who requested the practice to be done in his or her name or in the name of someone who has passed away or who is in trouble. In such cases, light rays focus on that particular person, but they also shine on and benefit all other sentient beings as well. Then, at the end of the Hundred-Syllable mantra, we add three lines for the hell realms (narak), hungry ghosts (preta), and animals (tirya) respectively:

> OM DAHA DAHA SARVA NARAKA GATE HETUM HUNG PHAT
> OM PACA PACA SARVA PRETAKA GATE HETUM HUNG PHAT
> OM MATHA MATHA SARVA TIRYAKA GATE HETUM HUNG
>   PHAT

With that, Vajrasattva, who is the wisdom being in the heart center of every single deity, says, "You yogis who have conceptual obscurations, breaches, miserliness, and evil habitual tendencies, all such obscurations, by reciting the hundred syllables, the quintessence of all tathagatas, all your breaches and conceptual obscurations will be purified, and you will be liberated from the karmic obscurations of falling into the lower realms. In addition, in this lifetime, all the buddhas will guard and protect you, regarding you as their noble child, and when you die, without a doubt, you will become the chief child of all the sugatas."

This absolves us of our failings and affirms that all our obscurations are purified.

STIRRING THE DEPTHS OF SAMSARA

Next, while chanting the hundred syllables, together with the previous three lines for the lower realms, and three more for the higher realms, wisdom light shines forth from the deities' place of union, which burns away the seeds of the six realms—AH, SU, NI, TRI, PRE, and DU—in every single sentient being, together with their habitual tendencies for taking rebirth among the six classes. Due to this, all sentient beings become sugatas of the six classes.

How you do this is as follows. Recite the Hundred-Syllable mantra, and at the end of the hundred syllables, say:

> OM SARVA TATHAGATA ADHISHTHANA ADHISHTHATE SARVA
> PAPAM AVARANA BHASHIM KURU SVAHA

Repeat the above three lines of DAHA and so on as well as the three additional lines for the higher realms—human, demigod, and god:

> OM CACHINDHA CACHINDHA SARVA NRI GATE HETUM
> HUNG PHAT
> OM TRATA TRATA SARVA ASURA GATE HETUM HUNG PHAT
> OM BHRITA BHRITA SARVA SURA GATE HETUM HUNG PHAT

OFFERING AND PRAISES

After completing each section of mantra recitation, we always repeat the offering and a set of praises. At this point, for the offerings in the *Ocean of Amrita*, you first say the Sky Treasury mantra, followed by a mantra for the four offerings, which are incense, flowers, lamp, and perfume:

> OM NAMAH SARVA TATHAGATA BHAYO VISHVA MUKHE
> BHYAH SARVA TEKHAM UTGATE SAPHRANAHI MAM
> GAGANA KHAM SVAHA
> OM AHARA AHARA SARVA VIDYADHARA PUJITE NAMAH
> SAMANTA BUDDHA NAM GAGANA KHAM SAMAYE
> SVAHA
> OM SHRI VAJRA RAGA DHUPE DHU
> OM SHRI VAJRA RAGA PUSHPE PU
> OM SHRI VAJRA RAGA ALOKE HRIH

OM SHRI VAJRA RAGA GANDHE GAN

After that, the praises for all the deities are combined in a single four-line verse:

OM ̥

Everything without exception, Body, Speech, and Mind, ̥

Great nature of Body, Speech, and Mind, ̥

Everything is pervaded by Body, Speech, and Mind, ̥

Great sphere of Body, Speech, and Mind, ho! ̥

THE APOLOGY

Everything is already pure as the nondual dharmakaya—whatever appears, whatever exists, since the very first is one overarching unity of the single sphere of dharmakaya. There is no exception; nothing is excluded from the single sphere of dharmakaya. Yet out of ignorance, we have ignored and denigrated this natural purity, resulting in granting concrete existence to things that don't really exist. Due to forming such concepts, we have created disturbing emotions and karma, leading to all different kinds of experiences of pleasure and pain. This is our state as ordinary sentient beings, and in order to reverse this flow of samsaric deluded mind, the different yogas all have various samayas related to the individual, the deity, the mantra, thatness, and so on. Although, having accepted such vows out of our desire to no longer perpetuate samsara, due to our ignorance of the true nature of body, speech, and mind, together with being careless and inattentive, we have strayed and broken our samayas. So, you visualize emanating a replica of yourself who asks all the mandala deities to forgive all that we have done that goes against the intent of the victorious ones. Then, you chant the Vajrasattva mantra with one hundred syllables and ask for all our wishes for enlightenment to be fulfilled.

PERFORMING THE VASE RECITATION

From a lineage master, a disciple receives the four causal empowerments corresponding to the four aspects of original wakefulness, namely, the common vase empowerment and the three higher empowerments known as the secret, wisdom-knowledge, and precious word empowerments.[17]

These empowerments are then replenished by conferring the path empowerments upon oneself during one's own practice. Awakening to complete enlightenment and fully realizing the four empowerments is the final fruition empowerment.

Whenever an empowerment is given, two vases are to be used during the ritual. Before we pour anything special into a container, we always make sure that it has been cleaned first; similarly, before we receive the blessing of an empowerment, we have to be purified and prepared. The action vase is used first to rinse away all impurities. The main vase is then used to "replenish" the four aspects of original wakefulness and empower ourselves to enter the wisdom mandala.

First, we consecrate the main vase. From the syllable BHRUNG, the celestial palace appears within the vase. Inside this celestial palace are all the peaceful and wrathful deities as well as the knowledge-holders. Visible yet empty, like the reflection of the moon on water, they are vividly clear, crisp, and individually distinct, yet insubstantial.

Rays of light shining from the mantra in our own heart travel through the dharani cord into the vase. This offering light swirls around inside the vase, inciting all the deities to enter into union with their consorts. From the self-resounding syllables and mantras in their heart centers, the nectar of the blissful union of their waking state flows down through the place of their union and fills up the vase. While their various mantras resound within the vase, we chant "the mantras for the combined three kayas, the peaceful and wrathful ones, and the dakas with their consorts."

OM AMARANI JIVANTIYE SVAHA
OM MANI PADMA HUNG HRIH
OM AH HUNG VAJRA GURU PADMA SIDDHI HUNG
OM AH HUNG VAJRA GURU PADMA TÖTRENG TSAL VARJA
     SAMAYA JAH SIDDHI PHALA HUNG AH
OM BODHICITTA MAHASUKHA JNANADHATU AH
OM RULU RULU HUNG BHYOH HUNG

At the end, you present the inner offerings with OM AH HUNG, and then imagine that all the deities melt into light and merge indissolubly with the water in the vase.

To consecrate the action vase and the purifying nectar that it contains, we imagine that from the forehead, throat, and heart of all the deities, light rays of white, red, and blue, respectively, radiate in the form of wisdom nectar that fills up the vase and becomes inseparable from the water within it. Then we chant the Hundred-Syllable mantra followed by a mantra to purify the elements:

OM

E HO SHUDDHE SHUDDHE

YAM HO SHUDDHE SHUDDHE

BAM HO SHUDDHE SHUDDHE

LAM HO SHUDDHE SHUDDHE

RAM HO SHUDDHE SHUDDHE

A A SVAHA

ENTERING THE WISDOM MANDALA

If the practice is being performed to benefit another, whether living or deceased, then, at this point, it is necessary to confer the empowerment on them. To do this, whoever is giving the empowerment must first take the empowerment themselves, as in Vajrayana whatever is given to others is first practiced by the one who is going to give it. In that case, this would be chanted. If it is done for the benefit of someone who has passed away, if one is acting in that capacity, then it is also said. But for the general practice, repeating these verses is not necessary because the empowerment is not really being given there.

However, acknowledging and saying that the wisdom beings present in the sky before me are always indivisible from myself, we close this session. Through the development stage, the recitation of mantra, and the completion stage, through the samadhis of bringing this vividly to mind, this reality is stabilized, so I will compose my mind in the equanimity of the same nature. Then, take a break and engage in whatever daily activities are required.

Depending on where this drubchen is being practiced, the above would conclude the third morning session, and the participants would go for lunch. Sometimes however, the *solkas*, the petitions, are added in here; other times it is the first thing after lunch, and we will include it here for now.

TORMA RITUAL

Next, you make offerings to the guardians of the vajra dharma, the inde-structible truth, as well as to the dakinis and gods of prosperity. As the *Ocean of Amrita* belongs to the *Barchey Künsel* cycle revealed by the great treasure revealer Chokgyur Lingpa, these offering chants begin with a very special one written by Chokgyur Lingpa himself: *Lama Yidam*. Those who have received a lot of different teachings and empowerments from different termas and lineages may find it difficult to keep all the commitments to the various protectors. However, as the *Lama Yidam* includes all the different protectors who guard the teachings, it suffices to just recite it and make a single torma offering to all the protectors.

If you imagine a king who has a huge treasury filled with precious things, isn't it reasonable for him to have guards protecting it? Similarly, the teachings connected with the Three Roots—the gurus, yidams, and dakinis—are like an immense treasury of riches, and so they are guarded by special forms of the buddhas called dharmapalas, "Dharma protectors" in English. Although they appear *as if they are what are called haughty be-ings, drekpas,* meaning in wrathful forms, the Dharma protectors are not mundane beings but rather wisdom beings.

When you receive an empowerment, you are not only entrusted with the teachings and associated practices but also with one or more guard-ians, who have promised to look after the teachings and those who prac-tice them. In return for this service, one promises to give these protectors a torma offering in return.

Mending

PERFORMING THE ACTUAL MENDING
AND PURIFICATION OF BREACHES

We now come to one of the primary purposes of this drubchen: the actual mending and purification. This is comprised of preliminaries, the main part, and a conclusion.

The preliminaries involve visualizing the objects of apology, making mandala offerings and supplicating, apologizing for failings, retaking the vows, and pledging to keep the samayas.

To begin, even though they are in essence indivisible from your own buddha nature of nondual awareness, you should imagine your guru and all the masters of your lineage, the Three Jewels (Buddha, Dharma, and Sangha), and the Three Roots (gurus, yidams, and dakinis) all gathered in the sky before you. Then, before all these objects of refuge, chant what is known as *Om Yeshe Kuchok*. This text is taken from the Tantra of Apology and it begins:

> OM §
> Natural mandala of the supreme wisdom body, §
> Like the full moon, you possess no complexity. §
> However, your compassionate forms appear equally for all
>   beings, like the light of the radiant sun; §
> So please come here, consider me and take seat. §

OFFERING THE MANDALA AND SUPPLICATING

A simple and very effective method for perfecting the accumulations of merit is to present a mandala offering while visualizing the objects of refuge as an immense gathering. Most people prefer to use a special metal mandala plate made of gold, silver, bronze, or copper, but any plate, even of wood or stone, is fine. For the five or seven heaps of offerings that you place on the plate, of course, precious stones would be the best; next best are natural medicines; and third best are various kinds grains, as long as they are fresh and clean.

While performing the offering, you recite a famous verse composed by King Trisong Deutsen when he made a mandala offering to Padmasambhava during the latter's visit to Tibet. These four lines have been used over the centuries and are considered very blessed:

> The earth is perfumed with scented water and strewn with
>   flowers,
> Adorned with Mount Meru, the four continents, the sun
>   and moon.
> Imagining this as the buddha realm, I offer it,
> So that all beings may enjoy this pure realm.

Each single mandala offering should possess the six paramitas in their completeness. To begin with, sprinkle the plate with a few drops, "cow nectar,"[18] to symbolize saturating the ground with the moisture of the enlightened mind; this represents the first paramita, generosity. Then, to signify the purification of all that obscures our nature, wipe the mandala plate with your bare wrist; this indicates that you are purifying your own obscurations and represents the paramita of discipline. For the paramita of patience, be careful not to harm any sentient beings, such as small insects, while doing this practice, and gladly undertake any hardship that may be involved in presenting the offering. The paramita of diligence is expressed by exerting yourself in making the offering. Fifth, maintain your focus on what you are doing and do not get distracted by anything else; this is the paramita of concentration. The last paramita, of transcendent knowledge, is to embrace the practice with the threefold purity in regard to the giver, the recipient, and the act of offering itself.

Usually, when making mandala offerings, such as when doing the preliminary practices (*ngöndro*), we use two mandala plates. There is the one we hold to make the offerings, and another called the mandala of accomplishment (*drubpa*), which is placed on the shrine to symbolize the objects to whom we are making the offerings. This is a nice plate on which you set five heaps. In the case of a Guru Rinpoche practice, such as found in the *Barchey Künsel*, it would be one heap in the center representing Padmasambhava, one heap in front for the yidam deities, to the right side one for the buddhas, behind a heap for the sacred Dharma, and on the left a heap for the noble Sangha. However, in the drubchen we already have created a shrine with an impressive mandala, so that functions as a mandala of accomplishment.

Depending on the tradition, there are various ways of doing mandala offerings, but here I will just describe the way it is done in conjunction with the *Ocean of Amrita*. While reciting the first line, "The earth is perfumed with scented water and strewn with flowers," you sprinkle a few drops of nectar on the offering plate (*chop-pa*) and wipe it clean with your wrist. Then, you place seven heaps so that it is "adorned with Mount Meru, the four continents, the sun and the moon." You put one heap in the center of the mandala plate to symbolize Mount Meru. Mount Meru itself is immense with a flat area on top where the king of the gods, Shakra, together with the thirty-two vassal gods of that realm reside. In the four directions are the four continents. The first, the continent to the east, can either be placed on the side nearest you or on the side nearer those whom you are making offerings to. Then, place a heap in each of the other directions, and finally, one in the east for the sun, and one in the west for the moon. While doing this, imagine these offerings of the universe are multiplied by ten, one hundred, one thousand, one hundred thousand, and then a countless number filling all of space with identical Mount Merus and so forth. By giving away the entire universe in this way, we accumulate a tremendous amount of merit.

To examine the mandala offering from the *Tukdrub*,[19] "*Khamsum nöchü paljor dang*," *khamsum* means "the three realms," the realm of desire, the realm of form, and the formless realm. *Nö* is "the world," and *chü* refers to "the beings." We offer all that the universe contains and whoever is included among sentient beings. *Paljor* means their glory and riches, all wealth and splendor, all luxuries; we offer everything that is wonderful and enjoyable within the three realms. In the second line, *daglü longhop getsog kun* refers to my own body, my enjoyments, my wealth, and so on, as well as all the roots of virtue that I have created, am creating, and will create throughout the past, present, and future. I offer all of this to those who are endowed with great compassion, meaning all the gurus, yidams, dakinis, the Three Roots, the Three Jewels, and so on. Please enjoy it and bestow your blessings of body, speech, and mind. The mandala offering is mentioned in small writing, and then we make a request, a supplication.

These are the lines starting with great joy. "Sovereign teacher, lord of great joy, please pay heed to me." This is a request to be allowed into the mandala that leads to the city of the great liberation.

APOLOGIZING FOR DOWNFALLS

When it comes to apologizing for more general faults and failings, you begin by apologizing for all the ways that you have violated the three levels of precepts, followed by apologizing specifically for having broken any of the fourteen root downfalls of Vajrayana.

If you have committed a really severe transgression, like one of the major downfalls, before making the general apologies in the assembly, you must first confess it to the person from whom you took the precepts. In their presence, you should express your remorse: "I have done such-and-such, and I am really deeply sorry."

Apology for General Infractions against the Three Vows

With the objects of refuge still visualized in the sky before us, we beseech them from the core of our hearts, by these lines from the *Ocean of Amrita*, with deep-felt remorse:

Uhu hu laso! Guru, great vajra holder, all buddhas and bodhisattvas dwelling in the ten directions, and all pure members of the Sangha, pay heed to me!

Then you repeat the following three times:

I, by the name [*say your name*], since beginningless samsara till now, overpowered by the disturbing emotions of attachment, anger, and delusion, have committed the ten unvirtuous misdeeds, the five deeds with immediate result, and the five deeds associated with them. I have acted contrary to the vows of individual liberation, contrary to the trainings of the bodhisattvas, and contrary to the samayas of Secret Mantra. I have caused damage to the Three Jewels,[20] forsaken the sacred Dharma,[21] deprecated the noble Sangha, disparaged my parents, shown disrespect to my preceptors and masters, scorned my companions who practice similar wholesome conduct, and the like.

In short, the entire gathering of faults and downfalls that are hindrances for higher rebirth and liberation, and causes for samsara and the lower realms, in the presence of the guru, great vajra-holder, all buddhas and bodhisattvas dwelling in the ten directions, and pure members of the Sangha, I openly admit them all! I remorsefully apologize! I don't conceal! I don't hide!

When I openly admit and remorsefully apologize in this way, I shall be established in happiness. This will not happen when failing to admit and apologize.

Apology for the Fourteen Root Downfalls of Secret Mantra

Now we come to the specific apology for violating the fourteen root downfalls. The first root downfall is to disparage one's own vajra master. Since attaining the supreme and common accomplishments depends on one's relationship with one's master, to disparage or to criticize your personal root guru obstructs your progress.

The second is to violate the words of the Buddha. For example, thinking, "I am a Vajrayana practitioner; therefore I needn't concern myself with the ordinary precepts for monks and nuns." Turning one's back on the Dharma by considering certain teachings inferior is to go against the words of the Buddha.

The third is to be angry with a vajra brother or sister. Fellow practitioners are considered one's vajra siblings. The vajra master from whom one receives the empowerment is like the father, and the mandala into which one is initiated is like the mother. Therefore, those who take empowerments and teachings together are like brothers and sisters, and to fly into a rage against any of them, to abuse them verbally or physically beat them, is to be avoided.

The fourth is to forsake any sentient being, to exclude someone from your love. To hold such thoughts as "I don't care about that person!" not only breaks one of the fourteen root downfalls, but also the bodhisattva vow.

Fifth is to neglect the root of the Dharma, bodhichitta, the awakened mind.

Sixth is to belittle or disparage anyone's belief or philosophical system, whether it is Buddhist or not. To have an air of superior thinking, "My way is the right way; what others believe is wrong," is another way of breaking the Vajrayana precepts.

Seventh is to divulge anything that one has been taught in secret. This means to explain such things as the view, meditation, conduct, mantras, mudras, or sadhanas to people who have not been properly prepared, meaning ordinary people who have neither received empowerment, transmission, nor any preliminary teachings. Divulging these secrets doesn't help such people because they are not ready.

To disparage the body is the eighth downfall. The aggregate of form is the Buddha Vairochana, of sensations, the Buddha Ratnasambhava, of perceptions or conceptions, Amitabha, of formations, Amoghasiddhi, and of cognitions or consciousness, Vajrasattva. So, to disparage or criticize the body or any of its components, or abusing one's own or another's body in any way, is to forsake the view of natural purity.

Similarly, the content of our experience and perception is nothing other than the five female buddhas. If you ignore the fact that the nature of all phenomena is utterly pure, instead clinging to the idea that everything is just inanimate matter, then you are actually looking down on the five female buddhas. By doubting the pure nature of all phenomena, you commit the ninth root downfall.

The tenth is to maintain friendships with enemies of the true teachings, those who maliciously disturb practitioners, harm them, steal their possessions, and so on. Being friendly and supportive of such people is the tenth root downfall. This also includes preventing someone who has the intention of creating immense negative karma from carrying out the deed.

Things don't possess the qualities we normally attribute to them. All phenomena are by nature beyond constructs and transcend names and concepts. All concepts such as the various physical elements, horses, yaks, houses, trees, and so on, as well as the labels we apply to them, have no substantial basis. When you look closely at some "thing," you cannot actually find anything to attach a label to, and yet, in our ignorance, we persist in just such a habit. We even tend to form concepts about the Dharma that is beyond names; hence we commit the eleventh root downfall.

The twelfth downfall is more personal in nature: to cause others to lose faith. This is not just a Vajrayana precept but is applicable to the other vehicles as well. Being a practitioner means that one is now a representative of the teachings, so one should not carelessly behave in ways that will cause others to lose faith or distrust any true teacher. Instead, all Dharma practitioners should behave in whatever way is necessary to gradually guide beings, teaching whatever is appropriate to a specific individual, and to behave in a manner conducive to one's own progress.

The thirteenth concerns refusing the samaya substance, including the five meats and the five nectars, during a Vajrayana ritual. For example, if some wine and meat are being used as a samaya substance during a feast offering (ganachakra) and one refuses, on the grounds that the Buddha said monks and nuns should not eat meat or drink intoxicating liquids, one would be committing the thirteen downfall. Of course, if it is outside the feast offering, then even a Vajrayana monk or nun shouldn't drink even a drop of alcohol.

The fourteenth downfall is to criticize women as their nature is knowledge (Sanskrit: *prajna*; Tibetan: *shes rab*). In general, all Vajrayana teachings should be understood as the unity of means and knowledge, which comes in many contexts, including the union of male and female. The male has the nature of skillful means, and the female is said to be the nature of knowledge. So one should not harbor the idea that women are inferior or cause trouble by diverting our attention. Also, since the male is the nature of skillful means, to criticize men is also to commit this root downfall. In brief, being sexist is to break the fourteenth root precept of Vajrayana.

In other Buddhist teachings, for example, in the chapter on concentration in *The Way of the Bodhisattva*, there is a lot of laying blame on women and presenting a list of their bad qualities. However, this is only because attachment and desire are seen as obstacles to concentration, and the teaching was only given to a gathering of monks for whom women and desire were a distraction. But, if the teaching were being given to a group of women, then the same criticisms would have been made of the object of attraction for women, namely men. So it goes both ways.

So if a *ngakpa*, one who follows the Vajrayana,[22] avoids all fourteen downfalls, he or she will definitely attain both the supreme and common accomplishments (siddhi).

The Vows and Samayas

Having mended our breaches and failings, we can now retake the vows and recommit to the samayas with a clean slate. This has four parts: (1) pledging the vows of individual liberation, (2) taking the bodhisattva vow, (3) pledging the vows of Secret Mantra, and (4) abiding by the samayas.

Pledging the Vows of Individual Liberation

There are several differences in the condensed vows that one takes, depending on whether one is ordained or not. Nevertheless, a layperson should uphold these vows just like a monk or nun for twenty-four hours. First, you promise not to kill or steal. Then, if you are an ordained monk or nun who has taken a vow of celibacy, you reassert that you will not engage in sexual intercourse. If you are not ordained and have not taken a vow of celibacy, then you promise not to engage in sexual misconduct, such as adultery. Next, you promise not to lie, for example, pretending to have supernatural powers, clairvoyance, being able to see spirits and demons, and so on. You also promise not to drink alcohol, which is the source of innumerable faults, and to maintain humility by not putting yourself above others by sitting in a place of honor. According to pratimoksha, this is a seat that is higher than one cubit.[23] You also promise not to eat at improper times, which is important if one is ordained, as monks and nuns are not supposed to eat after twelve noon. Furthermore, you promise not to wear perfume or jewelry, nor to sing or dance. In brief, those are the basic vows of individual liberation.

Taking the Bodhisattva Vow

The bodhisattva vows must first be made in the presence of a Buddhist teacher. Later, to make sure that the bodhisattva vow is retained undamaged and that it develops, one should retake it each day, usually as part of one's daily sadhana, before a sacred representation of enlightened body, speech, or mind. The bodhisattva vow comes through two major lineages: the tradition of the vast conduct and the tradition of the profound view. This is because bodhisattva training is of two kinds: the bodhichitta of aspiration and the bodhichitta of application. In other words, first, one aspires for enlightenment, and then one applies oneself to actually achieving that aim. Another way of explaining it is that anyone can form the resolve to attain enlightenment by making the wish, "May I attain enlightenment for the sake of all beings"; however, the applied resolve only comes about when one has some genuine insight into the nature of emptiness.

All buddhas and bodhisattvas formed the resolve toward complete enlightenment, "For the sake of all beings, I will awaken to true and complete enlightenment." And they then began to engage in all the activities of a bodhisattva, such as the six paramitas,[24] the four activities of pacifying sickness, obstacles, mental obscurations, and ignorance; increasing merit, life span, wisdom, and so on; attracting the life force and energies of the three worlds; and subjugating outer and inner negative forces. By diligently applying themselves to such training, they eventually achieved their aim, therefore:

> In that same way, I shall, for the benefit of beings,
> Form the resolve towards enlightenment,
> And likewise, will engage
> In the trainings step-by-step.

Pledging the Vows of Secret Mantra

To repledge yourself to the Vajrayana precepts, you begin by attracting the attention of all buddhas and bodhisattvas, their children, and all dakas and dakinis. The children of the Victorious Ones include those of the body, of speech, and of mind. The children of the body are the shravakas; the children of speech are the pratyekabuddhas; and the children of mind are the bodhisattvas.

Just as in the previous vow, you now pledge that from now on, you will emulate all the buddhas and bodhisattvas by aspiring to attain supreme enlightenment and doing all that you can to generate the enlightened mind of bodhichitta.

Furthermore, you make commitments for each of the five buddha families. Starting with the buddha family, vow to maintain the three disciplines of abandoning the ten nonvirtues, of gathering the virtuous qualities by embracing the practices of the six paramitas, and to act for the welfare of others through the four activities. You also pledge to always observe the vows to the objects of refuge, namely the unsurpassable Three Jewels of the Buddha, the Dharma, and the Sangha.

For the samaya of the vajra family, you vow to correctly adhere to the mudras represented by vajra and bell. The samaya of the ratna family is to always engage in the four types of giving. These four types of giving are to provide material necessities, to give others confidence so that they won't be afraid, to share the teachings on relative truth, and lastly, to share the ultimate truth. The samaya of the lotus family, which represents the purity of the awakened state, is to uphold, without exception, all the teachings of the nine vehicles: the outer vehicles of shravakas, pratyeka-buddhas (Hinayana), and bodhisattvas (Mahayana); the inner vehicles of the three outer tantras of Vajrayana, namely the *Kriya, Upa,* and *Yoga* tantras; and lastly, the secret vehicles of the three classes of inner tantra known as mahayoga, anuyoga, and atiyoga. The samaya of the karma family is to perfectly uphold all of the different levels of precepts as well as making offerings and performing acts of worship as often as you are able to.

Then again, we take the bodhisattva vow to attain unsurpassable un-excelled enlightenment and to liberate all the beings of the lower realms who have not been liberated; to carry across all those who have not crossed over from samsara to nirvana, namely the shravakas, and so on; and to "reassure those who have not acquired reassurance," meaning bod-hisattvas with incomplete enlightenment. In this way, you vow to not rest until all sentient beings have been established beyond suffering.

Abiding by the Samayas

Having already committed ourselves, we now confirm the oath that we have taken by drinking a few drops of the water of the vajra samaya. The Tibetan word for samaya is *damtsig,* which is a compound of *dampa* and *tshig.* In this context, *dampa* means "sublime," because, when keeping the samaya, one is connected with the sublime state of enlightenment; and *tshig* means "burned," because, if one violates the samayas, one will be scorched by the flames of hell. Therefore, *damtsig* means either to be sublime or to be burned, which is reflected in the lines of the verse that is recited when you take the water:

> This is the water of the vajra samaya.⁏
> It will burn me if I violate the samayas.⁏
> If I keep the samayas, this water of the vajra-nectar⁏
> Will make me accomplish all the siddhis.⁏
> VAJRA SAMAYA UDAKA THA THA THA⁏

Peaceful Male and Female Buddhas

When drinking this, you should imagine that the wisdom being is present in our heart center in actuality, and that the drops of water dissolve into this wisdom being and will remain there as long as you abide by your original commitment. If you violate what you originally committed yourself to, then something inside of you will turn against you; this is described as the wisdom being turning into an iron scorpion that will eat you from within, this state of self-imposed suffering being none other than the hell realms.

Purifying

We now come to the main part of the mending and purification, which has six aspects: (1) purifying breaches, (2) general cleansing for yogis, (3) feast offering, (4) mending rituals, (5) concluding liberation, and (6) receiving the empowerments.

Vajrayana practice extends from the time you receive the four empowerments until the wisdom of the empowerments is perfected, namely complete enlightenment. During this time, acting contrary to developing the four wisdoms connected to the four empowerments will impede one's development and is considered to be a breach of samaya. The four empowerments are said to be like lion's milk, which cannot be poured into a normal vessel, as a normal vessel will just break, unable to contain it. Therefore, we must first purify ourselves and become proper vessels. A drubchen like the *Ocean of Amrita* contains both purification practices and the four empowerments. The general purification washes away the dirt containing the seeds for samsara and restores one to be a suitable vessel for receiving the blessings of the four empowerments.

To fully mend and purify all breaches requires several steps. The first is purifying the six realms; then there is a general cleansing of the practitioner, followed by a feast offering and further mending rituals.

PURIFYING THE SIX REALMS

There is more than one way of explaining how the six realms of samsara arise, but the general system says that acting out of anger causes rebirth in the hell realms; being stingy causes rebirth as a hungry ghost; dullness and stupidity lead to one being reborn as an animal, attachment and desire as a human being, jealousy and envy as a demigod, and pride as a god. Another explanation is that the strength of the emotion and the number of times it is experienced decides in which realm one will end up; for example, very strong anger causes rebirth in hell, medium-strength anger causes rebirth as a hungry ghost, and mild anger causes rebirth as an animal. Whatever the case might be, the causes for the six realms must be purified. Your body of karmic ripening[25] itself contains the tendencies for taking rebirth in each of the six realms of samsara. The root causes for each of these tendencies are present within your body as six seed syllables. Each of these seed syllables has the potential to blossom into one of the six realms; so, in order that rebirth will not sprout in the field of samsara, you burn them with the flames of wisdom, scatter the ashes with the wind of dharmata, and wash away any remnants with the water of awakened mind. The procedure for doing this is the same for each of them; therefore, I will describe the method in detail only for the hell realms, as you then just follow the same basic steps for each of the other syllables.

To begin, imagine that your body is marked with the black syllable DU on the soles of your feet, a pale red PRE at your secret place,[26] a green TRI at your navel, a light-blue NRI at your heart, a reddish-green SU at your larynx, and a white A at your forehead.

Next, on the fingertips of your right hand are the seed syllables HUNG, OM, SVA, ANG, and HA resting on sun disks that transform into the five male buddhas. On the fingertips of your left hand are the syllables MUM, LAM, MAM, PAM, and TAM resting on moon disks, and they transform into the five female buddhas. Join your palms and say, OM SURATA SATVAM. Then put the fingers of your right hand together with those of the left, hence bringing the five male and female buddhas together, and say BENZA ANDZALI. Now imagine that the male and female buddhas are united and say BENZA BANDHA BAM. Then recite the following:

> NAMO, homage to the Three Jewels! By the truth of the words of the Three Jewels, by the truth of the pure innate nature (dharmata), by the truth of the unfailing cause and effect of conditioned things, by the truth of the magical display of the peaceful and wrathful deities, by the truth of the emanations, reemanations, and attendants, and by the blessings of the great truth, may all misdeeds and obscurations created by means of the disturbing emotion of anger, the cause of hell, be totally purified.
> NARAKA SHUDDHE CHAKSHU PRABESHAYA PHAT

NARAKA is the Sanskrit term for the hell realms, and SHUDDE means "to be purified," therefore the mantra means "may the hell realms be totally purified." Then, while grinding the palms of your hands together, flames of wisdom blaze forth from the heart center of the vajra master as well as from the place of union of the five male and female buddhas, totally consuming the black DU syllables on the soles of your feet.

Now, the wind of the unconditioned nature known as dharmata blows away any remaining defilements. To do this, you toss sand and mustard seeds that have been consecrated by special mantras, while saying the mantra, OM SARVA TATHAGATA ADISHTHANA ADISHTHATE SARVA PAH-PAM AVARANA BHASMI KURU SVAHA.

This mantra means, "By the blessings of the past and present moment, may all obscurations be totally purified." Follow this with OM DAHA DAHA SARVA NARAKA GATE HETUM HUNG PHAT, WHILE IMAGINING THAT EVEN IF SOME ASHES REMAINED AFTER THE SYLLABLES HAD BEEN DESTROYED BY FIRE, THESE ARE NOW BLOWN AWAY.

FINALLY, PURIFYING BY MEANS OF THE WATER OF AWAKENED MIND HAS THREE PARTS. FIRST IS APOLOGIZING WITH DEEP REMORSE. THIS VERSE BEGINS WITH *kyema kyehu*, an expression of deep regret:

> *Kyema kyehü*, Vajra Holder!
> Lord of beings, protect me with your compassion.
> Proclaim the king of the supreme empowerment.
> Henceforth, I shall neither hide nor conceal anything!

Next, the vajra master guides all those in attendance into the place of empowerment, saying,

> Child of a noble family, come here!
> I shall give you the supreme empowerment
> To protect against falling into the abode of Narak
> Through your violations and transgressions.

Now comes cleansing with the water of awakened mind. For this, as described earlier, imagine that the celestial palace of the auspicious vase contains all the peaceful and wrathful deities of the three roots dissolved into the rinsing water, which becomes the nectar of wisdom that embodies the nature of patience. Anger directly causes rebirth in the hell realms, and, among the six paramitas, patience is the remedy against anger and aggression. Therefore, the water of patience washes away the defilement of anger.

In this way, we have burned, scattered, and washed away the causes for rebirth in the hell realms embodied by the syllable DU on the soles of our feet.

Lastly, recite the Dharani mantra, then say, "Through this may all the negative karmas and obscurations and tendencies for rebirth in the hell realms be totally pacified, SHINTAM KURU SVAHA."

The procedures for purifying the remaining realms are exactly the same, except that the syllables are different, and the cleansing water takes on a different quality to counter the disturbing emotion that is the cause of each realm. For the hungry ghosts, we have the syllable PRE in our secret place, and with the water of generosity we purify the disturbing emotion of stinginess. The syllable TRI at our navel represents our habitual tendencies for taking rebirth as an animal. This time the water has the quality of intelligence in order to purify dullness. The syllable for rebirth as a human being is the NRI in the heart center, and, in this case, the nectar from the peaceful and wrathful deities has the quality of discipline and ethics, to purify the defilement of unethical behavior.[27] Next comes the syllable SU in the throat for the demigods known as ASURAS. The asuras suffer from laziness, which is purified by the water of diligence. Finally, we imagine that the white syllable AH in the forehead is purified by water that has the quality of concentration, because distraction is what makes us take rebirth as a god. Thus, all the habitual tendencies giving rise to the six realms of samsara are totally purified.

GENERAL CLEANSING FOR YOGIS

Purifying Body, Speech, and Mind

Once the purification of the six realms has been completed, you perform the general cleansing and purifications of body, speech, and mind. Each section includes an apology for mending breaches of samaya followed by a purification.

To purify our body, we bow down in front of the entire assembly of the Three Roots and the hundred peaceful and wrathful deities. The visualization is the same as before, with all the deities gathered in the sky before you. You should do full prostrations, not just touching the five points of the body to the ground, but actually stretching out flat on the ground. While doing this, imagine that it is not just you alone bowing, but countless replicas of you, as well as all other sentient beings bowing together, as many as atoms in the universe. If you have memorized the verses of homage, or can follow along while the others chant, then you should recite the verses while bowing down. Otherwise, just imagine that you are bowing, and recite the homages while filled with respect and devotion for each of the deities. Each verse addresses one of the hundred peaceful and wrathful deities, beginning with Buddha Samantabhadra and continuing in almost the same order as during the visualization of the mandala.

After paying homage to all the peaceful and wrathful deities, they emit rays of white light from their foreheads. This light becomes a liquid that then enters through the top of your own head, as well as those of all other sentient beings and replicas of yourself. As this healing nectar enters your body, you recite a few lines confirming that all of your breaches of samaya are mended, followed by the mantra of purification:

> HUNG§
> By cleansing with the wisdom nectar§
> Springing from the Vajra Bodies§
> Of the Three Roots, and the assembled peaceful and
>   wrathful deities,§
> Violations of the body's samaya are purified.§
> Arising with the appearance of a deity,§
> May the Vajra Body be accomplished.§
> OM AH HUNG VAJRA GURU DHEVA DHAKINI SHANTIKA
>   MAHA KRODHA KAYA ABHISHEKATE SAMAYA SHRI YE
>   HUNG§

As for the mantra of purification, GURU DEVA DAKINI refers to all masters, yidams, and dakinis. SHANTIKA refers to the peaceful deities and MAHA KRODHA to the wrathful deities, and KAYA ABHISHEKATE SAMAYA SHRI YE HUNG means, "May my body be totally purified of any breaches of samaya."

Lastly, you repeat the hundred-syllable mantra of Vajrasattva, followed by a mantra to purify the five elements:

> OM E HO SHUDDHE SHUDDHE, YAM HO SHUDDHE SHUDDHE,
> WAM HO SHUDDHE SHUDDHE, LAM HO SHUDDHE SHUDDHE,
> RAM HO SHUDDHE SHUDDHE A A SVAHA.

Purifying speech has three parts: visualizing and reciting the mantra of Vajrasattva, chanting the lamenting apology, and finally the purification.

The first part is the same Vajrasattva practice found in the preliminary practices. For purifying negative karma and obscurations, it is generally taught that we must have four remedial powers. The first, the power of the support, is to visualize Vajrasattva. Vajrasattva is the support for purification because it is in his presence that we form the attitude of the second remedial power, the power of remorse. Recalling all the negative karma we have committed during our innumerable past lives, we should feel great regret. This regret should be no different than if you discovered that you had swallowed a deadly poison. Third is the power of resolution, the intention to never again commit any negative karma, even at the cost of your own life. Lastly is the power of the applied antidote, which is to chant the Hundred-Syllable mantra while imagining the downpour of purifying nectar. It is said that whoever chants the Hundred-Syllable mantra with a pure mind just 108 times will become a pure child of all the buddhas. At first, your visualization may not be so clear, but it will improve with practice. Furthermore, using your voice to chant mantras and dharanis purifies karmic patterns of lying, harsh words, slander, and idle gossip, and also forms the circumstances for being able to realize the speech of all the victorious ones.

Just knowing these four powers, however, is not enough—you actually need to apply them. To do this, you visualize "the wisdom form of all buddhas," Vajrasattva, seated on a lotus and moon seat above your head. He is immaculate like the radiant autumn moon, and he holds a vajra in his right hand and a bell in his left while joyfully embracing his consort, Vajratopa, who is simply his own light. He is adorned with silk garments and gold jewelry, and is seated in full lotus within a sphere of bindus and rainbow lights. In the heart centers of both Vajrasattva and his consort is the syllable HUNG standing on a moon disk. Within Vajrasattva's heart center, the mantra is written counterclockwise around the HUNG and re-volves clockwise, while within his consort, Vajratopa, it is written clock-wise and revolves counterclockwise. While chanting the mantra, it slowly revolves, while colored rays of light radiate from the seed syllable HUNG and from the syllables of the mantra. These multicolored light rays shine out in all directions and to all buddhas. Making pleasing offerings, the rays return, fulfilling the twofold purpose for self and others. Emanating to the buddhas and bringing back blessings is for oneself. Radiating out to all sentient beings, pacifying their suffering, and removing all their negative karma and obscurations is for others.

Then again, all the light gathers back into the heart centers of Vajrasattva and Vajratopa and melts into nectar that flows from every pore of their bodies, from their place of union and from the soles of their feet; sometimes the big toe is specified. The nectar flows very strongly and then moves down into the crown of one's own head through entering what is known as "the aperture of Brahma." By descending into our body, all diseases, wrongdoing we might have committed in past lives, breaches of samaya, failures to keep any of the precepts, and so forth, as well as all negative influences, spells, curses, and so on leave our body. The wrongdoing is said to take the form of liquid coal; any diseases we have flow out as pus and rotten blood; all negative influences scatter in the form of nasty small creatures such as scorpions, snakes, tadpoles, and so on. All of this doesn't simply exit the body, but the earth below opens up and it all flows down into it in a big stream. Below are those to whom we owe karmic debts, beings we have killed for food, others we have robbed—all standing below with open mouths happily devouring what flows from us. Imagine that this satisfies them, and your debts are cleared. At the end, being totally purified, your body becomes transparent, as though it were made of hollow crystal filled with white nectar, much like a bottle of milk. In that way, we are totally purified.

The word *meshak*, translated as "lamenting apology," means to sing out with sincere remorse. As explained in the setting for the original Vajrayana teachings, long ago, after committing innumerable evil acts, Rudra was skillfully subjugated by the buddhas. Upon recollecting what he had done, Rudra felt great remorse and sang the following lament. When you sing it, you should not think that you are just singing along with someone who lived many aeons ago, but that you actually are Rudra. For Rudra is the ignorant, deluded mind that clings to the mistaken belief in a self, and, by giving rise to the disturbing emotions, creates negative karma that causes not only oneself to suffer but others as well.

OMȯ

Great compassionate Bhagavan Vajrasattva,ȯ
Immaculate color of conch, most excellent form,ȯ
Pure and brilliant, spreading the light of a hundred-
    thousand suns,ȯ

Hero, resplendent with a thousand rays of light,⸳
Knower of the triple existence, renowned as the teacher,⸳
Only friend of all the beings of the three realms,⸳
Loving protector, god of compassion, please listen to me.⸳

Since time without beginning, I have taken wrong paths,⸳
Lost my way, and wandered in the rounds of existence.⸳
In former lives, I was mistaken in committing wrong
    actions and misdeeds.⸳
For all these evil deeds, whatever I have done, I feel strong
    remorse and regret.⸳

Increasing and intensifying the power of this proud karma,⸳
I have sunken into the ocean of samsaric misery.⸳
The burning flames of anger have scorched my stream of
    being.⸳
The dense darkness of delusion has blinded intellect.⸳

My consciousness is submerged near the banks of the ocean
    of desire.⸳
The mountain of intense pride has pressed me down into
    the lower realms.⸳
The raging gale of envy has tossed me about in samsara.⸳
The demon of believing in an ego has tied me down
    tightly.⸳

I have fallen into the abyss of craving like into a pit of
    embers.⸳
Intense suffering has burned me like unbearable flames.⸳
These miseries are difficult for me to bear.⸳
With the intense fire of the power of evil deeds burning
    me,⸳
The sprouts of consciousness and sense organs have
    suffered.⸳

Since this is overwhelming my illusory body of aggregates,⸳
Compassionate and loving protector, can you bear it?⸳
I am foolish and deluded, a great sinner with evil karma.⸳
By the power of karma, I am reborn as Rudra in the realm
    of desire.⸳

I feel remorse for this rebirth! This karma is exhausting!§
I feel weary and I regret, but the karma cannot be changed.§
The force of karma is like the flow of a river.§
How can the river of karmic power be immediately
    reversed?§

All these ripenings result from my own karma.§
Although I entered the teachings, I have been unable to
    follow them.§
My body, speech, and mind have fallen prey to evil deeds.§
Forced about by the fierce storm of karma,§
I have, for countless former aeons,§

Wandered through the dark dungeons of samsara.§
So, protector, through your compassionate blessings,§
May you purify my obscurations of karmas and kleshas§
And establish me right now in your presence, like a loving
    mother.§

Brilliant, like the sun, and radiant, like the moon,§
Your compassionate face is captivating to behold.§
Since beginningless time, blinded by the cataract of
    ignorance,§
My physical eyes have been unable to perceive you.§
So where do you stay right now, protector of beings?§

By karma's most overwhelming and fierce power,§
I am completely terrified, afraid, and fearful.§
So, as I utter this lamentation of pure yearning,§
And make a destitute cry of great loss,§
Loving protector, unless you regard me with compassion
    right now,§
At some point, when I die, pass away, and my mind parts
    from my body,§
Separated from my spiritual friend and companions, I will
    be taken away by Yama.§

At that time, without being accompanied by my world and
    relatives,§
Alone I am carried by the power of karma.

Since I will be then without protector and refuge,⁑
Without any postponement or any delay of time,⁑
Assiduously, right this moment, perform your liberating
    activity.⁑[28]

After singing this lament, imagine that the hundred peaceful and wrathful deities emit rays of red light from their throats that enter our own throats. While this light shines toward us, it becomes red nectar, and drinking it purifies all our breaches of samaya. Then, request that the wisdom nectar that issues forth from the vajra speech of all the peaceful and wrathful ones purifies our speech samaya; request to hear all sounds as mantra, empty yet resounding; and to realize the vajra speech of all the buddhas. You then recite the same mantra as before, except instead of "KAYA" (body) you now substitute "VAKA", which means speech:

OM AH HUNG VAJRA GURU DHEVA DHAKINI SHINTAM KA
MAHA TRODHA VAKA ABHISHEKATE SAMAYA SHRI YE HUNG

This is followed by the Hundred-Syllable mantra and the mantra for Purifying the Elements.

Purifying Mind

Generally, when apologizing, we perceive our wrongdoing, approach the person we have wronged, and then say, "I am sorry; I was wrong." Obviously this involves a strong sense of duality, based as it is on distinctions of subject, object, and action. However, when performing the Apology of the Expanse of the View, all concepts, including those of right and wrong, are dispensed with. Instead, we acknowledge that all phenomena, including our misdeeds, the act of apologizing, and even the witnesses to our apology do not really exist. In short, all phenomena are totally unconstructed emptiness. So, recognizing this fact, we sing the apology:

AH⁑
Dharmadhatu, itself, is devoid of fabrications.⁑
How mistaken we are to regard it as duality, like good and
    bad!⁑
How deluded to attribute characteristics to things!⁑
I apologize for this in the expanse of great bliss free from
    fabrications.⁑

Samantabhadra is devoid of being good and bad.⁞
How tiring to regard him as duality, like good and bad!⁞
How pitiful it is to hold him as pure or impure.⁞
I apologize for this in the expanse free from good and bad.⁞

Equality is devoid of large and small.⁞
How mistaken to regard it as being a buddha or a sentient
     being!⁞
How tiring to hold it as being large or small!⁞
I apologize for this in the expanse of the great bliss of
     equality!⁞

Bodhichitta is devoid of birth and death.⁞
How tiring to regard it as being now and later!⁞
How deluded to hold it as being born or dying!⁞
I apologize for this in the expanse of unchanging
     immortality.⁞

The great sphere is devoid of sides and corners.⁞
How tiring to regard it as having form and substance!⁞
How deluded to hold it as the duality of sides and corners!⁞
I apologize for this in the ever-circular great sphere.⁞

The state is nothing but unchanging throughout the three
     times,⁞
How tiring to regard it as having beginning and end!⁞
How deluded to hold it as the duality of transformation
     and change!⁞
I apologize for this in the unchanging great sphere.⁞

The self-existing wisdom is not to be sought for.⁞
How tiring to regard it as the duality of cause and effect!⁞
How deluded to hold the duality of effort and attainment!⁞
I apologize for this in the self-existing expanse of
     effortlessness.⁞

Awareness wisdom is devoid of permanence and
     interruption.⁞
How tiring to regard it as the duality of permanence and
     interruption!⁞

How deluded to view it as existence or nonexistence!॰
I apologize for this in the wisdom space free from
permanence and interruption.॰

The pure dharmadhatu is devoid of center and edge.॰
How tiring to project or dissolve partiality to center or
edge!॰
How deluded to hold it as having center or edge!॰
I apologize for this in the pure dharmadhatu free from
center or edge.॰

The celestial palace is devoid of outside and inside.॰
How tiring to regard it as having outside and inside!॰
How deluded to hold it as the duality of being wide or
narrow!॰
I apologize for this in the space free from being wide or
narrow, outside or inside.॰

The space of the mother is devoid of high and low.॰
How tiring to regard it as the duality of above and below!॰
How deluded to hold the duality of high and low!॰
I apologize for this in the bhaga free from being wide and
narrow.॰

Dharmakaya is devoid of divisions.॰
How tiring to regard it as objects and mind!॰
How deluded to hold the duality of world and beings!॰
I apologize for this in the space of nondual wisdom.॰

Whatever is done or experienced is nothing but the display
of the father.॰
How tiring to regard it as individual thoughts!॰
How deluded to misapprehend it with names!॰
I apologize for this in the space free from fixating on the
display.॰

Awareness wisdom has not arisen from within.॰
How sad is this ignorant and deluded mind!॰
It perceives the formless phenomena as concrete and having
attributes.॰

I deeply apologize for this in the natural space of wisdom.

When not realizing the nature of nonarising,
How miserable is the mind of the mistaken individual!
It apprehends the nonarising phenomena as ego and self.
I deeply apologize for this in the nonarising space of great
 bliss.

When the nature of dharmata is not cognized in the mind,
One does not understand that appearance and existence are
 illusory
And gives rise to attachment to material things and wealth.
I apologize for this in the unattached dharmata of
 nonarising.

Not understanding that samsara is devoid of a self-nature,
One apprehends concrete and attributed phenomena as
 being permanent,
And fixates on attributes out of unvirtuous karma.
I deeply apologize for this in the space of faultless
 enlightenment.

When not realizing the equal nature as being equality,
One apprehends friends and deluded companions to be
 permanent.
How mistaken is this mind of an ignorant person.
I deeply apologize for this in the space of the nature of
 equality.

When not facing the true nature of dharmata,
One abandons the true nature and endeavors in unvirtuous
 actions.
Discarding the Buddha's words, one is deceived by
 mundane distractions.
I deeply apologize for this in the dharmata space of great
 bliss.

When awareness wisdom is not liberated in itself,
One abandons the self-cognizant nature and endeavors in
 distracted actions.

How pitiful is such a meaningless sentient being!§
I deeply apologize for this in the space free from
    approaching or keeping distance.§

Wisdom deities and protectors possessing the samaya,§
If this yogin who practices the samayas correctly§
Happens to have the delusion of not realizing the view,§
I deeply apologize for it with deep remorse and regret.§[29]

At the end, imagine that deep blue rays of light radiate from the heart centers of all the deities. The rays of light become nectar and enter your own heart center, purifying all of your mind's breaches of samaya. Recite:

By cleansing with the wisdom nectar,§
Springing forth from the vajra mind of the Three Roots,§
And the assembly of peaceful and wrathful deities,§
Violations of the mind's samaya are purified.§
By conceptual thinking arising as wisdom,§
May vajra mind be accomplished!§

In other words, rather than holding on to concepts and feeling, may everything be seen to be the nonarising nature of dharmadhatu, the expanse of emptiness. Once again you repeat the various mantras as found in the two previous sections, except this time replacing VAKA with CHITTA, which is Sanskrit for mind.

Purifying the General Violations of the Three Doors

The last purification before the feast offering is designed to purify any violations committed by a combination of the three doors of body, speech, and mind. The Apology of the Twenty-Eight Samayas belongs to the inner tantra and refers primarily to the samayas of mahayoga. The first three are for the body, speech, and mind of the guru, and then, there are five samayas of what is not to be discarded, five samayas of what is to be adopted, five samayas of what is to be engaged in, five samayas of what should be known, and five samayas of what should be practiced. Altogether, these are known as the Three Roots and twenty-five branch samayas that we break, out of ignorance, whether knowingly or unknowingly. So, again, in the presence of all the peaceful and wrathful deities, you must apologize for violating all these, and ask that they be purified and restored.

HUNG𗀀
There are numerous scriptures and tantras𗀀
Taught by the teacher, Vajrasattva.𗀀
But, in short, having entered the gate of the mahayoga of
    the secret mantra,𗀀
One should abide by the permanent pursuit, the vajra
    samayas,𗀀
That are not to be transgressed, and observe them
    correctly.𗀀

This has been stated in the tantras of the secret teachings.𗀀
But due to ignorance, laziness, recklessness, and indolence,𗀀
I have transgressed the commands and dissipated the
    samayas.𗀀
I now deeply apologize with deep remorse and regret.𗀀
Please forgive me in the state of nonconceptual
    equanimity.𗀀

As for the root samayas of body, speech, and mind;𗀀
Because of weak respect and devotion,𗀀
I have gone against the mind of the vajra master.𗀀
Because of lacking affection and modesty,𗀀
I have gone against the minds of my Dharma brothers and
    sisters.𗀀
Having interrupted the mantras and mudras with laziness,𗀀
I have gone against the samaya of speech,𗀀

The four general, the eight intermediate, and the secret
    samayas, and so on,𗀀
The secrets that I have divulged, and so forth,𗀀
What ought to be secret and what was entrusted to secrecy,𗀀
Whatever root samayas I have transgressed,𗀀
I now deeply apologize with deep remorse and regret.𗀀
Please accept me with your compassion, all-pervading like
    the sky.𗀀
Let all my defects and faults be purified as I apologize for
    them,𗀀
And bestow upon me the siddhis of body, speech, and
    mind.𗀀

As for the five samayas of "what is not to be discarded":ༀ
The five wisdoms of desire, anger, and stupidity,༔
As well as arrogance and envy,༔
Are to be enjoyed in the unexcelled secret mantra.༔
They are the adornment of the supreme display of Samantabhadra༔
And of the nature of the five families and five wisdoms, from the beginning.༔
But, I did not realize this.༔
Please forgive what I have discarded due to wrong thinking.༔

As for the five samayas of 'what is to be adopted:༔
The mamsa, zhang, chi, kuwa, and rakta,༔
Are of the nature of the five nectars, from the beginning.༔
They are the sadhana substance of all the buddhas of the three times,༔
And the journey traversed by all of the countless victorious ones.༔
While primordially of a pure nature,༔
Due to concepts of pure and impure and through lack of yogic discipline,༔
I did not realize them to be the dharmata state of equality,༔
So, please forgive me for not adopting the substance of samaya.༔

As for the five samayas of "what is to be engaged in":༔
The view of realizing the absence of birth and death,༔
The place, time, and clear samadhi,༔
Delivering all of the three realms from their abodes,༔
The view of absence of meeting and parting throughout the three times,༔
The mantra, mudra, and maintaining clear samadhi,༔
The uniting of the true activities of means and knowledge,༔
Skillfully taking in the form of light rays what is not given,༔
The food and wealth of those fettered by avarice,༔
And making offerings to the noble ones for the welfare of beings,༔

Telling lies because the view and conduct of secret mantra⁚
Are not understood by others and are hard to fathom,⁚
Cutting the core of the ten objects, the mantras of wrathful
 conduct.⁚
As these have been stated in the teachings and scriptures,⁚
Please forgive me for what I have not engaged in and
 applied in practice.⁚

As for the five samayas of "what should be known":⁚
The five skandhas, the five consciousnesses and faculties,⁚
The five elements, the five sense pleasures,⁚
The five colors, the five medicines, and so forth,⁚
Are of the nature of the five families and five wisdoms,⁚
As is stated in the words of the victorious ones.⁚
They should be known as the five family consorts,⁚
But out of feeble intelligence, I did not realize that.⁚
Please forgive me as I have gone against the teachings and
 scriptures.⁚

As for the five samayas of "what should be practiced":⁚
All that is outer and inner, the world and beings, all that
 appears and exists,⁚
Is primordially of the nature of the five buddhas.⁚
Although they don't exist apart from my own nature,⁚
I have a feeble power of understanding and awareness.⁚
Please forgive my failure to reach perfect realization.⁚

Neglecting feast-offering for months and years,⁚
Having scant amounts of feast, foods, and provisions,⁚
Opposing the wish of the vajra master,⁚
Discounting the mending of samaya, defying the bond of
 the dakinis,⁚
And disregarding the precepts and sublime words – for all
 these I deeply apologize.⁚

I have failed to accomplish the view,⁚
And I have faltered in resolving the conduct.⁚
Retribution for violated samayas is unbearable—⁚
Drinking my heart-blood, Vajra Rakshasa will⁚

Shorten my life-span, worsen my health, deplete my wealth,
    bring enmity and fear,⚎
And the Hell of Incessant Pain is extremely dreadful.⚎

All these agonizing experiences are intolerable,⚎
So I apologize for any samayas I have violated.⚎
May I repair those I have damaged or broken,⚎
And attain the fruition of the great state.⚎
May the victorious ones of the three times bestow their
    blessings!⚎
May my samayas be mended and the dakinis protect me!⚎

Radiating light from the secret space of nonduality,⚎
You are as pure as the sky and possess no thoughts.⚎
Even so, may you safeguard me as you earlier promised,⚎
Reveal to me your wish-fulfilling bodily forms,⚎
And, from the basic space, bestow upon me the siddhis of
    the knowledge-holders.⚎

As for the devas, asuras, and yogis of the ten directions—⚎
The vajra samayas that are difficult to transgress, and
    should be permanently kept,⚎
The three basic and the twenty-five branches,⚎
All of these have I, through my ignorance, knowingly and
    unknowingly damaged.⚎
Thus, I am tainted by the defect of violation defilements.⚎

With this deep-felt apology for what I have violated,⚎
May the damaged samayas of this practitioner be mended,⚎
And may the fruition of the great state be attained.⚎

May all the beings of samsara's three realms, without
    exception,⚎
Be established in the vajra rank of equality.⚎
May I be protected by the compassion of the dakinis.⚎
May my faults of violations be permanently purified.⚎
Bestow the siddhis of your Body, Speech, and Mind!⚎[30]

After reciting the apology, imagine that *"white, red, and blue lights, the nature of amrita, radiate from the three places of all the assembled deities."* By striking and entering your own forehead, throat, and heart, these rays of light totally purify all the breaches of samaya committed by your body, voice, and mind:

> HUNG⦂
> By cleansing with the wisdom nectar⦂
> Springing from the body, speech, and mind of the Three
>   Roots⦂
> And the assembled peaceful and wrathful deities,⦂
> Violations of the samayas of the three doors are purified.⦂
> May all appearances arise as deities, all sounds as mantra,⦂
> And all thoughts as wisdom.⦂
> Thereby, may we realize the three vajras.⦂

We conclude with the mantra for body, speech, and mind combined:

> OM AH HUNG VAJRA GURU DHEVA DHAKINI SHINTAM KA
> MAHA TRODHA KAYA VAKA CHITTA ABHISHEKATE SAMAYA
> SHRI YE HUNG
>
> OM AH HUNG VAJRA GURU DHEVA DHAKINI SHINTAM KA
> MAHA TRODHA VAKA ABHISHEKATE SAMAYA SHRI YE HUNG

This is followed by the Hundred-Syllable mantra and the mantra for Purifying the Elements.

Feast

We have reached the third section, which is to offer a feast to ensure that every single breach of samaya has been purified, followed by a ritual for mending the samayas.

In Tibetan the word for feast is *tsok*, which literally means "many," but can refer to a gathering or accumulation; for example, the two accumulations—the accumulation of merit with reference point, and the accumulation of wisdom without reference point—is *tsoknyi*. Here, in the context of making a feast offering, tsok should be understood in terms of four kinds of gatherings. The first one is the delighted gathering of the many deities whom we have invited to partake of the consecrated articles of the feast. The next is the fortunate gathering of people, all the yogis and yoginis with whom we share the same samaya, and do this practice with. The third kind of gathering is the abundance of the gathered articles of the feast, all the food and drink and so on, which is consecrated as wisdom nectar. The last is gathering the two accumulations: the accumulation of merit by making offerings and the accumulation of wisdom without reference point by giving every aspect of the practice the seal of emptiness.

There are actually various kinds of feast offerings, depending on who is present. The basic version in which we gather is called a *tsok chop-pa*, which we usually just refer to as a feast offering. A gathering of just men is called a daka feast, and if just women, then it's a dakini feast. A proper ganachakra (*tsok kor-lo*) requires more than one hundred people—one for each of the deities. To perform a ganachakra, you should also have someone present who has sufficient miraculous power to revive the dead.

CONSECRATING THE FEAST ARTICLES

For a feast offering, you should gather as much good food and drink as you are able, including the five meats—human, cow, dog, horse, and elephant—and the five nectars—feces, urine, blood, semen, and flesh. Sacred medicine, mendrub, contains something called the remnants of five meats and five nectars consecrated by past great masters, such as Padmasambhava. To prepare a feast offering, we add some of it to the wine, so that the five meats and the five nectars will be present in the feast.

We also consecrate all the offerings, avoiding all our normal concepts of food and drink by giving everything sacred names. This belongs to what is called "courageous discipline" or "yogic discipline," in which there are no normal concepts of clean and unclean, pure and impure. Just the same, the feast articles should be pure, in the sense of being free from the eight worldly concerns: loss, gain, happiness, sorrow, slander, praise, pleasure, and pain. One should be free from such ordinary notions as the conceit that "I am sponsoring a great feast." Such attitudes taint the feast articles. Another meaning of purity here is flesh that people usually don't eat and which comes from beings who have died of natural causes. In the context of a feast offering, the five meats are considered pure because they are not normally eaten in our countries and the animals have died naturally. On the other hand, the meat from animals that have been slaughtered against their will is not considered pure and cannot be used in the feast.

The key point in all of this is to go beyond concepts of pure and impure by dissolving everything into the state of equality. It doesn't mean to indiscriminately eat everything, like a dog or a pig does. Nor does it mean to eat like a rishi, ingesting only what is considered pure according to certain scriptures. That is not being free of concepts either. Instead, it means that if we have meat that comes from a sheep, and next to it, meat from a dog, we shouldn't form any preference or judgment. Purity and impurity are not found in the meat itself, but rather within our own concepts and attachments.

If a separate liberation offering is going to be done, a small portion of the feast offerings should be set aside for this purpose before consecrating everything. If they haven't been separated before, then it can be done later, but you would need to remember that the feast articles are no longer normal foodstuffs at that point. In essence, they are then wisdom nectar, and in the form of offering goddesses proffering enjoyable offerings. Therefore, if a portion wasn't set aside before the consecration, the essence of the offering goddess should be absorbed into one's heart center before making the liberation offering.

Having gathered feast articles, food, and drinks that are not tainted by stinginess or miserliness, as we still have some clinging to them as something that can be enjoyed in a concrete way, we purify this misconception by saying the mantra RAM YAM KHAM, by which we acknowledge that we are not suddenly making them empty, but that everything is naturally empty already. Then, still visualizing yourself as Guru Rinpoche, from your heart center send out these three syllables. One after the other, they burn, scatter, then wash away any notion of concreteness in the offering articles. After that, the light of these three syllables consecrates the articles into wisdom nectar, multiplies them, and turns them into all kinds of wonderful things. Then, we repeat the three syllables OM AH HUNG many times. The syllable OM becomes white nectar, the syllable AH red nectar, and the syllable HUNG blue nectar that is sprinkled all over the articles, transforming them into an immensity, like a cloud bank, of wonderful offerings filling the sky. With that, the offering articles are now consecrated.

INVITING THE DEITIES TO JOIN THE FEAST

Having prepared the feast, now you need to invite the buddhas of the three kayas headed by Padmasambhava as nirmanakaya, Avalokiteshvara as sambhogakaya, and Amitabha as dharmakaya, surrounded by the twelve Manifestations, the dakas and dakinis, and so forth, as well as an ocean-like amount of buddhas and bodhisattvas to come and join in. Request them not to remain as basic space, the luminosity totally devoid of any mental constructs, but rather to manifest in forms that are like wisdom magic in order to enable everyone to accumulate vast amounts of merit and to purify their obscurations. Wisdom magic refers to the indivisible unity of appearance and emptiness. We conclude by summoning the vajra samaya by saying, VAJRA SAMAYA JAH JAH.

OFFERING THE FEAST

The actual feast offering is comprised of three parts: offering the pure portion, mending and apology, and finally the deliverance or liberation offering.

Offering the Pure Portion of the Feast

First, a small portion of the offerings should be set aside for the residual feast. You might think that making a feast offering is a very elaborate affair, but it does not need to be. Purifying obscurations and gathering the accumulations of merit and wisdom depend primarily on our attitude, not the objects we arrange and use. If our offering articles are not contaminated by wanting to show off in front of others or by stinginess, then even a single biscuit will suffice to make a complete feast offering. You simply use one biscuit as a support for the visualization. For the residual offering, simply break off a small piece, and use a small piece for the liberation offering. Practices of this type are designed to be mainly mental. You should never think that you are unable to make a feast offering because you don't have this or that. Simply imagine that all masters of the lineage, all the buddhas and bodhisattvas, are present in the sky before you, and then use a biscuit or two, and, in a small cup, sprinkle a little mendrub for the five meats and five nectars, and put some clean water in another cup for the amrita. That is all you need.

By means of the enjoyment of undefiled or unconditioned great bliss, totally uncontaminated by any concepts of plentitude or scarcity, we request all the deities of the mandala of the Three Roots—gurus, yidams, and dakinis—to be totally pleased:

> OM AH HUNG꞉
> The essence of the feast-offering is a cloud bank of wisdom
>   nectar꞉
> In the form of goddesses carrying desirable objects filling
>   the sky.꞉
> May this enjoyment of unconditioned great bliss꞉
> Please you, assembly of mandala deities of the Three
>   Roots.꞉
> SARVA GANA CHAKRA PUJA HOH꞉

The mantra at the end means, "May you joyfully partake of this feast offering." Then, you offer the first pure part and place it on the shrine.

Mending and Apology

The mending and apology has three parts: mending samayas with the vidyadharas, mending samayas with the peaceful and wrathful deities, and the apology.

First comes the mending samayas with the vidyadharas. You begin by acknowledging that your surroundings, body, and so on are a pure realm:

The splendor and wealth of existence and peace are
> assembled in the vessel of the animate and the
> inanimate.

The bhandha of my body is filled with the nectar of the
> aggregates and elements.

The lotus vessel of the dhuti is brimming with the great
> rakta of bindu and prana.

The great torma of awareness is arrayed on the tray of
> space.

The desirable objects of the four visions shine within the
> sphere of the six lamps.

Then, as the *Ocean of Amrita* is based on the mandala of the *Barchey
Künsel,* you chant a few lines for each of the deities specific to that mandala. After that, you mend the samayas with each of the peaceful and
wrathful deities, following the same sequence as when we visualized
them earlier in the peaceful and wrathful mandalas. The Tibetan term,
translated as "to be mended," is *tukdam kangwa,* also meaning "to be fulfilled." For example, if someone gives you a very nice present and you
are happy and satisfied, you have a feeling of being fulfilled. Of course,
the deities themselves, being free of attachment, can be neither satisfied
nor displeased by being offered something or not. However, from our
perspective, if we feel that we have been separated from the deity, then by
making an offering we can clear away such mistaken views.

After you have mended your samayas, you then apologize:

> HOH$\frac{\circ}{\circ}$
> For the misdeeds, veils, faults, and failings created since
> > beginningless time,$\frac{\circ}{\circ}$
> And especially for the infractions and violations$\frac{\circ}{\circ}$
> Of the root and branch samayas,$\frac{\circ}{\circ}$
> I apologize and mend them by offering this feast of
> > desirable objects!$\frac{\circ}{\circ}$
> SAMAYA SHUDDHE AH$\frac{\circ}{\circ}$

"Misdeeds" (*digpa*) refer to the normal ten nonvirtuous actions; "veils"
(*drip-pa*) refer to the different kinds of obscurations; "faults" (*nyepa*) refer to the general precepts; and "failings" (*tungwa*) refer to the root and
branch samayas, such as the fourteen root downfalls, the samayas for the

body, speech, mind, and so on that we discussed earlier. "Infractions" (*gyalwa*) means "to have acted contrary to," and "violations" (*nyampa*) means "to have violated" or "to have broken." So, you apologize by proffering this great offering of desirable objects, and ask that all of your failings and so on be mended. The mantra at the end, SAMAYA SHUDDE AH, SIMPLY MEANS "May the samaya be pure."

After reciting the mantra, place the second portion of the feast offerings on the shrine.

Liberation Offering

You begin the deliverance or liberation offering with the mantra, PADMA MAHA SHRI HERUKA KOH HAM, which means, "I am the great Lotus Heruka." With that, you should assume the vajra pride that you actually are the wrathful Lotus Heruka. You then say:

> *Namo*, homage to the Three Jewels! By the truth of the words of the Three Jewels, by the truth of the pure innate nature, by the truth of the unfailing cause and effect of conditioned things, by the truth of the magical display of the peaceful and wrathful vidyadhara deities, by the truth of the emanations, reemanations, and attendants, and by the blessings of the great truth, may all incorrigible beings who are fit to be liberated be present in this support—the material linga.
>
> NRI YAM JAH NRI VAJRA ANGKUSHA JAH TRI YAM JAH TRI VAJRA ANGKUSHA JAH
>
> DZAH HUNG BAM HOH

In the mantra, NRI is the seed syllable of human beings, whom we first summon, and then bind; and TRI is for animals and other lower beings. DZAH HUNG BAM HOH are used to respectively summon, bind, tie down, and intoxicate the beings to be liberated.

Upon having subjugated them in this manner, innumerable beings, called *gingkara*, emanate from the heart center of the Great Glorious One, Palchen Heruka. There are various types of gingkara, including those who arrest the incorrigible forces and those who "deliver," meaning kill them. There are other gingkaras who proffer the offerings, like servers. What is actually liberated is an evil spirit that is simply our own dualistic fixation conceiving of a perceiver separate from whatever is perceived. Those erroneous conceptions are the demons and the obstructors that are being symbolically rounded up. Once they are dissolved into the luminous state in which no concepts whatsoever are held in mind, disturbing emotions may still linger; however, they no longer have any foothold due to acknowledging that not only does the perceived object possess no existence, but the perceiving mind is insubstantial as well. The verse of deliverance in the *Ocean of Amrita* is:

HUNG

Vajra Gingkara, heart emanation of Palchen Heruka,

Summon and dissolve the hordes of demons and
    obstructors, dualistic fixation!

Freeing them into luminous space, their meat, blood, and
    bones

I present to the assembly of mandala deities of the Three
    Roots.

SARVA BIGHANAN SHATRUN MARAYA KHA KHA KHAHI
    KHAHI

HA HA HI HI HUNG HUNG PHAT

The word translated here as "freeing" is *drelwa*, which means "deliverance" or "liberation." What is liberated is the rigid "lump of ignorant ego-clinging" that is the main enemy of all sentient beings. No enemy can do worse to you than what your own ignorant ego-clinging has already made you suffer. This is what the dagger of the knowledge-that-realizes-egolessness must kill. Once wisdom strikes ignorance, any "obstructions," never having had any true existence to begin with, simply dissolve back into basic space. After that, you simply let be, composing your mind in the equanimity of the natural state. That is the essence of the deliverance offering, and how we should understand it.

In the mantra, the word SHATRUN is composed of three syllables: *sha* ("flesh") symbolizing dullness, *trak* ("blood") symbolizing passion or attachment, and *ru* ("bones") symbolizing anger. These three substances are left behind as offerings and presented to the mouths of all the deities of the Three Roots. Thus, in sum, the mantra could be translated as "All dullness, attachment, and anger are liberated; please enjoy them!"

Opening the Eyes

Now that we have mended and cleaned our vessel, we are ready to fill it with blessings by receiving the empowerments. To receive empowerment means that you become empowered to take charge of your own situation. The traditional example is of a prince being enthroned as king. Without an enthronement ceremony, the prince is not the king and does not yet have the power to rule. But, once the prince has been formally enthroned, from then on, he has the power to rule the country. In the same way, once we receive empowerment, we are authorized to study and practice the profound Vajrayana teachings. It is taught that, without having received empowerment, one is not allowed to even glance at the tantric scriptures, much less engage in actual sadhanas and other practices.

Practicing Vajrayana without empowerment yields no result, like trying to squeeze oil out of dry white sand. Vajrayana practice is a bit like farming. Before planting any crops, the field needs to be fertile and the soil properly tilled; otherwise the harvest will be poor. Similarly, we must till the field of our own stream-of-being by reflecting on the four mind changings: the preciousness of the human body, the fact of impermanence and our mortality, the consequences of our actions, and the painful nature of samsara. Then, we fertilize the ground by taking refuge and forming the bodhisattva resolve. Once everything is prepared, then receiving the four empowerments can sow the seeds of enlightenment. In order to ensure that the seeds blossom into complete enlightenment, they must be nurtured through the various practices. Then, with proper care and diligence, one is sure to become a perfect buddha.

To reiterate, there are four empowerments: the vase, secret, wisdom-knowledge, and precious word empowerments. Another way to talk about empowerments is according to the empowerments of the ground, path, and fruition. First, one must receive the ground empowerment. The ground empowerment introduces the qualities of abandonment and realization during the series of four empowerments. It does not give you something that you don't already possess; it merely points out the qualities that are already present in everyone, from Buddha Samantabhadra down to the tiniest insect. All sentient beings have the exact same buddha nature; it never differs in size or quality. However, simply having this essence does not help much if it is not acknowledged. Without knowing the qualities that are intrinsic to one's own nature, one remains confused, clinging to all kinds of erroneous assumptions. Having fallen into such an ignorant state, a technique is required to reintroduce us to our own true nature. That is the purpose of the empowerment we receive from our glorious root guru. It is the ground empowerment in that we are being introduced to qualities that are already innate to us. Afterward, we can practice various sadhanas, and so on, in order to develop and perfect the wisdoms of the four empowerments. During these, we often also imagine that we receive the four empowerments again, for example, during the guru yoga practice in the preliminary practices (ngondrö). The empowerment we receive for our daily practice is known as the path empowerment. Lastly, upon attaining complete enlightenment, one receives the fruition empowerment confirming that one is now a fully manifest buddha.

ENTERING THE MANDALA

In order to obtain the empowerments, one must first enter the mandala, which has five parts: (1) supplication, (2) bringing down resplendence, (3) tossing the flower, (4) opening the eyes, and (5) disclosing the mandala.

Supplication

First, you must present a mandala offering and request the empowerment. In the *Ocean of Amrita* it states that you must make the thirty-seven-point mandala offering.[31] After that, you put on a blindfold to symbolize that, although you have already entered the natural mandala of what is, you are still blind to the fact. This is accompanied by saying the mantra CHAKSHU BHANDHA VARMANAYA. You are also given a flower to hold between your joined palms, symbolizing the purity of your motivation in making the request. You take the flower, saying AKHAM VIRA HUNG. Then, palms joined, you make the supplication to the vajra master:

> KYE HO!°
> We are liberated from samsara°
> By the master, the essence of compassion.°
> We implore him to make us completely enter°
> The sublime sphere of great liberation.°

Bringing Down Resplendence

Bringing down the resplendence is a way of being consecrated. The vajra master is of course the chief figure of the mandala, but you should not consider yourself an ordinary being, but visualize yourself as a deity as well, "without focusing on the concreteness of the three doors." This means that our normal body, usually thought of as flesh and blood, should be recognized as being utterly indivisible from emptiness. This emptiness takes the form of Hayagriva, *haya* meaning "horse" and *griva* "head," as Hayagriva is a heruka with a horse head attached to the top of his own head. This great powerful heruka is deep red in color, and in dancing posture holds a curved knife in his right hand, and a skull cup filled with blood in his left. In your own heart center is a swastika, spinning counterclockwise, upon which dances Vajra Varahi, who is also red. The vajra master should be regarded as Padma Tötreng Tsal, which is another name for Guru Rinpoche, in person.

Maintaining this confidence, invoke deep-felt devotion from the very bottom of your heart. Through the power of this devotion, rays of red light stream out from your heart center into the ten directions, invoking the samaya of all the buddhas, peaceful and wrathful ones, the masters, yidams, dakinis, and so forth in all buddha fields. They respond by showering down a rain of blessings of their body, speech, and mind in the forms of deities, mantric symbols, and the emblems that they hold in their hands, respectively. These blessings enter into you, not only through your senses, but through all the pores of your body as well, totally filling your form as Hayagriva and being absorbed into Vajra Varahi in the heart center, like a sponge soaking up water. This causes original wakefulness and overwhelming great bliss to blaze forth.

Imagining thus, burn the incense of resplendence. At the end of Tötreng Tsal's and the Peaceful and Wrathful Ones' mantras, append:

OM JNANA SARVA SIDDHI PASHAM KURU HO. JNANA
AHBESHAYA A AH. SATVAM BHAYA HA HA HA HA HE HE
HE HE RA RA RA RA CHALAYA CHALAYA HRIM HRIM PHEM
PHEM HUNG AH HA JHEM

Thus, recite fiercely while playing the damaru, thighbone trumpet, and various kinds of music, gently yet rapidly, mixing together, again and again, until the blessings arrive.

Vajrayana always employs a combination of three components: material substance, mantra, and samadhi. In this context, samadhi refers to the visualization and meditation; the mantra is as described; and the material substance is a specific incense made from frankincense and other substances specially formulated for the downpour of blessings or resplendence. While chanting the mantra, the vajra master and the other gurus play the damaru, blow bone trumpets, and so on, and a censer is carried around spreading this fragrant smoke. Those who have complete devotion may have some signs occur at this point. Physical signs are things like making involuntary dance movements; the sign of speech would be that one spontaneously utters Sanskrit words or syllables; and as a sign of blessings entering one's mind, the three meditation experiences of bliss, clarity, and nonthought might suddenly blaze forth in one's stream of being.

To signify that the resplendence and blessings that have been brought down should remain in your stream of being until you attain supreme enlightenment, you say, TISHTHA VAJRA, while touching the vajra to the crown of your head.

Tossing the Flower

Holding the flower that we received earlier, we now imagine that we are at the eastern gate of the mandala. Although the deities do not differ in quality, there are differences as to which buddha family we are more karmically connected with from former lives, so in order to discover which family this might be, recite the following, and with no concern whatsoever, toss the flower on the mandala tray to see where it lands.

> By offering this flower of wisdom awareness:
> To the exalted deity of previous connection,:
> I accept him as the yidam.:
> May it fall on whoever he may be.:
> PUSHPE GRIHANA HO

After tossing the flower, you should then examine where it has landed. If the flower falls in the center, that's the best. If it falls inside the palace, that's next best, and if it falls on the surrounding wall, that's the least auspicious. If your flower happens to be blown elsewhere by the wind, that's a sign that you have been unable to mend the breaches of samaya, and you must mend those and try again. After seeing which buddha family you are connected with, to signify that you are blessed, imagine that the vajra master places the flower on the top of your head again, and recite:

> HOH:
> By the blessing of offering the flower of awareness:
> To the sublime deity with whom:
> I am linked throughout previous kalpas,:
> And having truly met the self-arisen wisdom deity,:
> May the siddhis of body, speech, and mind be obtained!:
> PUSHPE PRATI KRIHANA SIDDHI HUNG:

Opened Eyes

As you are still wearing the blindfold to symbolize that you have not yet seen the mandala in actuality, in order to restore your eyesight, imagine that the vajra master, who is inseparable from the chief figure of the mandala, says:

> HOH:
> Just as the royal optician opened eyes,:
> On this day my cataracts of ignorance are cleared away:
> By means of the golden scalpel of wisdom-awareness,:
> And I am blessed by all the victorious ones of the past.:
> JNANA CHAKSHU PRABESHAYA PHAT:

With a scalpel he removes your blindfold.

> Thus it is said that by opening the eyes with the golden
> scalpel, the wisdom-eye will be attained.

Revealing the Mandala

After that, the vajra master shows the mandala of the three kayas, saying,

> This is the example illustrating the mandala;
> The real meaning of the mandala abides within oneself.
> By now meeting the great mandala of the unexcelled self-
> aware wisdom,
> This inexpressible, wondrous, and spontaneously
> accomplished profound nature of the deity—

Four Male and Female Gatekeepers

Nothing whatsoever, yet arising in every possible way—
Aeons of accumulated misdeeds and obscurations are surely
    washed away.
Therefore, humble yourself and rejoice sublimely.

"The example illustrating the mandala" means that what he is showing everyone is merely a superficial picture of the mandala; the real mandala of unexcelled self-aware wisdom is within each of us. Inexpressible,
the real mandala is beyond thought, word, and description. You can experience it, but it is ineffable. In itself, it is no concrete thing whatsoever, and, yet, it manifests in every possible way according to necessity.
Becoming reacquainted with one's own buddha nature purifies aeons of
accumulated misdeeds and obscurations.

Acknowledging the Purity

Actually obtaining the empowerments has four parts: (1) supplicating, (2) the four empowerments, (3) the empowerments of body, speech, and mind, and (4) performing the torma empowerment.

SUPPLICATING

First, we make a mandala offering and follow that by repeating three times the following request, in which Vajrabodhi symbolizes the indestructible, awakened state:

> Just as Vajrabodhi made a lavish offering⠿
> To the Awakened One,⠿
> Bestow upon me the vajra of space today,⠿
> In order that I may be protected.⠿

RECEIVING THE FOUR EMPOWERMENTS

The *Ocean of Amrita* is a marvelous way of restoring and purifying all the breaches of samaya that may have occurred in connection with the four empowerments. As explained earlier, receiving the four empowerments actually means being introduced to the four levels of wisdom, or to original wakefulness. Inevitably, the habitual tendencies prevent us from maintaining our commitment in regard to these, and so, the four empowerments need to be mended and restored. The process for restoring each of these is essentially the same and involves three aspects: (1) an apology for violating the samayas related to each particular empowerment, (2) mending those broken samayas, and (3) actually receiving the empowerment.

The original empowerment we receive from our root guru is called the ground empowerment. Later, to develop that fundamental understanding, we practice the path empowerments. We begin with the vase empowerment, which is connected with the development stage practices, and then, because the next three are related to the completion stage, they are known together as the three supreme empowerments. In this sense, the vase empowerment is like the preparation, and the three supreme empowerments are the main practice.

Nowadays, the four empowerments are all conferred during the same session, unlike how it was done in the tradition of Vajrayana as originally practiced in India. Back then, disciples would first request just the vase empowerment, and then embark on mastering the three fields of the development stage. Only once they had shown signs of mastery to their guru's satisfaction would they be allowed to receive the secret empowerment in which the three main nadis and the five chakras are described and instructions are given on how to do the yogic exercises known as *tsa lung trul khor*. After attaining a sufficient degree of proficiency in these exercises, the guru would examine the disciple, asking them to describe their practice and understanding. Only if a disciple had shown that they had mastered the skillful means of their own body would he or she be allowed to receive the third empowerment, which involves the mudra of another's body. That's how it was then, but who practices with such dedication and diligence these days?

THE VASE EMPOWERMENT

The vase empowerment provides you with the blessings required to master the three fields of development stage. The first is the field of mind, meaning that the practitioner must be able to visualize the entire mandala with all the deities, ornaments, attributes, and mantras clearly, vividly, and distinctly. Next is the field of the senses, in which one's environment is not only imagined as a mandala but is truly seen to be the mandala in actuality—one's dwelling place is a celestial palace, the environment is a buddha field, other beings are deities, and so forth. The third field is the field of objects, meaning that one can touch the celestial palace in reality, and, moreover, when other people look at you, they see a deity.

Here the perspective is of critical importance, for we are not training in transforming something impure into a state of purity; we are training in acknowledging that everything already is in a state of purity. It is only because of our delusion that we do not see that all that appears and exists is already a buddha field and deities. All enlightened beings see reality like that; it is only confused beings who, through their own projections, experience reality as different than it is. In other words, we experience disharmony between things as they are and things as they seem. In order to overcome our confusion, the vase empowerment allows us to train in seeing things as they actually are. The deities, buddha fields, and so on are all qualities of buddha nature; they are already spontaneously and originally present. It is only due to our own delusion that they appear otherwise, and if you practice faithfully and diligently, it is only a matter of time before you will perceive things as they actually are and actualize these qualities in your own life.

Apology for Violating the Samayas of the Vase Empowerment

When receiving the vase empowerment, we are committing ourselves to regard everything, the entire universe, all beings and phenomena, as pure. We pledge to regard the universe as a divine palace and all the beings within it as deities, all sounds as divine mantra, and all thoughts as the play of wisdom. Instead of maintaining this pure perception, we stray into the habit of regarding things as ordinary objects such as stones, mountains, water, trees, men and women, and so on. Moreover, instead of regarding our own body as the vajra body, which is the palace of the peaceful and wrathful deities known as the three seats of completeness,[32] we have regarded this body as just an ordinary human body of flesh and blood. In addition, we do not maintain a state of equanimity, seeing the true nature that pervades all things. Rather than regarding everything as the unity of appearance and emptiness, we regularly stray into one of the two extremes, either clinging to a materialist view of solid appearances, or else clinging to the nihilistic view of nothingness. Seeing things in all these erroneous ways violates the samaya of the vase empowerment, and so, we must apologize for these failings, for which the apology found in the *Ocean of Amrita* is extremely profound.

> OM
> Within my body, the celestial palace,
> At my crown, throat, heart, navel, and secret place,
> The purity of the five aggregates is the five families and
>   their consorts.
> I apologize for failing to bring them into the path of the
>   development stage of form!
>
> Though body and mind are primordially a unity,

I have failed to acknowledge the unity of the apparent and
 empty aspects,⸻
And thus have been unable to sustain the practices of
 meditation and post-meditation.⸻
I apologize for this within the expanse of the view of the
 threefold essence!⸻

While samsara and nirvana are primordially indivisible,⸻
I have failed to perceive the world and its contents as the
 celestial palace,⸻
And thus failed to master material phenomena.⸻
I apologize for such a philosophical view within the
 continuity of undivided samsara and nirvana!⸻

Failing to understand the primordial transcendence of birth
 and death,⸻
I die unrealized, unable to transform the experience at the
 time of death⸻
And incapable of transmuting the sphere of light through
 sound.⸻
I apologize for this within the state of fearlessness at the
 verge of death!⸻

Failing to acknowledge that the chief and common nadis of
 my body⸻
Are primordially the nirmanakaya,⸻
I have been unable to cultivate the nadis as the yoga of
 form.⸻
I apologize for this within the spontaneously present
 fruition, the primordial nirmanakaya!⸻

Failing to understand that the body and the nadis are the
 vase empowerment,⸻
I have been unable to practice the development stage of
 Mahayoga.⸻
I admit and apologize for these violations of the samayas of
 the vase empowerment!⸻[33]

Mending by Means of the Torma of Sense Pleasures to Rectify the Violations of the Body and Channels

Having apologized for violating the samayas related to the vase empowerment, together with those taken while progressing on the path of mahayoga, we now mend the samayas by means of the torma of sense pleasures. Within the vajra body are the subtle channels known as nadis, which are mended by the torma offering. Earlier, it was explained that the torma symbolizes the universe and the beings within it, in that the torma plate represents the universe, while the torma itself represents sentient beings.

Conferring the Vase Empowerment

The actual vase empowerment begins with an invocation:

> From the heart center of the master, who is inseparable from the mandala's main figure [Padmasambhava], hook-like rays of light shine forth, summoning all the empowerment deities of the three seats of completeness in the sky before me. VAJRA SAMAJAH.

You then make offerings, saying OM VAJRA ARGHAM PADYAM PUSHPA DHUPA ALOKE GANDHE NAIVIDYA SHABTA PRATISHTHA SVAHA, and imagine that "The empowerment deities filling the sky confer empowerment with the precious vase endowed with numerous auspicious emblems and replete with a stream of nectar." This is the vase that was consecrated earlier, within which all the peaceful and wrathful deities have dissolved into wisdom nectar. You should imagine that they are all present in innumerable forms packed together as densely as sesame seeds packed in a full jar.

Placing the vase at the crown of the practitioners' heads and then drinking some of the water from it, the wisdom nectar confers the empowerment. This is summarized in the word *abhishencha*, which means both "to scatter" and "to pour," in that pouring out the wisdom nectar anoints the practitioners and scatters their disturbing emotions. Furthermore:

> Having thus been conferred empowerment with the stream of nectar possessing the nature of the five wisdoms poured from the excellent vase, the five disturbing emotions are purified, the five

179

aggregates are transformed into the five buddhas, and the five wisdoms are realized. As the sign of empowerment, I am crowned with the five families of tathagatas.

Thus, by having been given the vase empowerment, the defilement of my body is purified; I am authorized to practice the path of the development stage; and I have realized the wisdom in which whatever is seen is manifest as the mandala of the deity. Thus, I am provided with the fortune to attain the fruition of nirmanakaya.

THE SECRET EMPOWERMENT

The second empowerment is the secret empowerment, which the vajra master introduces by revealing his own body as the mandala. It employs a skull cup filled with consecrated wine or beer. A special ingredient called mendrub is added to the wine or beer. Mendrub originally came from Guru Rinpoche and has been passed on through the lineage. Now it is prepared using some of the original as a starter, and it contains the five meats and five nectars. It is then dissolved in the wine or beer.

The secret empowerment points out that within the hollowness of our vajra body are three main channels and five chakras. By doing various yogic exercises in which you manipulate the channels and energies, you can ignite the blissful heat and recognize that the essence of bliss is emptiness. You also dissolve the twenty-one thousand circulations of the ordinary karmic winds into the central channel. By employing such skillful means, you can attain perfection in your own body. Here your own body possesses the skillful means to realize blissful emptiness through practices such as *tummo*. Through diligent practice, one can gain some personal experience of what this actually means.

Mending by Means of the Rakta of the Great Redness to Rectify the Violations of Pranas and Speech

After the apology, the violations of speech and pranas are rectified by means of the rakta of the great redness. *Rakta* means "blood" but can also refer to the color red; in this context, however, it represents one of the three poisons: passion.

To do this, you mentally offer all the vidyadharas, the Three Roots, the peaceful and wrathful deities, the dakas and dakinis, and the guardians of the Dharma different skull cups (bhandha) at the five chakras filled with various types of rakta: the skull cup of great bliss at the head is filled with the rakta of suffering and thoughts; the skull cup of enjoyment at the throat is filled with the rakta of myriad thoughts; the dharmadhatu skull cup at the heart-center is filled with the rakta of the mind's thoughts; the emanation skull cup at the navel is filled with the rakta of disturbing emotions and the root of existence; and the bliss-sustaining skull cup at the secret place is filled with the rakta of blissful essence. You then ask the gathered deities, "May our samaya be mended, may our breaches be mended, may our conceptual obscurations be purified. Please bestow upon us the empowerments and siddhis."

Conferring the Secret Empowerment

For the actual empowerment, imagine that "all the gurus and the peaceful and wrathful deities engage in passionate union so that the *kunda* bodhichitta, the support for the coemergent wisdom that is of one taste with the nectar in the skull cup, can be placed on your tongue." Then, place a few drops of the nectar from the skull cup on your tongue and chant:

> AH§
> With this elixir of bodhichitta from the union§
> Of all the victorious ones and their sons, filling the sky,§
> May the secret empowerment of great bliss be conferred§
> In order to accomplish the vajra speech of the buddhas!§
> OM SARVA TATHAGATA VAKA VAJRA ABHIKHENCHA AH§

After that, imagine that you receive the nectar of all the peaceful and wrathful deities. By tasting the nectar, the three nadis and five chakras are filled with the wisdom nectar, thoughts of the three times are brought to a halt, and the wisdom of bliss arises. Due to this, the four kinds of bliss—bliss, supreme bliss, desireless or transcendent bliss, and coemergent or innate basic bliss—are all experienced. With the conferral of the secret empowerment, the defilement of speech is purified. With this you are then empowered to practice the path of the great bliss of your own body by means of visualizing the central channel within the vajra body, like a pillar in an empty room, and so on. Through the downpour and blazing of the inner bliss, you actualize the wisdom of self-consecration that everything is like a magical illusion and the moon in water, and you are empowered with the ability to attain the fruition of the Sambhogakaya.

THE WISDOM-KNOWLEDGE EMPOWERMENT

These days, to confer the third empowerment, the master shows the student an icon depicting a consort and explains that this illustrates how one is supposed to practice. To do this correctly, one must abandon ordinary concepts. The practice of the third empowerment is based on an important principle: recognizing original wakefulness as the unity of bliss and emptiness, and acknowledging that this empty blissful wakefulness is intrinsic to oneself. When the bindu descends from the crown of the head to the throat, the heart, the navel, and finally the secret place, one must recognize the wisdoms of the fourfold joys. As before, you begin by sincerely apologizing for being unable to properly practice and for having broken the samayas connected to the empowerment. You mend the breaches of samayas by means of the nectar medicine to rectify the violations of mind and bindus.

Conferring the Wisdom-Knowledge Empowerment

Having mended your samayas and purified yourself, you now retake the wisdom-knowledge empowerment. While still imagining yourself as the chief figure, Padmasambhava, imagine that Vajra Varahi in the form of a beautiful young consort (*phonya*) with exquisite charm sits on your lap. This is what is illustrated by being shown the mirror with sindhura power or by being handed the icon of the consort. If using the mirror, take a bit of the bright crimson sindhura powder and make a spot on your chest.

Then, through possessing the threefold notions and entering the union with the consort, through the gradual succession of the four joys, the innate bliss is stabilized. The four joys are joy, supreme joy, desireless joy, and intrinsic or coemergent joy. The three notions are (1) the man and woman are the male and female deities, (2) the union of their two secret places produces the major mantra, and (3) the sensation that is produced is regarded as the original wakefulness, in which bliss and emptiness are indivisible.

The words of the mantra mean the following: *om sarva tathagata*, "all the tathagatas" or buddhas; *maha*, "great"; *anuraga*, "the great passion"; *jnana*, "wisdom"; *vajra*, "indestructible"; *svabhava*, "the nature"; *atma koh hang*, "that is me." In other words, "I am the indestructible wakefulness which is the passion of all the buddhas."

That was the actual conferral of the empowerment. The benefits from doing the practice are now described:

> Thus, by having received the wisdom-knowledge empowerment, the defilement of my mind is purified. I am authorized to practice the path of the phonya, and I have realized the wisdom in which the nature of all phenomena is seen as great bliss. Thus, I now have the good fortune to attain the fruition of dharmakaya.

THE PRECIOUS WORD EMPOWERMENT

The fourth empowerment is the word empowerment. Here *word* simply means that through a few words or a gesture, the nature of wisdom is pointed out and transmitted. There is a citation from one of the tantras saying, "The fourth empowerment is also like that," meaning like the nature of the third. Recognizing the unity of bliss and emptiness in the third empowerment, the same thing is being pointed out in the fourth empowerment: nothing other than the nature itself.

The Apology for Violating the Samayas of the Fourth Empowerment

First, you apologize for not having maintained the view of the great perfection of the nature of all things, both samsara and nirvana, which is the view of atiyoga totally free from any assumptions or mental constructs. This view is perfected through the paths of *trekchö* and *tögal*. In the following verses, we acknowledge that we have failed to practice properly and have not perfected our practice.

> HRIH⁝
> Though both means and knowledge are intrinsic to me,⁝
> I have failed to train perfectly in the tantra of means,⁝
> The tantra of knowledge, and the tantra of both.⁝
> I apologize for this in the state of the threefold path of the
>   vajra waves.⁝

Not recognizing that what benefits body, speech, and
    mind,§
And both body and mind are intrinsic to me;§
I have failed to recognize the qualities of similar-to-the-
    cause, ripening,§
Acting cause, and the immaculate.§
I apologize for this in the state of the view of the purity of
    all things.§

Not experiencing the view intrinsic to me,§
Signs of the supramundane principle have not appeared,§
And I have failed to realize the principle of vast empty
    bliss.§
I apologize for this in the state in which all phenomena of
    samsara and nirvana are the single empty bliss.§

Failing to realize that there is nothing to purify, cultivate,
    nor train in,§
I have neither trained, practiced, nor become capable,§
And have failed to gain mastery in the prana-winds.§
I apologize for this in the state of the mahamudra of
    passing.§

Though everything originally is the essence-body,§
I have not trained nor realized the fact of the natural state,§
And I have failed to practice the path of the vajra waves,
    the principles of the path.§
I apologize for this in the state of the fruition essence-
    body.§

From the nature of the fivefold life-and-effort,§
I have failed to actualize the primary aggregates, subsidiary
    consciousnesses, and so forth,§
As well as the ten winds in the way of the life-pillar.
I apologize for this in the expanse of great bliss.§[35]

Mending by Means of the Illuminating Lamp to Rectify the Violations of the All-Ground Wisdom

To offer lamps is considered the most eminent way of mending breaches of samaya, and so to mend the violation of the all-ground wisdom, we offer butter lamps or candles, reciting an incredibly profound prayer. Just look at a few of these verses:

HUNG૱

....

The vessel of the indestructible bindu૱
Is filled with the oil of nonarising wakefulness.૱
The flame of self-existing awareness burns૱
On the wick of twelve minor nadis.૱
This, as well, is a self-existing lamp૱
Which I offer to the vidyadhara gurus, the Three Jewels,૱
The all-encompassing peaceful and wrathful ones, the
    dakinis,૱
And to all the deities of the mandala including the ocean of
    vow-holding protectors;૱
May our samaya be mended!૱
Mending the violations and breaches, may my conceptual
    obscurations be purified!૱
Grant the empowerments and siddhis!૱

The vessel of the fivefold wisdom૱
Is filled with the oil of the twenty-one white a.૱
The flame of fivefold knowledge letters burns૱
On the wick of the light rays of wisdom.૱
This, as well, is a self-existing lamp૱
Which I offer to the vidyadhara gurus, the Three Jewels,૱
The all-encompassing peaceful and wrathful ones, the
    dakinis,૱
And to all the deities of the mandala including the ocean of
    vow-holding protectors;૱
May our samaya be mended!૱
Mending the violations and breaches, may my conceptual
    obscurations be purified!૱

The vessel of the supreme luminosity᠄
Is filled with the oil of radiant light.᠄
The flame of fivefold wisdom burns᠄
On the wick of the shining bindus.᠄
This, as well, is a self-existing lamp᠄
Which I offer to the vidyadhara gurus, the Three Jewels,᠄
The all-encompassing peaceful and wrathful ones, the
    dakinis,᠄
And to all the deities of the mandala including the ocean of
    vow-holding protectors;᠄
May our samaya be mended!᠄
Mending the violations and breaches, may my conceptual
    obscurations be purified!᠄

The vessel of the vast all-ground᠄
Is filled with the oil of dharmadhatu.᠄
The flame of spontaneously present five kayas burns᠄
On the wick of awakened mind.᠄
This as well is a self-existing lamp᠄
Which I offer to the vidyadhara gurus, the Three Jewels,᠄
The all-encompassing peaceful and wrathful ones, the
    dakinis,᠄
And to all the deities of the mandala including the ocean of
    vow-holding protectors;᠄
May our samaya be mended!᠄
Mending the violations and breaches, may my conceptual
    obscurations be purified᠄
DIPAM PRATICCHA SVAHA᠄[36]

Conferring the Precious Word Empowerment

To illustrate the main principle of the highest Vajrayana teachings, one can't do much except simply show a crystal. Nothing more can be shown because our basic nature of self-existing wakefulness is beyond thought, word, and description. A crystal is transparent, which symbolizes the primordial purity, and illustrates the related practice of *trekchö, cutting through*. However, if you hold a crystal in a ray of sunlight, the light naturally refracts into a spectrum of five colors. This reveals that the purpose of applying the key points of the practice of *tögal*, direct crossing, can be utilized. By practicing tögal, one progresses through four levels of experiences, known as "the four visions," and will ultimately reach the perfection of complete enlightenment. Therefore the main practices of Dzogchen can be effectively illustrated with a crystal.

While beholding the crystal that signifies self-existing wakefulness, cognizant and yet thought-free, say:

AH§
Emptiness, the nature of bliss,§
Great power of the unified state,§
In order to realize the awakened wisdom,§
May the inconceivable empowerment be conferred!§
OM SARVA TATHAGATA JNANA VAJRA ABHISHINCHA A A AH§

By this utterance, remain briefly in equanimity while sustaining the natural radiance of self-existing coemergent wisdom, cognizant yet thought-free, which is realized at the end of the third empowerment:

Thus, by being conferred the fourth empowerment, the defilement of habitual tendencies is purified. I am empowered to practice the path of trekchö and tögal. I actualize the utterly pure wisdom of coemergent great bliss, and am instilled with the fortune to attain the fruition of svabhavikakaya.

The instruction in small writing is to sustain the natural radiance of self-existing coemergent wisdom, which is cognizant, awake, and yet free of thought, and which was recognized at the end of the third empowerment, the wisdom knowledge empowerment, and to remain in equanimity for a short while. By having received this fourth empowerment, the word empowerment, the defilement of habitual tendencies is purified.

Just like sugar is by nature sweet and water is wet, the nature of all phenomena, including bliss, is emptiness. This is simply how it is, and that is the fourth empowerment. The mantra means, "May the empowerment of the vajra wisdom of all the tathagatas be conferred."

Through receiving the word empowerment, the defilement of habitual tendencies is purified. Habitual tendencies (*bakchak*) are much more subtle than ordinary thoughts and concepts. Mistaken concepts or normal thinking are purified by practicing the development stage. But, the latent tendency to be confused needs to be purified by the three supreme empowerments, in other words, the practices connected with the completion stage, both with and without attributes.

Habitual tendencies are very subtle and linger even after other defilements have been purified. In fact, habitual tendencies are what prevent even the greatest bodhisattvas from becoming buddhas. It is said that for the bodhisattvas who are just about to be fully awakened, only the practices connected with the fourth empowerment will successfully overcome the habitual tendencies.

Honestly, from the beginning all sentient beings are already buddhas and in essence are primordially pure. But not recognizing this original purity, being an obscured buddha does not help much—just like the sun's full potential is not displayed when it is hidden by a thick cloud. Temporary obscurations occur from moment to moment, and as they have various densities, the four empowerments are used to remove them, starting with the most blatant, coarse obscurations and ending with the subtlest. The first empowerment deals with coarse concepts of things, people, places, and so on. Then, the various completion stage practices, with and without attributes, that are associated with the three supreme empowerments remove ever more subtle obscurations, until remaining in the state of trekchö and the practice of tögal removes the subtlest habitual tendencies.

To reiterate, the practices connected with the fourth empowerment remove the final obscuration. When you have musk in a glass jar, a smell remains even after it's removed. It's very subtle and invisible, but something is still there, and it obscures. Receiving this fourth empowerment purifies the defilement of habitual tendencies. One is authorized to train in trekchö and tögal practice and to actualize the wisdom of great bliss, the innate or intrinsic utterly pure wisdom. That is the actuality. *What is pointed out through the third empowerment only illustrates the example.* This is the real thing. Through this empowerment, we are installed with the fortune to attain the svabhavika body, the essence body as the fruition, the fourth of the four kayas.

It is only after all these momentary obscurations are purified that one is truly a buddha. Never forget: every single sentient being, without exception, has this potential. Sentient beings are merely those who do not yet recognize their true nature. We possess the potential but are unaware of owning such a wish-fulfilling jewel until someone points it out to us and says, "You already possess it. Why don't you just clean off the dirt, rinse it, and polish it?" One polishes it by living in a smoother and softer manner until the buddha nature shines forth in all its radiance. Make no mistake: this is not an act of transformation, improving one's state from being impure to being pure—our basic nature always has been pure and never changes. Our efforts on the path only remove the obscurations temporarily veiling our essence.

This is the unique perspective of Vajrayana practice, unlike the general teachings of the Buddha, where attaining complete and total enlightenment is said to take thirty-seven incalculable aeons. Due to the skillful means employed in Vajrayana, if you simply keep your samayas pure, even without doing any practice at all, it never takes longer than sixteen lifetimes to achieve enlightenment. If you do practice, then following kriya yoga it will take seven lifetimes, upa yoga, five lifetimes, yoga tantra, just three lifetimes. If you have the good fortune to follow the path of Dzogchen, then, without hardship, you can attain enlightenment in this very body and life.

Sowing the Seeds

THE EMPOWERMENTS OF ENLIGHTENED BODY, SPEECH, AND MIND

After receiving the four empowerments, there are some additional empowerments for enlightened body, speech, and mind, and one more for mending the ultimate view of emptiness.

Empowerment of Body

Imagining the vajra master as the chief figure of the mandala with the peaceful deities in his heart center and the wrathful deities inside "the bone mansion" of his skull, the deities replicate and, just like holding an unlit wick to flame, a new set of one hundred peaceful and wrathful deities appears from those already present. They traverse the space between you and the vajra master and enter the crown of your head, indivisible from the peaceful and wrathful deities already present within your own heart and "bone mansion," where they dwell "brilliantly, vividly, and unobscured," exactly like the visualization we described earlier.[37]

Empowerments for the Peaceful Mandala

First comes the empowerment for Samantabhadra and his consort, Samantabhadri. The two AH seed syllables are those of Samantabhadra and Samantabhadri: Samantabhadra, the unceasing, in union with his consort, Samantabhadri, the nonarising. By conferring the empowerment of the nondual lord and lady, may grasping, meaning actually perceiver and perceived, subside into dharmadhatu, into basic space.

Here, Samantabhadra represents rigpa, which never ceases. He is indivisible from his consort, the nonarising quality of everything, emptiness. Being empowered with this nonduality, concepts of perceiver and perceived subside into basic space. The "perceiver" is the concept of a subject apprehending what is being experienced, and the "perceived" is the notion of objects of experience such as sights, sounds, smells, tastes, and textures. The mantra is AH A ABHIKENCHA OM AH AH.

AH, out of the innate nature of suchness, which is "pure like space," meaning the dharmakaya totally devoid of intellectual constructs, the first samadhi naturally manifests the self-existing forms of five colored lights. These are the five buddhas—Vairochana, Akshobhya, Ratnasambhava, Amitabha, and Amoghasiddhi—in union with their consorts. The first five syllables of the mantra, OM HUNG TRAM HRIH AH, are the seed syllables of the five male buddhas; the next five, MUM LAM MAM PAM TAM, are those of the five female buddhas. ABHSHINCHA AH means "May the empowerment be conferred." Reciting this, you should imagine that the five buddhas and their consorts dissolve into their respective places within your own body, which was described earlier.

HUNG is the seed syllable for the enlightened mind. Although the male and female bodhisattvas are in essence indivisible from the awakened state of all buddhas, due to their "vow of great compassion," they act as if they remain on the stages of the bodhisattvas known as bhumis. "Appearance" (nangwa) refers to what is perceived, and "mind" (sem) to all the thoughts of perceiving. As for the mantra, SARVA means "all" and BODHICHITTA, "awakened mind."

The male and female gatekeepers come next and are represented by two HUNG syllables. "In order to tame vicious forces," the incorrigible beings who are not tamed by ordinary methods, "you compassionately appear in skillful forms," meaning wrathfully, to subjugate those who cannot otherwise be influenced. "By conferring the empowerment of male and female gatekeepers, may enemies and obstructors of dualistic fixation be eliminated." Through this empowerment, the one true enemy—dualistic fixation—is eliminated. Dualistic fixation is clinging to the notion of a perceiving subject here, separate from a perceived object there. Dualistic fixation also leads to clinging to a disparity between entities and comparing one thing with another. JAH HUNG BAM HOH are the seed syllables of the four gatekeepers.

Next comes the empowerment for the six sages, known as munis, located in the throat; it begins with the seed syllable of the lotus family of speech, HRIH. "In order to guide the beings of the three realms, you display any type of emanated magic. By conferring the empowerment of the six munis, may the activities of taming the beings be fully perfected."

Existence can be divided into three realms: the realms of desire, form, and formlessness. The realm of desire can then be further subdivided into the six realms. The three lower realms contain the hell beings, hungry ghosts, and animals. The three higher realms contain the human realm, the asura realm, and some of the gods that live on the surface of the four mountains surrounding Mount Sumeru. These are the realms of the four kings who guard the world. At the top of Mount Sumeru itself is the abode of the thirty-three god kings headed by Shakra, king of the gods. Above that and in the sky are what are called the "tatra" devas, the gods who are free from fighting with the asuras; above them are the enjoying emanations, who enjoy the creations of others, the highest realm among the gods of desire. Each of the different god realms is more splendorous than the next, and the gods have progressively longer life spans, more pleasures, and so on.

Above the desire realm is the form realm, which includes seventeen god abodes. Simply being good and accumulating merit will not get you there; you have to cultivate a form of deep samadhi. The depth of your samadhi and how refined it is will determine which of the seventeen form realms you will enter at death. The first twelve form realms are divided into three groups of four corresponding to the lesser, medium, and higher levels of the four types of concentration (*dhyanas*). In addition are the five states of purity, the highest of which is Akanishtha. All of these form realms are inhabited by gods whose enjoyments and bodily forms are comprised of rainbow light. They are much more beautiful, luxurious, and desirable than the gods in the realms of desire, and it is because of their beautiful forms that these are called "form realms."

Usually described as above these, but not really above because they could be anywhere, are four extra realms called the four formless realms. They exist anywhere an individual has cultivated the samadhi that leads to that kind of state, called infinite space, infinite consciousness, nothing whatsoever, neither presence nor absence of conception. A person who has decided that one of these is the ultimate state of realization and cultivates that alone will be reborn as a god in the formless realms. This existence could last for as long as eighty major aeons until the power runs out, like a battery that has lost its charge. When the force of meditative concentration has been expended, whatever other karma that was created earlier and lies in the background will determine into which realm the individual will be reborn.

Being trapped inside samsara and endlessly migrating from one realm to another is like a bee trapped inside a jar: it can fly up and hover near the top for a while, but sooner or later it must fly down again, and even more importantly, it never escapes its prison. The six munis have vowed to help liberate all sentient beings from the prison of the three realms, and, to help facilitate this, they appear in whatever way is most beneficial. For example, in the human realm they will appear as a human being, and in the animal realm they might appear as any kind of animal. Depending on the circumstances, buddhas will "display any type of emanated magic," whatever form is necessary to benefit other beings, whether it be the form of the tiniest insect or a radiant sambhogakaya or dharmakaya buddha. By conferring this empowerment, "May the activities of taming all classes of beings be fully perfected. OM SARVE MUNI ABHISHINCHA AH.

This concludes the mandala of the forty-two peaceful deities, with them all now vividly present in our heart centers.

Empowerments for the Wrathful Mandala

We now move on to empowerment for the fifty-eight wrathful deities in the bone mansion of our skulls, starting with the six herukas. The two HUNG syllables are for the central wrathful deity, Chemchok Heruka and his consort. Chemchok Heruka is known as the "Truly Perfected King Heruka" (Ngöndzog Gyalpo) as he is "the one who is primordially totally perfected," in that he possesses the fourfold fearlessness, the eighteen unique qualities, the tenfold strength, and so on, from the beginning. As before, he is surrounded by his emanations in the forms of the male and female herukas of the five families. By receiving this empowerment of these five herukas, the five disturbing emotions of dullness, anger, stinginess, pride, desire, and jealousy are purified and "subside into basic space."

The next empowerment is for the eight yoginis of the sacred places and the eight mamos of the secret valleys. They represent "the natural purity of objects and senses," in other words all that is seen, heard, smelled, tasted, touched, and thought of. The natural purity of the sense faculties appears as the bodily forms (mudras) of these emanations. "By conferring the empowerments of the mamos of the places and valleys, may the projection and absorption of awareness display be fully unfolded." Since all sixteen of these female deities are nothing other than the display of awareness appearing and disappearing, may the power of awareness grow stronger. In the short mantra at the end, HA represents the eight women of the sacred places, and the HE represents the eight women of the sacred valleys.[38]

The four inner female gatekeepers come next. The bell woman summons, the hook woman pulls, the noose woman binds, and the shackles woman tethers. The four female gatekeepers are described as the natural forms of original wakefulness represented by "the wisdoms of the four immeasurables"—immeasurable love, immeasurable compassion, immeasurable joy, and immeasurable impartiality. By receiving the empowerment of these four, the movement of prana and the wandering of the mind are brought under control.

The last of the empowerments for the wrathful mandala is for the twenty-eight *ishvaris*. HUNG BHYO. "All of you in the state of being the play of dharmata..." means simply being the state in which your innate nature appears. Although appearing "in the form of activities," everything is "accomplished as wisdom" or original wakefulness. The countless different thought forms are represented here as the various women with animal heads; nevertheless they don't exist as anything other than our own thoughts, and so by receiving this empowerment they are all "freed into basic space."

Having completed the empowerment for enlightened body, we now move on to the empowerment of speech.

Empowerment of Speech

While reciting the combined peaceful and wrathful mantra, imagine that from the throats of all the deities appear mantra garlands that dissolve into your own throat. The peaceful deities send out garlands of the Bodhichitta mantra, OM BODHICHITTA MAHASUKHA JNANA DHATU AH, and the wrathful deities send out the Rulu mantra, OM RULU RULU HUNG JOH HUNG. These then dissolve into your own throat blessing your voice. "The sounds of the animate" refers to the voices of sentient beings, while the "inanimate" refers to the sounds created by the earth, water, fire, and wind. *Ah* is the first syllable. "By empowering ordinary speech by Vajra mantra, the source of all possible utterances, may all the sounds of the animate and the inanimate...." "The animate" means all the voices of sentient beings; "the inanimate" is the sounds of earth, water, fire, and wind. "May all this be realized to be the audible and yet empty voice of the victorious ones." OM SARVA TATHAGATA, all the buddhas, VAKA means speech, ABHISHINCHA AH.

Empowerment of Mind

The mind empowerment is to transform the incessant stream of deluded experience into the awakened state of the mind of all buddhas. So you should first "rest evenly within the innate state of luminosity, the nonduality of deity and thought." As describing the awakened state of all the buddhas is very difficult with words, the master will instead hold up a mirror and say, "Look!" While looking into the bright mirror, we recite verses that remind us that the awakened state is just "like a reflection appearing in a mirror." A mirror has no intention to reflect anything, and yet a reflection appears. The reflective brightness of the mirror cannot be pinpointed, yet though it is "ungraspable" as an object of reference, a reflection still vividly appears. Recognizing this, all thoughts are seen to naturally arise and dissolve of their own accord. "Ungraspable and yet vividly present. By empowering ordinary mind to be the mind of the victorious ones, may all thoughts be self-arising and self-liberated," arising out of oneself and dissolving back into oneself. OM SARVA TATHAGATA CHITTA, meaning mind, ABHIKENCHA HUNG."

Empowerment Mending the Ultimate View of Emptiness

When receiving the empowerment mending the ultimate view of emptiness, "rest in the innate state of luminosity. Thus, without any focus on the subject and object of the mending, rest evenly in the state devoid of the constructs of the three spheres," namely subject (the one doing the mending), object (the one that you are addressing), and the action of mending. Remaining in this state free from all correcting or modifying, recite the following:

> HUNG⦂
> May this mend, may it mend the primordial samaya!⦂
> May concreteness be mended in the expanse of dharmata!⦂
> May perception be mended in the expanse of original
> wakefulness!⦂
> May cognizance be mended in the expanse of knowledge!⦂
> May suffering be mended in the expanse of dharmata!⦂
> May it be mended in the expanse of nonarising!⦂

May it be mended in the expanse of nonceasing!༔
May it be mended in the expanse beyond both arising and
  ceasing!༔
May breaches be mended and conceptual obscurations be
  purified!༔
Bestow the empowerments and siddhis!༔

The Torma Empowerment

The supporting torma empowerment has three parts: (1) reminding of the fourfold significance of offering, deity, empowerment, and siddhi, (2) the actual empowerment, and (3) partaking of the siddhi.

Reminding of the Fourfold Significance

The torma is raised and you recite:

> The torma's substance is the offering of sense pleasures. The torma vessel is a celestial palace. From the three places of the peaceful and wrathful deities, visualized as the torma, white, red, and blue light-rays shine forth. They dissolve into my three places, conferring the empowerments of Body, Speech, and Mind. At the end, they melt into nectar and I partake of them as siddhi, thus possessing the fourfold significance.

The fourfold significance is torma as offering, as the deities, as nectar, and as the accomplishment.

Conferring the Torma Empowerment

The torma should be placed on a circular or round plate as it represents dharmadhatu, which is free from the sharp corners of mental constructs. The torma itself is awareness endowed with the five wisdoms: dharmadhatu, mirrorlike, equality, discriminating, and all-accomplishing. These five aspects of original wakefulness are indivisible from the basic space of dharmadhatu.

Now you should chant the Tötreng Tsal mantra and the mantra of the Peaceful and Wrathful Deities, then adding BALINGTA ABHIKHEN-CHA HRIH, which means, "May the torma empowerment be conferred."

Six Herukas

Partaking of the Siddhi

Third, by means of tasting the torma dough, imagine that your nadi elements are filled with nectar and that you hereby obtain the two siddhis.

By eating some of the dough from which the torma is made, imagine that the channels (nadis) running through your body are filled with nectar, and you obtain both the ordinary and the supreme accomplishments (siddhis).

Concluding Rituals

The concluding rituals related to the main part of the practice are (1) taking the pledge, (2) offering gifts and showing gratitude, and (3) making aspirations.

TAKING THE PLEDGE

Taking the pledge begins with expounding the Dharma in order to explain the key points of the samayas in regard to what should be adopted and what should be avoided; once these are understood one then takes the pledge to adopt certain behaviors and avoid others.

The four empowerments introduce the vital life force of the Vajrayana, but it is their related samayas that sustain that life. So, after receiving the four empowerments, it's very important that the exact nature of those commitments be explained. In short, all the samayas are contained within the three levels of precepts: the outer precepts of individual liberation, the inner precepts of bodhisattva training, and the innermost precepts of the vidyadharas. Teaching on these would fill a whole book itself, but the basics were outlined above in the section titled "Apologizing for Downfalls" under "Mending."

There are the fourteen root downfalls related to the four empowerments. Nine of them directly concern the vase empowerment: (1) to disparage one's own vajra master, (2) to violate the words of the Buddha, (3) to be angry with a vajra brother or sister, (4) to forsake any sentient being, (6) to belittle or disparage anyone's belief, (7) to divulge anything that one has been taught in secret, (8) to disparage the body, (10) to support the enemies of the Dharma, and (12) to cause others to lose faith. Two are connected with the secret empowerment: (5) disavowing bodhichitta and (13) neglecting the use of the samaya substances. Downfall 14, not to disparage women as they are of the nature of knowledge, is directly related to the third empowerment. The remaining two—(9) harboring doubt about the naturally pure teachings and (11) forming concepts about the dharma that is beyond names—are connected with the fourth empowerment.

If you have received all four empowerments, you have committed yourself to keep all fourteen. When you inevitably do break the samayas, you should go to a master who can act as a preceptor, apologize, mend and repair whatever samayas have been broken, and then receive the empowerments again.

The precepts of individual liberation are like a pot of clay or porcelain—once broken, they cannot be repaired—therefore, those samayas are given skillfully and very compassionately. The Vajrayana precepts, on the other hand, are considered to be like a vessel of pure gold: if they are dented, they can easily be straighten out. There are some minor infractions, for example, performing the activities of a master during a fire *puja* or a consecration but not completing the recitation. Although they may be minor, they are still breaking samaya. The fourteen major samayas listed above are the more severe precepts, and that's why they are called root downfalls. In either case, when you break any of the samayas, the most important thing is to acknowledge it immediately, apologize for it, and mend it fully. If you let one day go by, it becomes an infraction; if you let a month pass without repairing it, it becomes a violation; and by letting one year pass, it becomes a transgression. After three years, it becomes a true break, and if more than three years pass, it becomes irreparable.

However, it is possible to repair most breaches. Making a feast offering repairs an infraction. A violation requires offering all your possessions. For a transgression, the tantras say that one must offer one's children and spouse, and if three years go by, a true break demands one's own life. So it is imperative to know what samayas you need to observe, otherwise you won't be aware when you violate them. If, out of ignorance, you repeatedly break the samayas, such failings will grow stronger and stronger and become increasingly difficult to repair. Fortunately, Guru Rinpoche in his infinite wisdom provided us with the means to easily repair any breaches, from short daily feast offerings to great accomplishment practices like the *Ocean of Amrita*, in which we not only mend our samayas but also retake them.

OFFERING THE GIFT

After retaking the samaya vows, we offer a gift and then give thanks. If the master for mending the breaches is present, for the benefit of others you should offer him or her your children, spouse, wealth, possessions, and all that gives you pleasure, even your own body. You may not have the courage to actually do this, but as one's attitude and state of mind is the important factor, it is perfectly fine just to imagine that you are giving away all that you own. The vajra master replies:

> My child, henceforth,
> I will be your Vajrasattva.
> My child, you must therefore obey
> Whatever precept I give you.

Fully aware of the master's great kindness, the disciples accept,

> With an attitude of trust and devotion
> Toward you, the master, the Vajra King,
> Whatever precept you give me,
> I will accept with my body, speech, and mind.

With all breaches that have occurred between master and disciple cleared up, we now rejoice and show our gratitude by having a feast.

SHOWING GRATITUDE

Enjoying the Feast

The feast offering is an inner sublime form of a fire puja. By swallowing the food and drink, it is fed to the flames of the inner heat practice known as tummo. The offerings that you consume are burned and dissolved into wisdom nectar that permeates your entire body to the delight of all the wisdom deities present there. Everyone chants:

> OM AH HUNG
> By these offerings, everyone is pleased and satisfied.
> It is a medicine benefiting all.
> Through the yoga of the great nature,
> Everything is devoured and used for adornment.
> A LA LA HO!

> Eating, swallowing, drinking, and wearing,
> Endowed with the five desirable qualities,
> Heaped in the sky like billowing cloudbanks,

The mandala dissolves into the mandala.⁏

A LA LA HO!   .

Here, "everyone" refers not only to all those present, but to all the deities in the body as well. "The yoga of great nature" is to remain completely free of any preconceived ideas or conceptual thoughts. Seeing the purity of all things, they dissolve into the mandala, which is also pure, and you express your great joy with the phrase "A la la hoh!" and the following poem:

HO!
My body, aggregates and elements, and senses
Are, in essence, the three seats of completeness;
The mandala deities of the hundred sacred families.
All movement is the great bliss,
The unexcelled vajra samaya.
We enjoy a great cloud of bodhichitta
In the nondual state of equality.
Having perfected the accumulations of the path of yoga,
May we remain untainted by the obscuration of food.
May the benefactors, who are indeterminate,
Also enjoy the fruition of the greater vehicle.

"The three seats of completeness"—the aggregates (skandhas) and elements (dhatus), the senses (ayatanas), and the body and its various abilities (indriyas)—are the mandala of all the buddhas and bodhisattvas.

The aggregates and elements are the seat of the five male and female buddhas. This is clearly explained in the verses for the mending of natural purity that occurs earlier in the *Ocean of Amrita*:

May the samaya be mended with Samantabhadra,⁏
The natural purity of awareness, perceived as 'here'.⁏
May the samaya be mended with Samantabhadri,⁏
The natural purity of external perceived objects.⁏

May the samaya be mended with Vajrasattva,⁏
The natural purity of the aggregate of consciousnesses.⁏
May the samaya be mended with Dhatvishvari,⁏
The natural purity of the space element.⁏

May the samaya be mended with Vairochana,⁞
The natural purity of the aggregate of forms.⁞
May the samaya be mended with Buddha Lochana,⁞
The natural purity of the earth element.⁞

May the samaya be mended with Ratnasambhava,⁞
The natural purity of the aggregate of sensations.⁞
May the samaya be mended with Mamaki,⁞
The natural purity of the water element.⁞

May the samaya be mended with Amitabha,⁞
The natural purity of the aggregate of conceptions.⁞
May the samaya be mended with Pandara Vasini,⁞
The natural purity of the fire element.⁞

May the samaya be mended with Amoghasiddhi,⁞
The natural purity of the aggregate of formations.⁞
May the samaya be mended with Samaya Tara,⁞
The natural purity of the wind element.⁞

The following verses from the same mending ritual describe how the senses (*ayatanas*), which are comprised of the sense faculties and their objects, are the seat of the male and female bodhisattvas.

May the samaya be mended with Ksiti Garbha,⁞
The natural purity of eye consciousness.⁞
May the samaya be mended with Lasya,⁞
The natural purity of perceived form.⁞

May the samaya be mended with Akasha Garbha,⁞
The natural purity of nose consciousness.⁞
May the samaya be mended with Malya,⁞
The natural purity of perceived objects of smell.⁞

May the samaya be mended with Avalokiteshvara,⁞
The natural purity of tongue consciousness.⁞
May the samaya be mended with Girti,⁞
The natural purity of perceived objects of taste.⁞

May the samaya be mended with Vajrapani,⁞
The natural purity of ear consciousness.⁞

May the samaya be mended with Nirti,⁑
The natural purity of perceived objects of sound.⁑

May the samaya be mended with Lord Maitreya,⁑
The natural purity of the faculty of sight.⁑
May the samaya be mended with Incense Maiden,⁑
The natural purity of the concept of past. ⁑

May the samaya be mended with Nirvirana Viskambin,⁑
The natural purity of the faculty of hearing.⁑
May the samaya be mended with Flower Maiden,⁑
The natural purity of the concept of now.⁑

May the samaya be mended with Samantabhadra,⁑[39]
The natural purity of the faculty of smell.⁑
May the samaya be mended with Lamp Maiden,⁑
The natural purity of the concept of future.⁑

May the samaya be mended with Manjushri the Youthful,⁑
The natural purity of the faculty of taste.⁑
May the samaya be mended with Perfume Maiden,⁑
The natural purity of the concept of indefinite.⁑

May the samaya be mended with Yamantaka,⁑
The natural purity of the concept of touch consciousness.⁑
May the samaya be mended with Rolangma,⁑
The natural purity of the view of permanence.⁑

May the samaya be mended with Shengyi Mitub,⁑
The natural purity of the concept of the touched.⁑
May the samaya be mended with Invincible Maiden, ⁑
The natural purity of the view of nihilism.⁑

May the samaya be mended with Mighty Hayagriva,⁑
The natural purity of the concept of perceiving texture.⁑
May the samaya be mended with Tronyerma,⁑
The natural purity of the view of ego.⁑

May the samaya be mended with Amrita Kundali,⁑
The natural purity of the concept of touching.⁑
May the samaya be mended with Ralchigma,⁑

The natural purity of the view of characteristics.⟨

May the samaya be mended with Samantabhadra, the
　　Doer,⟨
The natural purity of mind consciousness.⟨
May the samaya be mended with Samantabhadri, the
　　Deed,⟨
The natural purity of the ayatana of mental objects.⟨[40]

Finally, the body and its various abilities (indriyas) are the seat of completeness of the male and female wrathful ones.

In this way, our entire mental and physical makeup is actually the mandala of the peaceful and wrathful deities, thus "all movement is the great bliss" and enjoying the feast offering in full awareness of this fact is "the unexcelled vajra samaya."

SINGING AND DANCING

Expressing our great delight in having purified samaya in combination with the feast offering, we sing and dance. The song that appears in the *Ocean of Amrita* is known as "The Song of the Vajra." It is from the *Union of the Sun and Moon* tantra, which is one of the Seventeen Dzogchen Tantras. It is in the language of the dakinis and is very profound.

The following verses, "Unborn and unceasing . . ." and so forth, are most probably the Tibetan translation of *Ema Kiri Kiirii,* and we sing that as well. The following verses roughly translate the meaning of the song:

Unborn, it is unceasing,⟨
Neither coming nor going, all-pervasive,⟨
Great bliss, supreme Dharma, immutable.⟨
Equal to space, free and untainted,⟨
Devoid of root and unsupported,⟨
Nondwelling, nongrasping, the great Dharma.⟨
Primordially free, spontaneously equal, great openness.⟨
Unfettered and beyond being untied,⟨
All-encompassing mansion, primordially present,⟨
Pervasive, equal, and fully beyond.⟨
So vast! So great! The expanse of space.⟨
Great Dharma, circle of the sun and moon,⟨

Spontaneously present, directly perceived,⁞

Vajra, mountain, great lotus.⁞

Sun, lion, son of wisdom,⁞

Music of the great sound, beyond compare,⁞

Partaking to the end of space.⁞

Buddhahood equal to all buddhas.⁞

Samantabhadra, vast summit of Dharma,⁞

Within the sphere of Bhadri, expanse of sky,⁞

Spontaneously present space of luminosity,⁞

Primordial Great Perfection!⁞

MAKING ASPIRATIONS

Everyone attending the great accomplishment ritual are our vajra siblings, for we all have the same father and mother in that our father is the vajra master and our mother is the mandala. Acknowledging this fact, everyone should raise a butter lamp or candle in their right hand, and with the left hand form a chain so that everyone is interconnected, and chant the lamp aspiration:

> HUNG⁞
>
> By embarking on the path of the essence of enlightenment,⁞
>
> Within the supreme mandala of the secret charnel ground,⁞
>
> May we not fall into the immense abyss of samsara,⁞
>
> May we not take rebirth in the canyons of attachment and
>   hatred,⁞
>
> May we not roll into the hellish copper cauldron of wrong
>   view,⁞
>
> May we not hear the vicious growling of the carnivores of
>   resentment, and⁞
>
> May we not be pierced by the treacherous spears of
>   disturbing emotions.⁞
>
> In this life and in all those that follow,⁞
>
> May we never be separated from those kind spiritual
>   teachers,⁞
>
> From the brother and sister practitioners with whom our
>   life-force is linked, nor⁞

From the three consorts to whom we are linked by means
    of the third empowerment.⸲
With the samadhi of keeping their undivided company,⸲
May we gradually journey through the special qualities of
    the ten bhumis.⸲

At some point, when the time comes to die and change
    bodies,⸲
And there is a chance that we will again return to the abyss
    of samsara,⸲
May this clear and radiant lamp that spreads illumination⸲
Show the way to accomplishing the vidyadhara levels.⸲

On the level of Great Lotus, may we be spontaneously
    perfected,⸲
And when we arrive at the level of Great-Assembly Wheel,⸲
May all the former victorious ones welcome us.⸲

On the level of Universal Illumination, may our being be
    purified,⸲
May the yidam deities support our life force from behind,⸲
May all the bodhisattvas surround us,⸲
May the offering goddesses lead the way,⸲
And may the gathering of mother ishvaris guard the rear.⸲

When reaching the level of the Braided Realm,⸲
Although we remain in the state of nonreturn,⸲
Vajra King of the Wrathful Ones, may we behold your
    countenance,⸲
May we be inseparable from all the vidyadharas, and
    accomplish the unsurpassable body, speech, and mind.⸲

THE CONCLUDING ACTIVITIES

At last we reach the seven concluding activities: (1) distributing the residual offerings, (2) invoking and offering torma, (3) propitiating the guardians of Tibet and Kham, (4) concluding the activities with the dance, (5) dissolving the vivid presence of the visualization, (6) engaging in the magic of unity, and (7) reciting aspirations and verses of auspiciousness.

DISTRIBUTING THE RESIDUAL OFFERINGS

Before being offered to the servants of Palchen Heruka, the remaining offerings must first be consecrated by sprinkling them with a little of the amrita and rakta and uttering OM SARVA PENTSA OM AH HUNG HA HOH HRIH. Saying this, we trust that "the sky is filled with the residual samaya substance, an inexhaustible mass of sense pleasures." All the servants of the Great Glorious One, Palchen Heruka, can now be invited to come and enjoy the leftover offerings.

There is a four-line prayer for this, concluding with a mantra; in the words of the mantra: MAMA are the ones whom we are calling on; HRING HRING increases the offerings; BALINGTA refers to the torma; and KHAHI means "help yourself."

INVOCATION AND TORMA OFFERINGS

To offer the tormas to the guardians of the dharma, first consecrate the tormas by purifying them with RAM YAM KHAM and then with OM AH HUNG. Imagine that it becomes the nectar of all sense pleasures. Now call upon the dharma protectors (dharmapala):

HUNG ⁸⁄

From the dharmadhatu palace of Akanishtha, and
From the mundane and supramundane charnel grounds,
Three Jewels, Three Roots, and Dharma protectors,
Armies of the eight classes of drekpas, manifest from space!
Now at the end of the age of degeneration,
I invoke your pledge to be the protectors and guardians of
    the teachings and beings.
Fulfill the four types of activities!

Drekpas are a particular type of malevolent demon. The Dharma protectors subdue obstructors and enemies of the Dharma by performing the four types of activities—pacifying, increasing, magnetizing, and subjugating. With that, you distribute the torma.

All the Dharma protectors are now reminded of their oath. To do this, imagine that this oath was written down in the distant past, when the earliest protectors, the guardians of the Dharma, vowed to protect the teachings into the future. You now read this pledge out loud and proclaim the covenant. "This is what you promised before, now please do it!"

"Dharmata" is our true innate nature. The "three lineages" are the mind transmission of the buddhas, the symbolic transmission of the vidyadharas, and the oral transmission of great masters. As we are successors in the lineage of Guru Rinpoche, "Lord Padma," who bound all the dakinis and guardians under oath in the charnel ground of Sitavana, and the protectors enjoying the torma belong to the same family as those gods and demons, we remind them that they remain bound by this original oath and must protect us.

As there are several tormas offered to different deities and guardians, you need to "place the general torma of the Three Roots, the dakini torma, and the tormas for the guardians and wealth gods in the treasury. Except for the tormas of Tseringma and the Three Kunkyil brothers, offer all the tormas outside."

PROPITIATING THE TENMA GODDESSES

Sprinkle the torma plate with nectar, and place the torma for the twelve tenma goddesses. There are three sets of four goddesses whose nature is that of the eight mamo dakinis of the wrathful mandala and the four female gatekeepers. Just as they were given the nectar of samaya in the past, ask them to accept this nectar of an offering torma and fulfill the activities to which they are bound by oath.

> HUNG:
> On the near side of the land of India and:
> On the far side of the country of Nepal,:
> Within the Asura Cave,:
> You were allowed to participate in the feast assembly:
> Upon the seat of a spread-out zhing skin,:
> Performed by vidyadhara Wrathful Vajra:
> And Master Vasudhara.:
> Twelve great Tenma Goddesses,:
> You were given the nectar of samaya.:
> In accordance with your oath and promise,:
> Accept this nectar of an offering-torma:
> And fulfill the activities this yogi demands.:

OM MAMAH LALAH LELAI TAM TAM TETAI KHARAKMA
MAMA SING DROMA HUNG BHYO HUNG॥

The vidyadhara Wrathful Vajra is the wrathful form of Guru Rinpoche known as Dorje Drakpo Tsal. The mantra is composed of the twelve seed syllables of the tenma goddesses.

CONCLUDING THE ACTIVITIES WITH THE DANCE

Next comes the horse dance. "Suppress the vajra-cross upon the torma vessel facing upside down...." The purpose of this is a kind of suppression, ensuring that after carrying out the four activities—pacifying, increasing, magnetizing, and subjugating—everything doesn't turn back and revert. The purpose of pacifying is to make the causes for the eight and sixteen fears, sickness, and other disturbances subside so they don't return. "Increasing" is to develop further merit, life span, splendor, prosperity, and so forth; "magnetizing" is to gain control over appearances, mind, samsara, nirvana, and all the different types of influences so they don't revert. The purpose of subjugating is to crush the enemies of the Buddha Dharma, of the enlightened masters, the teachings, and so on, preventing them from returning. Then, one performs this suppression. Outwardly, stamping down, "with the great yogic action of the horse—Hayagriva—dancing the awesome dance of the Mighty One, with the splendorous neighing and the awesome dance," the samaya violators of superficial dualistic fixation, attaching reality to what really doesn't exist. This is, for example, the notion that "I am here, you are there, that is such-and-such." All of this is only superficially true. All of that is stamped down, suppressed into the basic expanse of great perfection where no self-identity or ego exists and none may be formed again. The mantra summarizes just that: "I am the great Hayagriva that stamps down all concepts of self into basic space."

Receiving the Siddhis

At the end of your practice, whether alone or in a group, but whenever you have a particular special object on a shrine, you must receive the siddhis (*ngodrub len*). When practicing for many days in a row, as in a great accomplishment ritual, signs of accomplishment could occur at any time, and if they do, the receiving of the siddhis should be performed. However, if no particular signs occur that everybody can see or agree on, it should be performed at the conclusion on the last day.

After repeating the offerings, praises, and asking forgiveness, which were explained during the recitation praise, you should chant:

> HUNG HRIH⦂
> In the essence mandala of bodhichitta,⦂
> Gathering of deities reveling in wisdom magic,⦂
> Without departing, remember your vajra samaya,⦂
> And bestow blessings, empowerments, and siddhis!⦂
> GURU DHEVA DHAKINI KAYA VAKA CHITTA JNANA KARMA
> SARVA SIDDHI PHALA HUNG⦂

The inherent essence of all sentient beings is their buddha nature. Like the light of the sun pervading all of space, it shines as the nature of mind of all sentient beings. This is the mandala of awakened mind, within which all the wisdom deities reside, as they are indivisible from buddha nature, even though they appear as all the peaceful and wrathful ones and their manifestations. Prior to becoming enlightened, all buddhas took certain vows and aspirations to be present and to appear whenever they are needed. There is a proverb that a day may come when all the fish leave the ocean, but there will never be a day when the enlightened ones don't act in a timely manner. The mantra translates as "Gurus, deities, and dakinis, please bestow the siddhis of body, speech, mind, wisdom, and activities", GURU DEVA DAKINI means the gurus, gods, and dakinis; KAYA VAKA CHITTA is body, speech, and mind; JNANA, wisdom; KARMA, the activities; SARVA SIDDHI, all the accomplishments; and PHALA HUNG, please bestow.

Take the sadhana representation from the shrine and touch it to the crown of your head, and we "drink the nectar" of the blessings. While doing this, we imagine that "My nadis and dhatus are filled with the essence of nectar. I have realized the supreme siddhi." We imagine that the three main nadis and all our chakras are suffused with the nectar of original wakefulness, and that light radiates throughout your body and into the ten directions, and the common siddhis, the eight masteries, etc. are effortlessly accomplished. By doing so, you are "blessed to be forever inseparable from the great circle of the mandala," the emptiness endowed with all the supreme aspects, indivisible from the unchanging great bliss.

Now take a minute to rest in your true nature.

DISSOLVING THE MANDALA

Unfolding the mandala during the development stage, you must now dissolve it again. Before dissolving the mandala,[42] we consecrate the images on the shrine by saying,

> OM
> Remain here for as long as samsara exists,
> Inseparable from this image.
> Bestow upon me, in completeness, everything sublime
> As well as good health, longevity, and mastery.
> OM SUPRA TISHTHA VAJRAYE SVAHA

If you have a mandala of colored sand or powder, or have used heaps of grains to resemble the deities in the mandala, you should ask the deities to depart, as the mandala will be dismantled and swept away.

You don't need a fancy thangka painting or an elaborate mandala made of colored sand—you can always find appropriate means for creating a mandala and making feast offerings within your means, and that will be good enough. The main point is always the inner samadhi; the external details are not so important. For example, you can even use being served a meal in a restaurant as an opportunity for making a feast offering. Other people will think that you are simply out having a nice meal, but in your own experience you can be enjoying a lavish feast offering with all the deities and gurus.

Similarly, generosity is of three types: giving material things, giving protection against fear, and giving Dharma. So you might think, "The giving of Dharma means to give teachings to a great number of beings. I'm not doing any of that. Giving protection against fear means to protect others, to save lives. I haven't done that much either. Giving material things can be giving, great giving, and extremely great giving. Giving is giving of a lot of material things, great giving is to give one's spouse and children, and extremely great giving is to sacrifice one's own life. I haven't done any of these either. So I have no chance to practice generosity." But that is a totally wrong attitude. You can give something at any moment and in any situation, and, of course, you can always give all of the above mentally. Mentally, we can give our spouse or our children away, we can give all our possessions, we can even give our own life and so forth; at any moment, you just need to arouse your devotion and sincerely think, "I give all that I have to all buddhas and bodhisattvas." By training this way, repeating it many times in your imagination, you can perfect the act of generosity. Therefore, knowing the key points is vitally important.

Visualizing the mandala during the development stage corresponds to birth, while the completion stage of dissolving into the state of luminosity corresponds to the process of dying. At the end, since nothing lasts forever and no one lives forever, everything dissolves into the state of luminosity. In death, the elements dissolve one into the other: first, earth into water, then, water into fire, fire into wind, each accompanied by certain experiences, until the white and the red element meet together at the heart center. At that moment, there is a blackout and finally what is called "the ground luminosity of full attainment," which is the total dissolution of innate thought states. To prepare ourselves for going through this, we practice the completion stage.

To do this according to the *Ocean of Amrita* you chant HUNG three times and then say,

> The world and beings vividly present as deities dissolve into me. I too dissolve into the seed-syllable within my heart-center. Without focusing on even that, I rest evenly in the state of luminosity.

With this, imagine that the entire buddha field, the whole universe and all beings, dissolves into the celestial palace; the celestial palace dissolves into the retinue of deities, in this case the twelve manifestations, the gatekeepers, and so forth. Then, they too dissolve, the outer ones into the inner ones, and then the whole inner circle of deities dissolves into you as Guru Rinpoche. You, as Guru Rinpoche, then dissolve into the seed syllable HRIH in your heart center, so that nothing remains other than the HRIH. Finally, the syllable HRIH itself dissolves from the mark at the bottom called an *achung*, up until only a single point is left, and then it too dissolves; so that nothing remains other than the state of luminous emptiness totally beyond any mental constructs. You should then remain in that state for as long as you can.

Training like this is an excellent preparation for dying. Also, unless you dissolve the development stage into the completion stage, you can easily fall into the extreme of eternalism.

ENGAGING IN DAILY ACTIVITIES, THE ILLUSORY MAGIC OF UNITY

After remaining in the completion stage, you should again reemerge in the form of a deity in order to prevent against falling into the opposite extreme: nihilism. You do this by first saying PHAT three times, then:

Once more, like a fish emerging from water, I am vividly present as the chief figure, marked with OM at the forehead, AH at the throat, and HUNG at the heart-center.

A fish doesn't slowly rise from the water; it bursts forth in a single leap, and there's the whole fish. In the same way, imagine that you are suddenly vividly present as Guru Rinpoche. This method of visualization is called present as instantaneous recollection, as it doesn't require first imagining the seed syllable and then going through all the gradual steps one by one. You have a white OM on your forehead, a red AH in your throat, and a blue HUNG at your heart center. You now make a mudra while saying the mantra OM AH HUNG VAJRA KAVACHI RAKSHA HANG which means, "My body, speech, and mind are protected by indestructible OM AH HUNG.[43]

Throughout the rest of the day, you should always "*keep the view that sights, sounds, and awareness are deity, mantra, and wisdom, and make all your daily activities meaningful.*" Whatever you see is the divine forms of the mandala, the deities, and so on; whatever you hear, any sound no matter what, is the sound of mantra; and any movement of awareness is the play of the wisdom of original wakefulness. In this way, you don't just fritter your life away or further enmesh yourself in the suffering of samsara, but "make all your daily activities meaningful."

You should not feel that the practice is now all over and you can just stand up, go home, and carry on with your regular business. That is never the case in Vajrayana. Instead, during the breaks, you should always maintain vajra pride, in complete trust and confidence that you are the deity.

ASPIRATIONS AND VERSES OF AUSPICIOUSNESS

To conclude the practice, *"first seal the root of virtue with the dedication of the complete purity of the three spheres."* This means to dedicate the merit of your practice without any notion of merit to be dedicated, sentient beings to whom the merit is dedicated, or yourself as the one making the dedication. To do this, you should remain for a short while totally free of any concepts held in mind; this is what is meant by "the dedication of the complete purity of the three spheres."

Dedicating the merit to other beings is a special quality of Buddhist practice that distinguishes it from non-Buddhist spiritual practice. Dedicating the merit is like throwing a few drops of water into the great ocean: as long as the ocean exists, those drops will somehow still be there as part of it. Not only will they not vanish, they will also increase. If we don't dedicate the merit, then a moment of anger is said to be enough to destroy the roots of virtue, so we should always remember to dedicate the merit. You need to already have done something good in order to be able to dedicate it; however, you don't need to have done anything good before making an aspiration—you can make aspirations any time.

The dedication in the *Ocean of Amrita* is:

> HOH!§
> By the power of accomplishing the mandala of the
>   vidyadhara guru,§
> May I and all the infinite sentient beings, without
>   exception,§
> Spontaneously accomplish the four kinds of activities§
> And be liberated into the luminous space of dharmakaya!§

Scatter flowers, play music, and while chanting the verse of auspiciousness, imagine that the sky is filled with buddhas and bodhisattvas. All these deities scatter special *mandarava* blossoms, so that a rain of flowers slowly descends all around, dispelling all warfare, famine, sickness, and disharmony and bringing peace and happiness as well as prosperity for the Dharma.

> May the blessings of the root and lineage gurus enter my
> heart!
> May the yidams and dakinis accompany me like a shadow
> follows the body!
> May the Dharma protectors and guardians dispel all
> obstacles!
> May there be the auspiciousness of attaining the supreme
> and common siddhis!

The last lines we chant are to dedicate the merit. Whenever a great act of merit was being performed and it was asked to be dedicated for the benefit of another, then the Buddha and his retinue would chant these four lines, so please say them again now.

> By this merit may all the infinite beings
> Pacify the outer, inner, and secret obstacles.
> May they perfect the journey of the path of the two stages,
> And swiftly attain the state of the Lotus King
>
> May the blessings of the root and lineage gurus enter my
> heart.
> May the yidams and dakinis accompany me like a shadow
> follows the body.
> May the Dharma protectors and guardians clear away all
> obstacles.
> May there be the auspiciousness of attaining the supreme
> and common siddhis.

Peaceful
Mandala

Wrathful
Mandala

Appendices

Six Munis

Appendix 1

DETAILED VISUALIZATION OF THE TWELVE MANIFESTATIONS

The Twelve Vidyadharas

The palace is square with a gate centered on each side. A portal protrudes out over each gate. The eight main beams of the main hall are supported by eight pillars, with two pillars set near each gate; thus, the center of the palace is open all the way up through the three stories. In the center of the palace, a large raised platform made from a jewel is supported by eight lions and has eight sides. In the center of this platform is a lotus with four petals in the cardinal directions on which the four inner manifestations sit.

To the east is the successor of the conquerors, the protector of beings, Gyalwey Dungdzin. Sometimes he is described as standing, but here he is sitting in half-vajra posture. He is white and holds a sword in his right hand and a hook in his left. He wears a tiger-skin skirt, bone ornaments, and a crown of dry skulls.

To the south, the lion of speech, Mawey Senge, who has perfect knowledge, sits in vajra posture. He is radiant white, and his hands are in the mudra of expounding the Dharma. He holds two lotus flowers, and on each of the blossoms, which are blooming near his shoulders, is a book. The book on the right contains the sutra canon known as *The Three Baskets* (*Tripitaka*), and the one on the left is the eminent Vajra Kilaya scripture titled *Supreme Knowledge*, which embodies all the Vajrayana teachings. He wears a hat and the traditional three layers of Dharma robes.

To the west is Kyechok Tsülsang, who has attained supreme siddhi, also sitting in vajra posture. He is yellow and holds a vajra in his right hand and a casket in his left. He wears a red *pandita* hat and the three Dharma robes.

To the north is the slayer of mara, Dukyi Shechen, who tames heretics. He is light brown in color and stands in a striding stance, one foot slightly in front of the other. In his right hand he holds the recitation dagger (Sanskrit: *kilaya*; Tibetan: *phurba*), which he supports on his thigh. With the action kilaya in his left hand, he stabs at the obstructors. He wears a lotus crown, a brocade gown, and Dharma robes.

Around the lotus, on each side of the eight sides of the platform, are the remaining eight vidyadharas:

To the east is the ornament of the world, Dzamling Ghenchok, who is indivisible from the yidam. He is blue and bears a wrathful expression. He stands in striding stance with a dagger in each hand and another tucked in his sash. He wears a brocade cloak as well as the eightfold charnel-ground attire.

To the south, sitting in vajra posture, is the lotus-born, Pema Jungney, who is radiant clear blue. He holds a vajra in his right hand and a bell in his left. On his right sits his consort, the white princess. They both wear silks and jewel ornaments, and he has bone ornaments as well.

To the west is the supremely exalted one who wields all (*kun tu 'chang*), the white Kyepar Phakpey Rigdzin. He stands, pointing a vajra with his right hand, and with his left, he holds a khatvanga as a walking staff. He wears a lotus crown, a blue cloak, and Dharma robes.

To the north is the annihilator of obstructing spirits (drekpa), the dazzling reddish-maroon Dzutrül Tuchen. He is sitting on a lotus and is dressed like a monk, but also wears a garland of heads as well as bone ornaments. He holds a vajra in his right hand and a dagger in his left.

To the southeast is the master of samsara and nirvana, the red vidyadhara of wrathful power, Dorje Drakpo Tsal. He holds a vajra in his raised right hand and a scorpion in his left. He wears the charnel-ground attire of a wrathful deity. He is embraced by the dark-blue Vajra Varahi, who holds a knife in her right hand and a skull cup in her left.

To the southwest is the lord of the nine spheres of wisdom, the great glorious one, Chemchok Heruka, who in this context is called Kalden Drendzey. Dark blue, he is standing in striding stance and blazing with flames. He holds a vajra in his right hand and a skull cup in his left. He is dressed in "the glorious attire," which refers to the eight charnel-ground ornaments typically worn by wrathful herukas, together with his vajra wings and flames. The precise list can differ from one sadhana to another, so you should stick to the list particular to the practice that you are doing. He embraces his consort, the sky-faced one, Namshelma, who holds a curved knife in her right hand and a skull cup in her left.

To the northwest stands the subjugator of rakshas, Raksha Tötreng, who is an awe-inspiring maroon in color. He wears the charnel-ground ornaments and holds a vajra in his right hand and a skull cup filled with blood in his left. He is embracing his consort, Ting-Ö Barma, who is blazing light-blue in color. She holds a skull cup in her left hand and a curved knife in her right. They are stomping on a corpse that lies beneath their feet.

To the northeast is the radiant clear-red king of great bliss, Dechen Gyalpo, who is the indivisible nature of the three kayas. He and his consort are in dancing posture with one leg bent and the other extended. He holds a vajra in his right hand and a bell in his left hand, which are crossed in front of his chest, embracing his consort. He wears both jewel and bone ornaments. He and his consort are smiling wrathfully. His consort is pink and holds a vase in her left hand and a small hand drum known as a damaru in her right.

Appendix 2

DETAILED VISUALIZATION OF THE PEACEFUL AND WRATHFUL DEITIES

Chokgyur Lingpa had a cycle of termas called the *Seven Profound Cycles* (ZAB PA SKOR BDUN), each of which was decoded from dakini script engraved on different metals. Each cycle was named after the material on which the original dakini script was inscribed. The most extensive of these was inscribed on iron; the most profound on copper; a very profound one on turquoise; others were written on silver and gold; and one was even found on a deep-red gemstone called CHONG, which is probably a special kind of agate. The particular colors of the peaceful and wrathful ones found in the *Ocean of Amrita* are those described in the terma that was inscribed on the profound copper plate. Jamgön Kongtrül included this particular cycle of peaceful and wrathful deities (ZHITRO) in his famous *Treasury of Profound Termas* (*Rinchen Terdzo*).

The Peaceful Mandala

The Lord of the Mandala and the Buddhas of the Five Families

The raised platform in the center of the peaceful palace is square, with its four sides in the cardinal directions. This platform is decorated with a golden Dharma wheel with four spokes pointing in the cardinal directions.[44] On the center of this wheel, the seed syllables OM and AH sit on a lion throne. The OM becomes dark-blue Samantabhadra and the AH transforms into his consort, Samantabhadri, who is a slightly lighter shade of blue. Samantabhadra has three faces: his middle face is blue, his right face is white, and his left face is red. He has six arms. He holds a vajra in his top right hand and a bell in his top left hand. His middle hands form the mudra of enlightenment, meaning the gesture that symbolizes teaching the Dharma, and the bottom pair are in the mudra of equanimity, which is formed by resting one hand, one on top of the other, on one's lap. His consort, Samantabhadri, embraces him with her left hand, in which she holds a vajra, and, like all the consorts, she holds a bell in her right hand.

Next come the buddhas of the five families. Each of the male buddhas is seated in vajra posture and has three faces and six arms. They all hold the same six symbolic attributes, but the one that signifies the family to which they belong is always held in the top right hand. For example, as he is from the vajra family, Vajrasattva holds a vajra in his upper right hand; whereas Amitabha holds a lotus in his upper right hand, symbolizing that he is from the padma (lotus) family. So, if you memorize the order for Vajrasattva, then for each of the others, it is simply a matter of swapping the vajra and the symbol appropriate to the respective family. All of the consorts are sitting on the laps of their partners, with their legs wrapped around him in the lotus posture. Each consort holds a bell in her right hand and embraces her male partner with her left hand, in which she holds her family's attribute.

So, with the above in mind, on the spoke that points to the east, directly in front of Samantabhadra, a blue HUNG and MUM sit on another lion throne. These transform into Vajrasattva and his consort, Dhatvishvari, respectively. Vajrasattva is blue. His right face is white, his left face is red, and his central face is blue. In his three right hands, from top to bottom, he holds a vajra, a Dharma wheel, and a jewel; and in his left hands, from top to bottom, he holds a bell, a lotus, and a sword. He is embraced by Dhatvishvari, who is a lighter shade of blue and is holding a vajra in her left hand and a bell in her right.

Farther to the east, directly in line with Vajrasattva, at the point where the spoke meets the rim, is an elephant throne on which sit the two white syllables OM and LAM. These syllables become white Vairochana and his consort, Buddha Lochana, respectively. Vairochana's right face is blue, his left face is red, and his middle face is white. As he is from the buddha family, he holds a Dharma wheel in his top right hand, then a vajra in his middle right hand, and a jewel in his bottom right hand. Like Vajrasattva, in his three left hands, from top to bottom, he holds a bell, a lotus, and a sword. He is embraced in union by Buddha Lochana, who is known as Sangye Chenma in Tibetan. She is also white and holds a Dharma wheel in her left hand and a bell in her right.

Moving clockwise around the rim, on the spoke pointing to the south, the two syllables SVA and MUM sit on a horse throne. These syllables transform into Ratnasambhava, who is in union with Mamaki. They are the lord and lady of the ratna family. He is yellow, as is his middle face, while his right face is white and his left face is red. He holds a jewel (Sanskrit: RATNA) in his top right hand, a Dharma wheel in his middle right hand, and a vajra in his bottom right hand. In his left hands, he holds the same implements as Vajrasattva and Vairochana. Mamaki is pale yellow and, of course, holds a jewel in her left hand and a bell in her right.

Continuing clockwise, on the spoke pointing west, is a peacock throne on which sit a red AH and TAM. They transform into Buddha Amitabha and his consort Pandaravasini, respectively. Amitabha's middle face is red, his right face is white, and his left face is blue. He holds the same six symbols as Vajrasattva, the only difference being that he holds the lotus with his upper right hand and the vajra with his middle left hand. Pandaravasini is a lighter shade of red, and in addition to the bell in her right hand, she holds a lotus in her left, as she too is a member of the padma (lotus) family.

On the last of the four main spokes of the wheel, the one pointing to the north, a green HA and TAM sit on a shangshang[45] throne. These seed syllables transform into Amoghasiddhi and his consort, Samayatara. These two are of the lord and lady of the karma (activity) family. Like the rest of his body, Amoghasiddhi's middle face is green. His right face is white and his left face is red. In his upper right hand, he holds a sword. He holds a wheel in his middle right hand and a jewel in his lower right hand. In his left hands, from top to bottom, he holds a bell, a lotus, and a vajra. He is in union with Samayatara, who is a lighter shade of green and holds a sword in her left hand and a bell in her right.

The Eight Pairs of Bodhisattvas

The first four pairs of bodhisattvas sit cross-legged on sun and moon disks that rest on top of lotuses. These are located on the rim of the wheel where it is intersected by the four intermediate spokes.[46] Each bodhisattva arises from one of the seed syllables KSI HING TRAM TRAM HRIM HRIM JRIM AH and holds their symbolic attribute in their right hand and a bell in their left. They retain the color of their seed syllable, with the female a lighter shade than the male.

First, to the southeast are the first two syllables, KSI and HUNG, which are white. These syllables transform into the personification of merit, Ksiti Garbha, and the goddess of beauty, Lasya, respectively. Ksiti Garbha holds a jeweled seedling, and Lasya holds a mirror.

Moving clockwise around the rim to the southwest, two yellow TRAM syllables transform into the personification of the blessings of enlightenment, Akasha Garbha and the garland goddess, Malema. He holds a sword, and she holds a garland of jewels.

To the northwest, two red HRIM syllables transform into the embodiment of compassion, Avalokiteshvara, who holds a white lotus, and the goddess of song, Girtima, who holds a lute.[47]

To the northeast, the blue syllables JRIM and AH give rise to the embodiment of enlightened power, Vajrapani, who holds a vajra, and Nirti, who displays different dance mudras.

The other four pairs of bodhisattvas are also sitting on sun and moon disks on top of lotuses in the intermediate directions, but they are just farther out in the corners of the platform beyond the rim of the wheel. They arise from the syllables MAI JAH THCHIM HUNG HUNG BAM MUM HOH.

In the southeast corner, the two syllables MAI and JAH give rise to the personification of enlightened love and activity, Maitreya, and the goddess of incense, Dhupa. They are white with a yellow glow. Maitreya holds a *naga* branch, and Dhupa holds an incense holder.

In the southwest corner, the syllables THCHIM HUNG transform into the personification of the qualities of enlightenment, Nirvirana Viskambin,[48] who purifies wrongdoing and obstructions, and the goddess of flowers, Pushpa. He holds a jeweled wheel, and she holds a flower. They are yellow with a reddish glow.

In the northwest corner, the syllables HUNG and BAM give rise to the personification of enlightened aspirations, Samantabhadra,[49] and the goddess of light, Aloka. They are red with a green glow. He holds a jewel, and she holds a lamp.

In the northeast corner, the syllables MUM and HO transform into the personification of enlightened wisdom, Manjushri, and the goddess of perfume, Gandha. They are green with a white glow. He holds a blue lotus flower (utpala), and she holds a conch containing perfume.

> On the east and west side of the hall,
> On jeweled thrones with lotus, sun, and moon seats,
> Are sky-colored Samantabhadra and his consort.

They are both sitting cross-legged and form the gesture of equanimity (the samadhi mudra) with their hands.

In each of the four corners of the palace and in the intermediate space to the north and south is a lotus flower on which sits the seed syllable that will become one of the six munis. Although there are only six munis, there are seven syllables: KRIM SRUM KSHAM BRAM HUNG TRUM YE. This is because the muni for the demigod realm has two syllables, HUNG TRUM. Each of these six buddhas retains the color of their seed syllable and stands on single lotuses, and:

> Wearing the attire of unattached, supreme nirmanakayas,⸸
> They stand in the manner of benefiting beings.⸸

This means that they all wear the three layers of Dharma robes.

In the southeast corner, the white syllable KRIM becomes the buddha of the god realms, Indra,[50] who holds an Indian lute called a VINA.

To the south, the yellow syllable SRUM transforms into the buddha for the human realm, Shakyamuni, who holds a staff and a begging bowl.

In the southwest corner, the dark-yellow syllable KSHAM becomes the buddha for the hungry ghost (preta) realm, Jvalamukhadeva.[51] He has fire blazing from his mouth and holds a casket.

In the northwest corner, the dark-red syllable BRAM turns into the buddha for the animal realm, Shravasingha,[52] who holds a book.

To the north, the dark-blue syllables HUNG TRUM become the buddha of the demigod (asura) realm, Vemachitra,[53] who holds armor.

And in the northeast corner, the black syllable YE transforms into the buddha of the hell realms, the lord of death, Dharmaraja. He holds a flame in his right hand and a conch filled with water in his left.

The Gatekeepers of the Peaceful Palace

At each of the four gates of the peaceful palace is a sun seat on which rests a pair of seed syllables from which the gatekeepers will arise. The seed syllable for all four male gatekeepers is HUNG, and the syllables of their four female partners are DZA HUNG BAM HO.

All the gatekeepers wear the complete attire of the wrathful ones, the charnel-ground accoutrements, such as skull necklaces, garlands of severed heads, winding sheets, and so on. Assuming a striding stance, they stand on the sun seats and are enveloped in swirling flames. All eight gatekeepers hold skull cups filled with blood in their left hands and their individual implements in their right hands.

At the eastern gate are the dark-brown seed syllables HUNG and DZAH. The HUNG transforms into dark-brown Yamaraja, who wields a club made with a human head.[54] The DZAH transforms into his consort, the hook goddess known as Chakyuma.

At the southern gate is a pair of the dark-yellow HUNG syllables. One transforms into dark-yellow Mahabala, who holds a spear. The other transforms into his consort, the lasso goddess known as Zhakpama.

At the western gate are the dark-red syllables HUNG and BAM. The HUNG transforms into dark-red Hayagriva, who has the head of a horse protruding from his skull. He holds a club made from a skull with snakes entwined around the handle. The syllable BAM transforms into his consort, the shackles goddess called Chakdrokma.

At the northern gate are the dark-green syllables HUNG and HOH. The HUNG transforms into dark-green Amrita Kundali, who holds a vajra cross. The syllable HOH transforms into his consort, the bell goddess called Drilbuma.

THE WRATHFUL MANDALA

The Lord of the Mandala and the Herukas of the Five Families

In addition to the description of the wrathful palace that is found in the commentary, here are a few more specifics; any further details can be sought in other sources. The beams are made out of the corpses of Brahma, and the eight pillars are made from the corpses of Mahadeva. Both of these have various symbolic ornaments such as tortoises hanging from them. The supports for the pillars are made of the eight types of Rahula. The banners hanging down the pillars are made from the eight great nagas. Those are just some of the details to paint a rough picture; there are many more details that you can learn elsewhere.

As the general details for the six main herukas can be found in the main commentary, here we shall just provide further specifics for those who would like to be able to generate a more detailed visualization.

On the central bear throne, a pair of dark-blue HUNG syllables transform into the king of herukas, Ngöndzog Gyalpo, and his consort, Dhatvishvari. Ngöndzog Gyalpo is dark blue and has three faces. His central face is dark blue, his right face is white, and his left face is red. With his upper right hand he holds a nine-pronged vajra, with his middle right hand he holds a five-pronged vajra, and in his lower right hand he holds a three-pronged vajra. In each of his three left hands, he holds a skull cup filled with blood. His four feet stamp down on Ishvara, who lies across his prone consort. Ngöndzog Gyalpo is embraced by the sky-faced one, Dhatvishvari, who has two arms and two legs. She holds a vajra in her right hand, and, with her left, proffers a skull cup filled with blood.

To the east, directly in front of Ngöndzog Gyalpo, is another bear throne. The pair of blue HUNG syllables becomes the wrathful form of Vajrasattva, Vajra Heruka, who is also known as Vajra Krodha, embraced by his consort, Krodhishvari. Vajra Heruka's body is dark blue. His central face is dark blue, his right face is white, and his left face is red. In his upper right hand, he holds a five-pronged vajra, in his middle right hand a nine-pronged vajra, and in his lower right hand a small corpse (*tira*). In his left hands, from top to bottom, he holds a bell, a skull cup filled with blood, and a tiny replica of the world that looks like Mount Meru. He is embracing his consort, Krodhishvari, who holds a bell in her right hand, and with her left proffers a skull cup filled with blood. Vajra Heruka "guides the kleshas" and devours passion and desire.

Farther to the east, where the spoke intersects the rim of the wheel, is a bull throne on which two maroon HUNG syllables transform into Buddha Heruka embracing his consort. His central face is dark brown, his right face is white, and his left face is yellow. In his right hands, from top to bottom, he holds a wheel, a vajra, and a tira. In his left hands, from top to bottom, he holds a bell, a skull cup, and a trident. His consort, Buddha Krodhi, holds a bell in her right hand, and with her left proffers a skull cup filled with blood. Buddha Heruka devours ignorance and delusion.

To the south, on an ox throne, the pair of yellow HUNG syllables transform into Ratna Heruka, who devours pride and arrogance, and his consort, Ratna Krodhi. His central face is dark yellow, his right face is blue, and his left face is red. In his right hands, from top to bottom, he holds a jewel, a vajra, and a small corpse. In his left hands, also from top to bottom, he holds a bell, a skull cup filled with blood, and a battle-ax. His consort, Ratna Krodhi, holds a bell in her right hand, and, with her left, proffers a skull cup filled with blood.

To the west, on a leopard throne, the pair of red HUNG syllables transform into Padma Heruka, who transforms attachment, and his consort,

Padma Krodhi. His central face is dark red, his right face is white, and his left face is yellow. From top to bottom, in his right hands he holds a lotus, a vajra, and a small corpse; and in his left hands a bell, a skull cup, and a small hand drum that he is playing by flicking it back and forth. His consort, Padma Krodhi, holds a bell in her right hand, and, with her left, proffers a skull cup filled with blood.

To the north, on a tiger throne, the pair of dark-green HUNG syllables transform into Karma Heruka with his consort, Karma Krodhi. Karma Heruka's central face is dark green, his right face is white, and his left face is red. From top to bottom, he holds in his right hands a vajra cross, a vajra, and a small corpse, and in his left hands a bell, a skull cup filled with blood, and a ploughshare. Karma Heruka devours envy and jealousy. His consort, Padma Krodhi, who holds a bell in her right hand, embraces him, and, with her left, proffers a skull cup filled with blood.

The Goddesses of the Sacred Places and Valleys

Next are the eight yoginis of the sacred places (mamos) and the eight mamos of the sacred valleys.

> The natural purity of objects and senses⣿
> All manifest as the mudras of emanations.⣿
> By conferring the empowerments of the mamos of the
>   places and valleys,⣿
> May the projection and absorption of awareness display be
>   fully unfolded.⣿

The eight goddesses of the sacred places are located in the corners of the platform at the ends of the minor spokes. They each arise from a *ha* syllable, which is the same color as they are. First come those in the cardinal directions: to the east is Gauri, who is blue and holds a fresh skull and a corpse; to the south is Chauri, who is yellow and holds a bow and arrow; to the west is Pramoha, who is red and holds a sea-monster banner; and to the north is Vitali, who is black and eats an infant and holds up a corpse. In the four intermediate directions are: to the southeast, Pukassi, who is orange and brandishes a baby's entrails; to the southwest, Ghasma, who is green and drinks blood from a skull; to the northwest, Smeshva, who is dark blue and eats a baby's heart; and to the northeast, Chanda, who is light yellow and is tearing apart the body of a corpse.

Around the periphery, similar to where the six munis were located, the eight goddesses of the sacred valleys arise from HE syllables.

In the four cardinal directions are "the four goddesses with faces": To the east is Singha, who is yellow, has the face of a lion, and holds a pair of crossed corpses in her mouth. To the south is Vyaghri, who is red, has the face of a tiger, and is looking down at her genitals, which she covers with her crossed hands. To the west is Srila, who is black, has the head of a fox, and holds a baby (*jipa*). To the north is Shvana, who is dark blue, has the head of a wolf, and looks down to where she is tearing the head from a body with her two hands.

In the four intermediate directions are the four goddesses with animal heads. To the southeast is Gridha, who is red, has the head of a vulture, and brandishes intestines. To the southwest is Kangka, who has the head of a bird, and has a rotten corpse wrapped over her shoulders. To the northwest is Kaka, who is black, has the head of a crow, and holds a corpse in her mouth. To the northeast is Ulu, who is dark blue, has the head of an owl, and holds many hooks.

The Gatekeepers of the Wrathful Palace

There are inner and outer walls to the palace, and the four female gate-keepers stand guard at the four inner gates. They wear the charnel-ground attire of a wrathful female deity and dance on fresh human corpses. To begin with, there is a PHAT syllable at each gate, which gives rise to a gatekeeper. Each of the four gatekeepers holds a skull cup filled with blood in their left hand and their specific implement in their right hand. Guarding the eastern gate is blue Horse-head, holding a hook in her right hand. Guarding the southern gate is black Sow-head, who bares her fangs and holds a lasso in her right hand. Guarding the western gate is red Lion-head, who carries shackles in her right hand. Guarding the northern gate is dark-green Wolf-head, joyfully ringing a bell.

The Twenty-Eight Ishvaris

The twenty-eight ishvaris (*wangchukmas*) are situated in the moats of blood and human grease that flow between the inner and outer walls. Along each of the four sides are a set of six, grouped according to which of the four activities they perform. In addition to these, there are four outer female gatekeepers standing guard at the outer gates. They all dance on seats composed of corpses and skeletons and wear garments made from human skin. They are also adorned with various bone ornaments and garlands of dried skulls and have a three-pronged iron vajra on top of their heads. Each of them makes a threatening gesture (mudra) with her left hand and holds her symbolic implement in her right hand. They all arise from the seed syllable BHYOH, which is actually twenty-eight identical seed syllables superimposed on one another.

To the east are the six pacifying goddesses: Rakshimi, who is dark brown and holds a fresh skull in her right hand; Bhrami, who is orange and holds a lotus; Mahadevi, who is light green and holds a trident; Tokdo, who is blue and holds a wheel; Kumari, who is red and holds a spear; and the female form of Indra, Shakri, who is white and holds a small form of Indra.

To the south are the six increasing or enriching goddesses: Vajri, who is yellow and drinks sandalwood nectar; Amrita, who is red and holds a lotus; Chandri, who is white and holds a white lotus;[55] Bechön, who is dark green and wields a club; Rakshi, who is red and drinks blood from a skull; and Zawa, who is dark green and has a handful of entrails in her right hand.

To the west are the six magnetizing goddesses: Mudita, who is red and brandishes a spear; Mahabali, who is white and holds a ploughshare; Vajri, who is yellow and slashes with a razor; Raga, who is red and holds a bow set with an arrow; Norsung, who is white and holds a vase; and Vayudevi, who is blue and raises a banner.

To the north are the six subjugating goddesses: Soje, who is white and carries a sword; Mimo (which means "human maiden"), who is red and holds a torch; the black Sow-faced one, baring her fangs and holding shackles; Genje, who is red and eating a child's corpse; Hastini, who is light green and drinks blood from a skull; and Water Devi, who is blue and holds a lasso made from a snake.

The last four are the outer gatekeepers: the eastern gate is guarded by black Vajri, holding a hook; the southern gate is guarded by yellow Vajri, holding a lasso; the western gate is guarded by red Vajri, holding her iron shackles; and the northern gate is guarded by dark-green Vajri, who joyfully rings a bell.

Notes to Section 2

ACCUMULATION OF MERIT: THE SEVEN BRANCHES

1. Ngari Panchen, *Perfect Conduct: Ascertaining the Three Vows*, with commentary by Dudjom Rinpoche (Wisdom Publications, 1999).

2. Ibid.

THE BODHICHITTA OF APPLICATION: THE FOUR IMMEASURABLES

3. This is known as the *Namkha Dzö* mantra.

BUDDHA NATURE

4. Also known as "intrinsic ignorance."

5. Known as the king of all confessions, it is from the tantras.

6. *Rakta* is a Sanskrit term refering to menstrual blood, which, being red, symbolizes passion and desire.

7. The five meats are those of humans, cows, dogs, horses, and elephants. The five nectars are feces, urine, blood, semen, and flesh. All of these are to be imbibed by the follower of tantra. A yogi who is able to transcend concepts of clean and unclean, pure and impure, will use these, but ordinary people don't have the courage and, typically, cannot even stomach the thought of eating such substances. [tr.]

MANTRA RECITATION

8. A longer more detailed description can be found in a text called the *Dzapkyi Köljang*. (The translation of this is forthcoming in the *Dispeller of Obstacles*, Rangjung Yeshe Publications, 2014).

9. OM A AH I IH U UH RI RIH LI LIH E EH O OH
KA KHA GA GHA NGA, TSA TSHA DZA DZAH NYA
TA THA DA DHA NA, TA THA DA DHA NA
PA PHA BA BHA MA, YA RA LA WA
SHA KA SA HAKSHA

10. OM YEDHARMA HETU PRABHAVA HETUN TEKEN TATHAGATO HAYA WADET
TEKEN TSAYO NIRODHA EWAM VADI MAHA SHRAMANA SVAHA

11. OM VAJRASATTVA SAMAYA MANUPĀLAYA VAJRASATTVA TENOPA TIṢṬHA
DṚIDHO ME BHAVA SUTOKAYO MEBHAVA SUPOKAYO MEBHAVA ANURAKTO
ME BHAVA SARVA SIDDHIṂ ME PRAYACCHA SARVA KARMASU CA ME CITTAṂ
ŚREYAḤ KURU HŪṂ HA HA HA HA HOḤ BHAGAVAN SARVA TATHĀGATA VAJRA
MĀ ME MUÑCA VAJRĪ BHAVA MAHĀSAMAYA SATTVA AH

12. Available from Rangjung Yeshe Translations in the new edition of the combined *General and Additional Chantbook*.

13. A mythological type of garuda, half-human and half-eagle, who plays cymbals as he flies.

THE SPECIAL MANDALA OF THE PEACEFUL AND WRATHFUL ONES

14. A detailed description can be found in Appendix 2.

DISSOLVING DUALITY

15. The five poisons or disturbing emotions are desire, anger, delusion, pride, and envy. [ed.]

CHANTING

16. *Rig pa,* as in "*rig pa, gsung,*" which is translated here as "knowledge speech," should not be confused with the same term in dzogchen terminology. *Rig-pa* is the Tibetan translation of the Sanskrit word VIDYA, which originally meant knowledge or science. Vidya mantras, or *rigs ngags* in Tibetan, are associated with specific deities of the outer tantras and were traditionally used to attain a particular aim. [ed.]

17. A detailed explanation of the four empowerments can be found in *Light of Wisdom*, Vol. 2, 35. [tr.]

MENDING

18. Five essences from a special cow. [ed.]

19. This is the mandala chant from the Tukdrub Barchey Künsel *ngöndro*. The entire verse reads: "The three realms, vessel and contents, glory riches, My body, luxuries, and all virtues, I offer to the lords of compassion. Accepting them please bestow your blessings." The treasure source of this mandala offering is the *Zabtik Drolma*.

20. Meaning the objects that represent the Three Jewels, like the three types of representations, shrine objects. [ed.]

21. Not believing that what the Dharma says is true. [ed.]

22. The most supreme Vajrayana practitioner is called a *bhikshu* (monk) vajra holder, second is a novice vajra holder, and the inferior type is a lay Buddhist Vajrayana practitioner. In this context, all of these are considered ngakpas. [ed.]

23. One cubit is approximately 18 inches or 46 centimeters. [ed.]

24. The six transcendent actions of generosity, discipline, patience, diligence, concentration, and discriminating knowledge. [ed.]

PURIFYING

25. According to Jokyab Rinpoche, the body of karmic ripening is produced by dualistic mind together with the conceptual states of the eight collections of consciousness (*Light of Wisdom,* Vol. 2, 184). [tr.]

26. "Secret place" refers to the region of the perineum and genitals. [ed.]

27. According to Lama Putse, this is the opposite of observing discipline, for example breaking the samayas of the Vajrayana. In the context of the Bodhisattva vows, if one simply thinks, "I don't care about that person," one has forsaken that person and hence the bodhisattva vow is broken.

28. Padmasambhava and Chokyur Lingpa, *Ocean of Amrita, The Ngakso Puja,* translated by Erik Pema Kunsang (Boudanath, Nepal: Rangjung Yeshe Translations & Publications, 1993–1998), 142–45.

29. Ibid., 149–53.

30. Ibid., 155–56.

OPENING THE EYES

31. This is the same mandala offering as in the ngöndro. [ed.]

ACKNOWLEDGING THE PURITY

32. "The three seats of completeness" means that the aggregates and elements are the seats of the male and female buddhas, the sense organs and objects are the seats of the male and female bodhisattvas, and the concepts and times and so on are the seats of the male and female gatekeepers.

33. *Ocean of Amrita,* 187–88.

34. The secret-place secretions released by the deities engaging in coitus. [ed.]

35. *Ocean of Amrita,* 202–3.

36. Ibid., 206–7.

SOWING THE SEEDS

37. See Appendix 2.

38. Exactly what form of purity each of these represents can be found in the verses by which one mends the samayas with the wrathful deities. [ed.]

CONCLUDING RITUALS

39. This is the bodhisattva Samantabhadra, and should not be confused with the deity of the same name.

40. *Ocean of Amrita,* 167–71.

41. Tibetan: *Nyida Khajor.*

42. If we have a mandala in a photograph, a painting, or on canvas, it is appropriate to do the tenshuk, the four lines above, asking them to remain in the image.

43. OM AH HUNG represents body, speech, and mind, vajra is indestructible, KAVACHI is a contraction of KAYA, VAKA, CHITTA which are body, speech, and mind, and RAKSHA means protect.

APPENDIX 2

44. Lama Putse follows the description of the wheel as found in another terma text, the *Kunzang Tuktig*, where the wheel only has four spokes pointing in the cardinal directions. However, the *Ocean of Amrita* clearly states that the first four pairs of bodhisattvas are sitting "on the intermediate spokes," (*Ocean of Amrita*, Rangjung Yeshe, 42), which clearly indicates that this is a typical Dharma wheel comprising eight spokes. Notes have been provided wherever Lama Putse differs from the root text itself. [ed.]

45. A mythological type of garuda, half-human and half-eagle, who plays cymbals as he flies. [ed.]

46. Following the description of the mandala according to the *Kunzang Tuktig*, Lama Putse describes an alternative approach in which the wheel only has four spokes in total. "In the *Ocean of Amrita* it says 'on the intermediate spokes,' however, this actually refers to the rim between the four main spokes. The first four pairs of buddhas are located where the four cardinal spokes meet the rim, while the male and female bodhisattvas are sitting on the rim stretching between the spokes." [ed.]

47. The goddess of song is more commonly known as Gita. It is also interesting to note that both the *Kunzang Tuktig* and the *Ocean of Amrita* reverse the usual pairings that are more popularly described as being Gita with Vajrapani and Nirti with Avalokiteshvara. [ed.]

48. Also known as Sarvanivaransviskambhin.

49. This is the bodhisattva and is not to be confused with the primordial buddha of the same name.

50. Also known as Shakra.

51. Tibetan: Khabar Dewa.

52. Also known as Dhruvasimha in Sanskrit and Senge Rabten in Tibetan.

53. Tibetan: Taksangri.

54. The *Ocean of Amrita* says that Yamaraja raises "a nri head." NRI is actually the seed syllable for the humans, and so it refers to a human head.

55. *Punda* is short for *pundarika*, which is a white lotus. [ed.]